**When The World Changes Its View Of Us
We Change Our View Of The World**

Nick Nelson is a Renaissance Man of the American West - prospector, scientist, inventor, storyteller, writer, artist and vortex celebrity. He lives in Gold Hill, Oregon.

Book & Cover Design
  Linda W. Hurst - Minerva Designs

Front Cover Photograph
  Lois Nelson

Back Cover Photograph
  Maria D. Cooper

The Golden Vortex

The Conscious Popular Library

The Golden Vortex

First Edition

© 2000 by Nick Nelson

All rights reserved

Library of Congress
Catalog Card Number 00-105858

ISBN 1-929096-01-1

Conscious Publishing

PMB #323
6663 SW Beaverton Hillsdale Highway
Portland, OR 97225-1403

Table of Contents

1 The Oregon Vortex 8

2 Portals To Anywhere 67

3 Portals To Anywhen 109

4 The Egyptian Vortex 156

5 The Motor In The Magnet 203

6 A Terraline Map 255

7 A Vortex Map 278

8 A Gold Map 313

9 The Open End.. 341

Illustrations

Chapter 1
- 1 29
- 2 42
- 3 46

Chapter 2
- 4 74
- 5 81
- 6 85
- 7 93
- 8 97
- 9 106

Chapter 3
- 10 135
- 11 137
- 12 141
- 13 143
- 14 151
- 15 154

Chapter 4
- 16 174
- 17 175
- 18 175
- 19 180
- 20 188
- 21 190
- 22 196
- 23 197
- 24 199

Illustrations

Chapter 5
- 25 211
- 26 221
- 27 224
- 28 234

Chapter 6
- 29 276

Chapter 7
- 30 282
- 31 286
- 32 291
- 33 293
- 34 294
- 35 295
- 36 296
- 37 299
- 38 302

Chapter 8
- 39 323
- 40 328
- 41 335
- 42 338

Chapter 9
- 43 372

1

THE OREGON VORTEX

There are localities on this planet where reality contrives a subtle shift from that which is considered normal, and it apparently does so simply because human beings are present. A natural condition exists one moment that should be the same in the next moment, except the memory of the two moments do not match.

These anomalous sites on the landscape are not scarce, for they exist in an encompassing global network of intertwining lines that lace through each other like a spider's web forming focal nexus points. Here, the mind interprets the products of the eyes as contradictory, and tends to ignore the experiences. Human reason carefully guards its hard-won description of reality, and since everything is formed from the same unsubstantial stuff, these creases, or lines through the body of the continuum can be easily disregarded. The discovery of these places, therefore, is rare.

For lack of a better descriptive term, these distortions on the face of reality are called, vortices, or as I prefer vortexes. A better term would be vortex *field*. When I ran across my first vortex field, it had to be shown to me. I doubt I would have recognized it on my own.

It was 1970, and I was holding down the passenger seat in a friend's car as we headed for home from Reno, Nevada. Forty-five minutes earlier we'd left California, and topped Siskiyou pass on Interstate 5. We were about ten minutes north of the city of Medford, Oregon, when, a half-mile or so from the exit to the town of Gold Hill, my friend pointed out a billboard in a pasture alongside the freeway.

VISIT THE HOUSE OF MYSTERY, the sign beckoned, AT THE OREGON VORTEX.

"I think I've heard of this thing," my driver said. "Wonder what it's like?"

"It's a roadside rip-off, John," I answered without enthusiasm. I'd not visited this place, but was certain I'd been to one just like it.

"Could be," he said, steering his '68 Mustang toward the highway exit.

John had never been to Reno, and he had talked me into going on this trip so I could show him around. I didn't care about seeing a tourist trap called the House of Mystery, but I decided I could use the break. We'd been on the road almost five hours, and there was another nine hours of pavement until we reached home in the northwest corner of Washington State. An hour or so on my feet, and away from the torture of a Ford bucket seat looked pretty good.

We crossed the Rogue River into Gold Hill, a small town the bypassing freeway on the other side of the river had made even smaller. Two miles on the other side of town, we turned up a country lane called, Sardine Creek Road. A sign informed that the "mystery" house waited four and a half miles ahead.

"It's a fake," I said.

"Could be," was John's laconic answer.

I settled back, thinking of a weekend over ten years in the past. It was 1959, and I was with a different companion in a replica Wild West saloon at Knotts Berry Farm. We were having a sarsaparilla, and taking part in a market survey of a new snack sensation called, Fritos Corn Chips. We were on the second day of our first liberty from Camp Pendleton in Southern California. Life wasn't too bad. After all, we'd survived Marine Corps Boot Camp.

I was 18, and exploring my young life, which had developed a strange glitch. I was right in the middle of learning that things are not always what they seem, and certainly not what I thought they should be.

We told some people with clipboards that the Fritos were good, but the sarsaparilla could easily have been replaced with a Pepsi. Outside, a fake cowboy gunfight was happening on the street of the fake Old West town.

The morning before, a Los Angles MTA bus had dropped me near Hollywood and Vine. I suppose a neophyte like me expected the place to be teeming with movie stars. At any rate, a simple urban street corner wasn't on my list of things to be found there. What a gyp!

That same evening, while attending a promotional dance inside Disneyland, I stood in a long line of other Marines and Sailors, waiting for a thirty-second dance with Annette Funicello. At last! A real movie star.

When my turn came, Annette, the obvious better dancer, pushed me around to the slow music. She asked my name, and I told her. Without much interest, I thought, she asked where home was, and I told her. How was the weather there, she wanted to know?

I said that home was about a thousand miles away, and that I hadn't been there in four months. How would I know what the weather was like? She shrugged and looked blankly over my shoulder. I realized that she not only didn't care about the weather in Washington, she wasn't terribly interested in me.

Her limp hand was slick with sweat, probably from all those other guys ahead of me, and there was something hard and flat at her waist. A girdle? She was a pretty girl, and no doubt I would have stood in line to dance with her no matter who she was, but I was wishing I'd left her up on the silver screen running around the beach with Frankie Avalon.

Just prior to ordering the bad soft drink in the fake saloon at Knotts Berry Farm, I ran across something that had ruined another memory.

In the early fifties, I used to tune in a weekly country music radio show that was broadcast from a place called, The Chuck Wagon Circle. My radio imagination had conjured up a picture of a group of covered wagons and cowboys on the lone prairie. The wagons were circled around a roaring campfire, ala Roy Rogers, and on the fire were a kettle of beans, a blackened coffee pot, and a spitted rack of ribs. My mind's eye even put in a moon-silhouetted coyote howling in concert with the fiddles and guitars. All this, of course, came from the legendary Knotts Berry Farm.

I had just found the Chuck Wagon Circle. It was a big cement hole in the ground with spectator's seats forming the sides. Ringed around the top edge of this small amphitheater were little fake chuck wagons looking down on the stage at the bottom of the hole. Just beyond this affront to a cherished memory was a line of planted trees along a sidewalk, then a parking lot full of automobiles. There were no horses stirring restlessly away from the light of the fire. I was not appreciating the lessons Southern California was serving up.

It was with some trepidation that I left the saloon to further explore this concrete and asphalt "farm".

The next thing that caught our attention was a poster at the ticket booth of what looked to be an interesting concession. For fifty cents, the sign promised to amaze and mystify with a trip through the, MINER'S HAUNTED SHACK. It was billed as a place where gravity was upside down, and the laws of nature were bent.

We paid the fare, waited for a tour group of ten or fifteen people to form, then followed a young male guide through a man-made tunnel of plaster and river rock. The first thing I noticed was that the tunnel entrance was smaller than the exit, which tended to throw off perspective. Part way through the thirty-foot tunnel, our guide warned us to beware of the "strange force" trying to hold us back.

I turned to my companion, and said, with what must have been a sneer, "Feels like the same strange force that holds us back on those hills we run up and down in Pendleton." I was a newly born skeptic, turning fast into a cynic.

Beyond the tunnel, we encountered a horribly twisted, longish building made from old, grayed boards. The "Haunted Shack". It was lying at about a 15-degree angle from plumb, and the concrete landscape looked like what it was— contrived. Inside the shack, water seemed to flow uphill, and we were allowed to roll a ball down a ramp only to have it roll back up toward us. I was impressed with the optical illusions, but in no way thought the ball, and water were actually defying gravity.

I sat in a chair that was propped against a wall, and then true to the guide's assertion that I would not be able to stand, was unable to do so. This presented no problem to my newly awakened scientific mind. The chair and the wall were leaning so far back that I was nearly lying on my back.

I was a little bothered by the guide's next trick, though. He stood a straw broom up on its sweeping end, and made it balance by itself on that steeply slanting floor.

When the guide turned to lead his flock out the door, I held back, pretending to tie a shoelace. I snatched the broom and sneaked a peek at its bottom. The straw was neatly shaved flat and slanted to match the angle of the floor.

Outside the shack, we took seats on benches that were fronted by a ten or twelve-foot long platform. Volunteers faced one another from either end of this small stage, and then changed places, apparently also changing height. I believe I laughed out loud. The background behind the demonstrators was so outlandishly slanted that I was forever cured of belief in magic.

So, eleven years later, when John pulled to a stop under the hand-carved wooden sign that announced our arrival at the HOUSE OF MYSTERY, I was certain we were about to be treated to another very bad magic show.

The price of admission was more than fifty cents, but the scenery at the Oregon Vortex was far better than at Knotts Berry Farm. A rustic footbridge crossed the four-foot, Sardine Creek to the ticket window. The green Oregon flora featured, red-barked Pacific Madrone, or Madrona trees, standing with Maple, Oak, and the occasional tall Douglas Fir, and Incense Cedar. Partway up a path from a flat yard, though, was what I expected to find. Obscured by a gray, barn-board fence on the side hill, was a slanted, and badly twisted old shack. The "House of Mystery", no doubt.

I hadn't forgotten the contrived cover story at The Miner's Haunted Shack. A miner, frustrated by lack of gold, was hanging around, even though dead, still hunting the elusive yellow metal, and messing up reality while he was at it.

The tale of the House of Mystery was less colorful, but at least more realistic.

The history of the slanted shack was told to us by our guide, an older man by the name of Ernie. This longish, obviously old, and very crooked building was once an assay shack, supposedly built around the turn of the Century by a gold mining company. Sometime later, in a rainstorm, the shack slid downhill getting into its present sorry condition naturally.

I listened politely, but paid little attention when Ernie had the small crowd make an estimate about how much higher the north end of the structure was than the south end. It looked a lot less than the number of feet most thought it was, but I knew all about perspective and screwy angles. Inside, there was no water flowing uphill, but there was a ramp outside the upper window on which a golf ball, when rolled down, briefly stopped, and then came back up.

Not only had I seen that before, but the old board which made the ramp looked so much like the one at the Haunted Shack, it could have been stolen from there. It was the exact same dumb trick.

Then Ernie threw me a curve. Not only did he admit that the golf ball demonstration was a fake, but he insisted we understand that it was no more than an optical illusion. He said the trick was only included in the tour to point out the kind of things done to unwitting tourists at many different imitations of the Oregon Vortex. Places like...Knotts Berry Farm!

While I was digesting this candor, Ernie balanced a straw broom on the slanted floor on its sweeping end. He did it quickly, and I must have blinked when the broom looked as if it had pulled itself from his hand and stood on its own. When I asked to examine the broom, he thrust it at me, and then stood by silent as I examined the straw bottom. It wasn't shaved flat, and appeared to be rounded and worn down by what were probably years of sweeping.

Something began gnawing at my smug certainty, and it may have been the same thing that caused me to be a little unsteady inside the crooked old shack. It felt as if the floor was moving, but looking around confirmed that terra firma was still firm. It wasn't the air, there was no wind, and even if there had been a breeze, it wouldn't have accounted for the feeling that something seemed to be churning through me rather than around me.

When we all moved outside into the fenced backyard, the feeling abated, so I blamed it on the old building. If the eyes feed unfamiliar signals to the brain, like crooked walls, the equilibrium is bound to get a little messed up. Still, I had been in the slanted environment of The Miner's Haunted Shack without queasiness. I was only a little worried, though. Given time, I was sure I'd figure out how Ernie was fooling us.

In the backyard, parallel to the rear of the building, was a wooden platform about ten feet long. Ernie put one person on each end of the platform, then had them change places. The effect was startling. It appeared as though the two demonstrators changed heights in relation to one another by as much as eight or ten inches.

Our guide placed a four-foot carpenter's level on the platform to prove it was even with the world. He didn't need to use the level. If the platform was so far out of plumb to cause the effect I had witnessed, I would have also easily seen its tilt. Also, the demonstrators would have surely felt themselves walking up and downhill as they went from one end to the other.

There were only two explanations: One, that the background provided by the slanting face of the shack caused a dramatic optical illusion, or two, that those people actually shrank and grew as they walked by one another on the level wooden planks.

As I was desperately rooting for number one, Ernie asked for a couple more volunteers. John grabbed my arm and dragged me toward the platform.

Standing on the east end of the platform, looking across at John, I realized that something else was not right. I knew that I was at least three inches taller than my friend, yet my eye level was squarely on the bridge of his nose. John claimed to be looking above my hairline. When we changed places, I got that funny feeling in my gut again. My line of sight had moved to a couple of inches above the top of his head.

Next, Ernie unhooked a huge brass plumb bob from the side of the old board fence. It hung from a tree limb high above the yard on a long chain. He pulled it back, then just let it swing east and west. For a few swings, all seemed normal, then the plumb bob began swinging off center until, in about a minute, it circled around and swung steadfastly north and south.

"The plumb bob will refuse to swing east and west," Ernie told us, driving a nail into the coffin of my skepticism.

I knew enough physics to realize that a swinging weight acts like a pendulum. Once the weight is set in motion, it must go in the direction of that motion until it stops. Even if Ernie had applied a covert twist to one side or the other of the plumb bob, causing it to circle, it would not have assumed a new back-and-forth motion. It would have continued to circle.

I had shed the inhibiting garb of skeptic, and came to a conclusion that should have been apparent long before tangling with Gold Hill's little vortex:

Just because a thing can be duplicated by slight-of-hand doesn't mean that everything is done by slight-of-hand.

The problem was, I wanted to learn what caused the things I had witnessed. I was instantly addicted, and without knowing it, I took on a quest that continues stronger than ever thirty years later.

During the seventies, I returned many times to the vortex. With different friends at different times, we spent at least twice a year wearing ruts into the pavement of I-5 on our way to Nevada. We would leave Washington, from up near the British Columbia border, drive in one 850-mile shot to Reno, and burn out the town in three days. On the more leisurely trips home, especially if someone was along who had never seen the vortex, I would stop in to pick Ernie Cooper's brain at the House of Mystery. He and I never became close friends, but did manage to get in a few hours of combined conversation over more than ten years of being acquainted.

I told him once that the Gold Hill Vortex was closely connected to the Bermuda Triangle anomaly. Ernie listened to my theory, and then said I should write it up. With that prodding, I put together a short book in 1980. Ernie sold a bunch of those booklets in the House of Mystery's gift shop, and he even posted excerpts from it on the information board in the yard.

While this was going on, an era was closing. The traveling cadre was breaking up, mostly because of marriage, mine included, but also because Reno was slowly becoming Las Vegas of the North. The old clubs were either being taken over, or simply remodeling into glitz. The old mechanical slot machines were giving way to electronic monstrosities where all one did by pulling the handle was trip a switch. When a perfectly good product is "new and improved" it generally loses me as a customer. We lost interest in Reno, and I spent a lot of time not traveling through Southern Oregon.

I did continue chasing and researching the kind of ideas that regular scientists normally disdain. My library of odd books grew, and my experimentation notebooks fattened up. I was no longer a fanatic wild-eyed ex-skeptic, but a more careful plodder who looked at everything with an open mind. I was also learning to have fun with the strange knowledge I was acquiring.

Most of my time, though, was spent in the mundane tasks of making a living, so all that fun came in fits and spurts with long droughts in between. It seems I spent a lot of time in those mundane tasks, and along about 1993, I managed to lose my mind. At least I consider buying an apple farm in North Central Washington, or anywhere else, an insane act.

For about three years I fooled myself into believing that next year I would actually make money growing apples. Then, after I retrieved my mind, I spent another two years sitting behind a for-sale sign hoping someone who really enjoyed growing apples to give away would come along and buy my really swell farm.

Then it finally happened - a farmer, who couldn't stand to be without hundreds of trees to prune, showed up with a bank in tow that didn't know any better. Through this small window of opportunity one more totally unexpected thing flew in. I got a phone call from out of my past.

It was from a television producer who was researching a segment for a Learning Channel program called, STRANGE SCIENCE, WEIRD PLACES. She had been told that I might know something useful about a place called The House of Mystery?

I knew a few things, and filled her in. How much they used of my vast knowledge, I don't know, but with my upcoming freedom from apple bondage, the call triggered a primal urge to revisit the good old Gold Hill Gravity Vortex.

The call came in the spring of 1998, and by September, me and my trusty '75 Datsun 280-Z were on the road to Southern Oregon.

It was a beautiful fall day when I parked my copper-colored steed beneath the old familiar hand-carved sign along Sardine Creek Road. The log house souvenir shop still spanned the slow moving creek, and all around the trees were just beginning to change color. As I approached on the steps down from the road level, the admission window slid open.

Two women peered out at me. After a pause, one of them said, matter of factly, "You're the guy who wrote the book." I was home.

I was loaded with new facts and research to pass on to my old acquaintance. I asked for Ernie, but the answer I received exposed a trail of leaves behind me. These were not leaves from Autumn Maples, but were calendar droppings. I was made to deal with what I knew; that it had been sixteen years since I had last been there. What I did not know, was that it had been ten years since Ernie had passed away.

The middle-aged lady who recognized me, I had met a long time ago. She was Ernie's daughter, Maria, who I quickly learned, was now managing the business. She invited me in to the gift shop where we proceeded to catch up on a large time gap. It was Maria, I learned, who I could blame for sending the TV producer after me. I was shocked to see that the excerpt pages of that old, long out of print booklet still graced the bulletin board in the yard outside. In some ways, the place hadn't changed a bit.

I hung around most of the day, and in between tours, Maria allowed me to wander the property to do experiments. When I wasn't engaged in arcane activities, like dangling magnets from a string, she told me about the day when the television people came to shoot the segment.

She talked about a man named Salvatore Trento who had come with the crew. He was a writer and expert in alleged strange places, but not a newcomer to the Cooper's Vortex. He'd been there a few years earlier, but in a book written right after that visit, he hadn't exactly given the place a five-star recommendation. The feeling is that, during this time, he had just come from one of the cheap copies that have been built as tourist traps, and perhaps had his view of such things influenced negatively. I knew a little something about that sort of thing.

On his latest trip, though, Mr. Trento was evidently more impressed. He prowled the area with a sensitive magnetometer, looking for funny goings-on, and reportedly, found a few. Almost four months after the film crew departed, Maria showed me the general place, just outside the souvenir shop, where Mr. Trento complained of not being able to calibrate his machine back to a zero setting. Evidently, such a thing needs to be done after each result in order to take a new reading. This sort of glitch with an otherwise healthy machine was not supposed to occur, and it bothered him greatly.

After hearing this, I charged out the door to investigate. It took about ten minutes of dangling my magnet to discover that the demarcation line marking the boundary of the vortex suddenly came to an impossible end. It is supposed to be a circle. If this spot on the ground had confused Trento, it was doubly confusing to me. I knew the circle could not just stop, so I kept looking. It took another ten minutes to find where the line picked up and kept going about 18 inches on a direct line toward the center of the vortex. This, however, left a gap I couldn't explain.

I marked the end and beginning of the line in the dirt with my boot toe, then stood back to think. I wondered if anything would happen if I bridged this gap with my body? When I stepped on the ends of each line simultaneously, some sort of subtle, but never-the-less rude force shoved me backwards. I tried this maneuver several times while my head played with a wild "what if". What if this gentle, but steady push were magnified a few thousand times?

Stargate?

From up the hill a tour group was heading toward me, so I backed off to let them pass into the gift shop. A man in full stride placed one foot squarely between my marks, lurched awkwardly sideways, but continued on without giving any sign that he had noticed.

Maria approached and inquired of my intense interest in the dirt. I explained the marks, and asked her to step on them. She did, and by action and voice confirmed that there seemed to be an active anomaly of some sort at work.

The man who had stumbled came back out into yard with his wife, and they got involved in the discussion about my discovery. The woman seemed more interested than the man, so I asked if she would step on the marks.

She stepped right up. "Oh..." she said, wavering backward, "there does seem to be something happening."

The husband's face held the look of a confirmed skeptic, but with prodding from his spouse, he took a position on the marks. The three of us watched his fists clench, his arms and shoulders stiffen, and his body incline from the knees about five degrees.

He turned his head, looked at us with an absolutely blank expression, and said calmly, "I don't feel anything."

With the sigh of someone who has been there before, his wife answered, "Honey, that thing you can't feel is about to knock you over."

Maria tolerated me for an entire day while I roamed around loose, retracing old steps, and learning new ropes. When she shut the gate, and chased me out, I took her business card and promised to stay in touch.

As my vintage sport car and I pointed our noses north to visit friends and relatives in Washington, I had plenty to think about. For five hundred miles of mostly driving through the night, I pondered exciting new ideas. Then, three days later, when I reached home, I began placing those ideas into a fantastic context. If I was right, the iceberg below water was about to be exposed.

Two months later, after I could no longer question the unconventional drift of my own work, I made a decision to change the direction of my family. I placed a call to Maria.

"When you open in March," I asked, "will you need help?"

She wanted to know if I was serious. I assured her I was.

"March first," she said. "If you can't make it, let me know."

It was the easiest job interview I ever had. On March first 1999, I reported for work as a fledgling tour guide at the Oregon Vortex, also known as the House of Mystery. It turned out to be the best job I ever had. Don't tell Maria.

Being in the vortex eight hours a day, five days a week, has allowed me many things, not the least of which has been the privilege to meet more incredibly interesting people in one short season than in the last forty years.

On the first day our only customer was a man dressed in buckskins, wanting to know if he could come in and play his Didgeridoo, a hollow, crooked stick carved and painted for him by an Australian Aborigine chieftain. He wanted to see if it sounded different inside the vortex. Maria, myself, and my trainee partner, an intense, somewhat unfocused, but very intelligent young woman named Bryton, showed him around. He aimed and tooted his stick at almost everything. We didn't learn if the instrument was affected by the vortex field, but for nearly an hour it sounded like a sick elephant was loose in the woods.

The first thing that Bryton and I had to learn was how to tell customers concisely what a vortex is.

In a strict classical sense, a vortex is any thing that whirls around. A tornado, hurricane or even a spiral galaxy is a form of vortex. The simplest example is water going down a bathtub drain. This explanation doesn't describe the precise nature of the whirlpool of force existing around the old assay shack, but it is a good analogy bridge, allowing a language leap from the third dimension to the fourth. The Oregon Vortex is not exactly like a tornado with a top and a bottom, because, it must be seen as spherical; an infinite energy sphere, with its genesis in the Quantum where three dimensions are not enough dimensions.

The vortex might also be considered an entity, because it has measurable boundaries. Its main boundary is delineated on the ground with a short line of bricks showing the beginning of a curve that goes on to make a circle. This circle constitutes a knife-edge mark, called the line of demarcation, and it was originally measured at 165 feet, four and half inches across its diameter. Another important feature is the corona, another circular line that surrounds the vortex like a thin donut. This line is 27 feet, six and five eights inches wide. The corona's width is precisely one-sixth of the vortex's diameter, a mathematical necessity that will be showing up frequently the deeper into the book we get.

#1

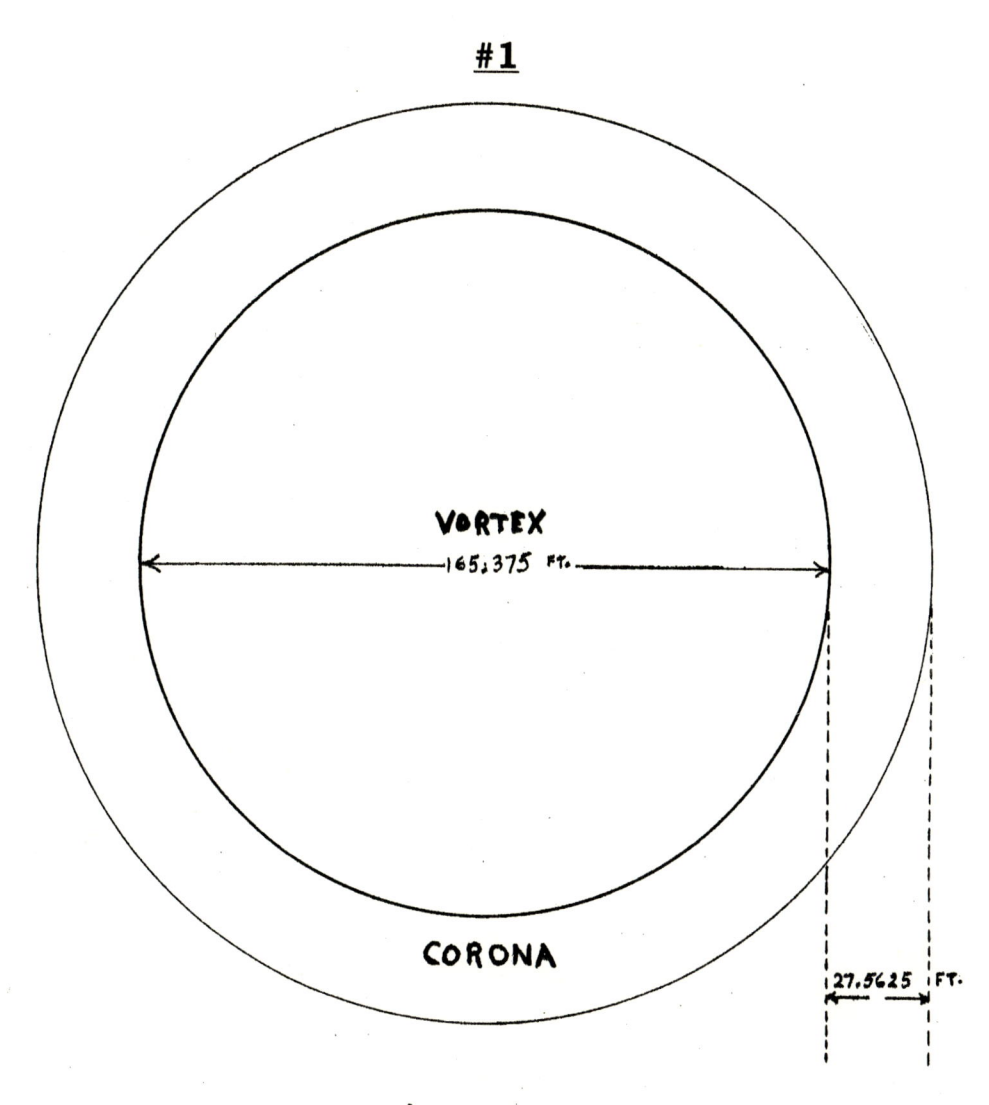

VORTEX
|—— 165.375 FT. ——|

CORONA

|27.5625| FT.

LITSTER'S
SIMPLE DIAGRAM OF GOLD HILL GRAVITY VORTEX

The vortex is only about three-quarters of an acre in area, but it stays in one place, and has done so for as long as its existence has been known. Its geographic position is rigidly stable, though from day to day, or even from hour to hour, its effects do change in intensity. These effects on the senses are what many consider disquieting, sometimes sobering, or even just uproariously funny.

Next, Maria stresses to her guides, the need to relate the true history of the area. She is aware of all those Miner's Haunted Shacks out there, and wants to make sure the staff doesn't pass out the same kind of silly stories as they do. The Oregon Vortex is the original vortex field to be open to the public, and she proudly points out that the many imitators, even if they sit on natural vortexes, copied the House of Mystery, not the other way around.

The first human contact with the vortex is uncertain, however, the Native Americans in the area must have known about it, if for no other reason than the animals they hunted were aware of it. Warm blooded, wild animals have an innate distrust of the field, evidently sensing something alien. The Indians might also have noticed that game trails went out of their way to go around this small area.

The most reliable story about the local Indians acknowledging the anomaly comes from the time when they got horses. If horses can be said to hate, then horses hate the vortex. Those who have risked their lives to ride or lead a horse beyond the line of demarcation can, at the very least, attest to an intense equine fear.

Birds will fly in, or fly through, but will rarely stop to visit. Birds don't perch in the vortex, and none have ever been seen to nest. I was startled one day to see a Robin land in the yard. I watched for about two minutes while it stood still, then it walked, almost staggered around in a tight circle, not even attempting to cock its head to check for worms. Finally it discovered it had wings, and escaped.

Humans and dogs get along with the area, but sometimes even that observation has to be revised. I've watched people try to pack a pet cat across the demarcation line, and it's not a pretty sight. Cats and horses have an equal dislike.

Cold-blooded animals like snakes, lizards, and frogs don't seem to have any problem with the area. Unfortunately, insects such as hornets and mosquitoes are also quite at home in the vortex.

After the 1849 gold rush in California, prospectors began breaking rocks all along the Cascade, and Sierra Nevada mountain chains. With few towns in those days, cartographers relied heavily on the placement of mountains, rivers, and creeks as reference points for maps, so an early first survey was conducted along Sardine Creek in 1858. It's not known if the surveyors noticed anything odd in the neighborhood of the vortex.

By the turn of the Twentieth Century, Southern Oregon was bustling with two main industries, sawmills, and gold mining. In 1904 an outfit called, The Old Gray Eagle Mining Company, established a large hard rock mine just up the hill from the vortex's position along the creek. A number ten stamp mill was built on the property, which was used to crush the gold ore into powder. Several other buildings were erected, including the assay shack that later came to be known as the House of Mystery. Everyone assumes the shack was originally constructed plumb, but since it was erected almost dead center in the vortex, and since all measurements in the vortex are suspect, no one can be certain.

This was a large mining operation, and it ran full-bore for the next seven years, employing many men. Certainly, some of the miners must have noticed that reality in their work area was a little out of whack. One of the things I point out to visitors is that the hill where the last demonstration takes place appears very steep when looking down, yet at the bottom, the incline looks like a gentle upward slope. The miners must have wondered how half a hill vanished when compared from one end to the other. A large bunkhouse was part of the complex, and still exists sixty or seventy feet from the line of demarcation. Working, and living at the site had to have generated some interesting letters to the folks back home. Unfortunately, the stories from this era are mostly word of mouth, and anecdotal.

One of those anecdotal stories relates that just before the mine closed in 1911, a rain storm loosened the side hill dirt, causing the assay shack to fall off its foundation and slide a short distance, where its progress was stopped by a small Maple tree; now a large Maple tree. The Company, knowing the gold was running out, didn't bother to straighten up the building, and for the short time remaining, moved the assay operation to a tool shed lower down the hill. Not being aware of the special nature of the area, they didn't know that this building was not in the vortex. Immediately, the story continues, it was noticed that the refined gold being assayed weighed a tiny bit more at the new location. The Company supposedly learned, to its horror, that it had been cheating itself, over nearly seven years, by a factor of about two per cent.

This is a fun story, but perhaps, one with a grain of truth backing it up. Experimentation has shown that under certain conditions, gold is the only substance that will weight differently on either side of the demarcation line. Everything else, people or lead, always weighs the same inside and outside the vortex. This is a consequence of relativity, which points out that a measuring device will necessarily change to the same degree as the object being measured.

I had long been aware of the aberration concerning of the weight of gold, which caused me to harbor a pet theory; underground, I thought, at the center of the energy sphere, was a huge gold nugget weighing several tons. This glob of gold, I reasoned, caused the abnormal effects in the area. After my 1998 trip, I disposed of this idea in favor of a more likely cause, which I will deal with in a later chapter.

After the Old Gray Eagle Mining Company ceased to exist, the property lay unused, though there may have been a little high grading going on. Old tailing piles, the leftover garbage rock of a mining operation, still contains extractable gold, and a few independent miners might have helped themselves to some of this booty. Even if this activity, with or without permission of the mineral rights owners, was going on, the history of the place has a gap until sometime in the late twenties, when a mining engineer by the name of John Litster came on the scene.

Litster grew up in South Africa as the son of a diplomat in the English Foreign Service. The Litster family moved around a bit, but later, John took his higher education in Scotland, and considered himself a Scotsman. By all accounts, he possessed a huge intellect, spoke nine languages fluently, and held at least one university degree, and that in Geology. He was a highly regarded geologist and mining engineer, and known to be something of a scientist by many people in the Southern Oregon area. Then he got himself all tangled up in the vortex.

    Here I have to make guesses. Perhaps Litster heard miners' tell campfire ghost stories about a world that just wasn't quite right, or he may have been asked by the owners to investigate the odd things going on up there in the woods. Maybe he just stumbled into the vortex, but I suspect he had heard about, or had visited another such area, and already had an interest in the phenomenon. He was in his forties, a man of the World, and he may have thought he'd be able to walk into whatever was going on along Sardine Creek, quickly figure it out, and then publish a blockbuster scientific paper. Instead, he got hooked. The place will do that to people. Ask me.

We know for sure that Litster bought the twenty acres on which the vortex sits. We know that after doing experiments, in 1930, he opened the vortex up to the public as an oddity roadside attraction. We know he lived on the property while showing it to tourists, and doing research. Folklore has it that over the thirty or more years he owned the place, he conducted some 14,000 experiments on the way to trying to explain the mystery.

    Folklore generally isn't too concerned with facts, and rarely bothers to run the numbers. If he really did 14,000 experiments, that would be about one and a third experiments per day, every day for the rest of his life.

There is little doubt that he did many, many experiments, but there is also little doubt that those experiments did not produce a satisfactory public explanation of what makes a vortex tick. Litster died in 1959, and by dying, he made himself a part of a greater mystery.

For a long time after his death, folklore spread another story. He went out in the yard behind the gift shop, lit a bonfire, and then fed the flames all his notes detailing those 14,000 experiments. The reason for this action was supposed to have come from his widow. She was believed to have said that he burned the research notes because he didn't think the world was ready for what he had found.

It has taken nearly thirty years to dig up the facts behind this myth, and oddly, there was a lot of truth buried. Evidently Litster's last will and testament directed his wife to destroy his notes and data. There was no bonfire out in the backyard. His widow, though, was in bad health, so she gave the records to her son to dispose of. The son, instead of burning the papers, stored them in his attic. A bad leak developed in the roof, soaked the documents for several days, and ruined them beyond recovery. Litster got his last wish, and the world is safe from his discoveries.

I think that's just great. Really. Now, I get to drive the world crazy. I'm on to old John Litster.

Even without his notes, he left a great many clues that a person who tends to ask off-the-wall questions can decipher.

By 1944, Litster was thought to have actually solved the mystery. Around that time, or a little after, he published a 30-page booklet, titled, *Notes and Data*, in which he described the vortex in rather arcane Nineteenth Century scientific jargon. The booklet was mostly diagrams of what he called Terralines, and a lot of photographs of the crooked building and short and tall people. Whether Litster meant to leave clues in this book, I don't know, but when matched with the placement of his demonstration platforms, that are still used to bend customers' minds, the book begins to make sense.

Notes and Data is still sold by the hundreds of copies a year out of the gift shop. People are hungry for any kind of explanation to help them understand what they have just experienced. It seems to me, though, that almost no one understands the book. I've had a copy hanging around since 1970, but didn't have a workable idea what it said until the last couple of years.

One of the first things Maria showed me after I came to work was a small sign left by Litster out in the yard. It's a piece of metal about six by eight inches, painted white, then hand-lettered in black. It was old, but easily legible and hanging on rusty wires from the roofline of a small canopy covering the first demonstration platforms. Situated between two other, larger information signs, it rather cryptically read:

The black line on which you are asked to stand is at an angle of 23 degrees, 27 minutes, 8 seconds (plus) from true north. (This is the equivalent to the Obliquity of the Ecliptic.) The magnetic declination at this point is approximately 20 degrees East.

Maria didn't have a clue. She wanted to know if perhaps she should take it down, because no one else probably had a clue either. This sign generated a lot of unanswerable questions, and patron's questions deserved answers.

I wondered how many times I had seen and read this sign since I first began showing up? Obviously, I'd never studied it, and at first glance, there didn't seem to be much point in trying to study it. For instance, there was no black line on which to stand. If there ever had been such a line, time and weather had long since erased it.

Magnetic declination, I understood. A compass on the Earth only points to Magnetic North, not to the axis of the planet, which is True North. The magnetic pole is north of Hudson's Bay, around Baffin Island, and compasses point toward this spot. If a compass isn't positioned directly in line with both the axis and the magnetic pole, the difference in degrees of arc is referred to as declination. The needle declines, or deviates, from the polar axis toward the magnetic source.

Even as I explained this part of the sign to Maria, I was puzzling over the rest of it. What in the world was the tongue twister, *Obliquity of the Ecliptic*? Then it hit me. 23 degrees, 27 minutes, and 8 seconds of arc had to be referring to the tilt of the Earth on its axis relative to the plane of its orbit around the Sun. Obliquity of the Ecliptic, I told her, was just a perplexing way to describe summer and winter.

The Boss' reaction to this was a kind of pensive, so-what shrug. So what does this have to do with anything? I could tell from this reaction that the more she knew, the more she didn't know, and I didn't blame her. She asked me to take the sign down.

At the time, it seemed like a good idea, but that little sign has since provided a huge insight. Its message dovetails neatly into my other research, and verifies to me that Litster knew what he was doing. I now know, as well, where the missing black line should be. Maybe we should get some new wire and re-hang the sign.

As the Spring progressed, both Bryton and I became more at ease dealing with the number of people, which came in larger groups the closer we got to the Summer season. I had come to the vortex for a variety of selfish reasons. I needed something to keep me busy, but beyond that I wanted to get experience in public speaking. Later, I hoped to get on a seminar circuit talking about the related subject of magnetic fields for health purposes. The biggest reason, though, was for the constant accessibility to one of the more interesting places on the planet, and how that aided my greater research.

With each bunch of people I showed around, I learned something about groups as single entities. I began to understand what entertainers mean when they refer to audiences as having personalities. What I wasn't prepared for was to be having so much fun, while at the same time being able to explore such a wondrous, open-ended universe.

I also wasn't prepared to have my tour groups inadvertently help me with the more critical research. One day, while standing in the front yard of the assay shack filling some folks in about the history of the building, I noticed a woman whispering in the ear of a friend. They were both looking at me and giggling.

I asked politely what they found so amusing?

"I'm sorry," the first lady said, "but you...well, you're crooked. And you just look funny."

A couple of others agreed, saying that they also noticed that I was standing leaning backward. Finally the whole crowd of 12 or 15 people pointed out that they too noticed that I was in a rather peculiar, and what looked to be awkward, stance. There was mutual agreement on the question of whether I was doing this on purpose?

I assured them I wasn't, and said I felt perfectly normal. Then, the lady who had started the whole thing asked if I would trade places with her?

After switching positions, I saw what everyone else saw. She was standing near the front of the building, and leaning opposite the direction of the shack's slant. It looked like she should fall over backwards. Someone asked her how she felt. Her response was that she felt just fine, and couldn't possibly be leaning. This turned out to be a slow tour. Almost everyone had to try standing in front of the shack, and many had their picture taken in that spot

After that, I began using other groups to test a theory. Finally, one day when I was sure of my findings, I asked Maria, "Did you know you have more than one vortex here?"

She had no idea what I was asking. The standard, every day, one hundred and sixty-five foot, four and a half inch vortex was plenty. What did I mean, "...more than one vortex...?"

I took her up in the front yard and showed her the leaning act, then explained that this result was possible because there is another line of demarcation encircling the old house. This primary vortex, as I call it, is exactly one-third the diameter of the larger vortex, a little more than fifty-five feet across, and the assay shack barely fits inside it.

I dragged my foot through the dirt to show her where the line was, then showed her something that I'd been trying on tour groups for more than a week.

#2

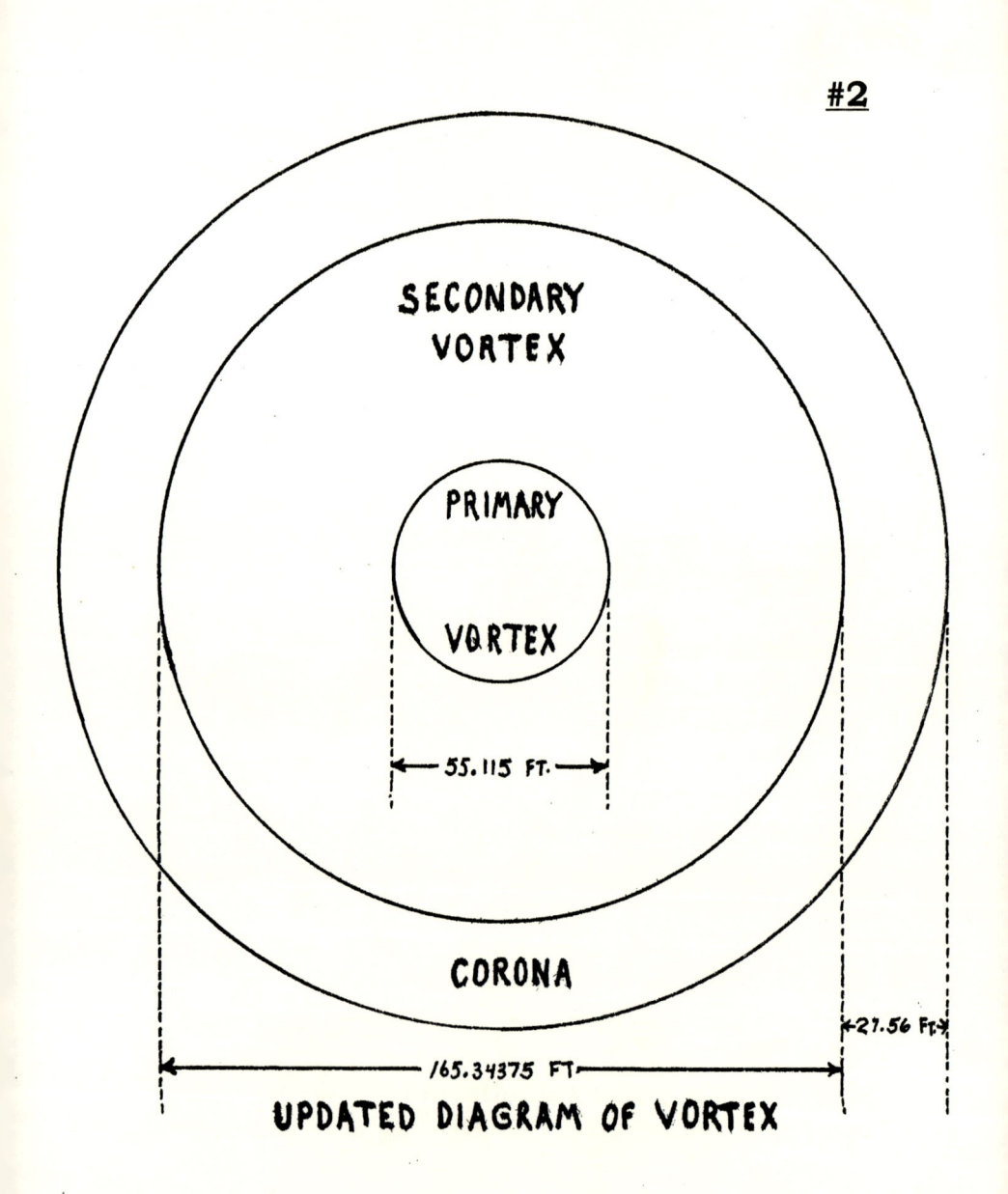

SECONDARY VORTEX

PRIMARY VORTEX

←55.115 FT→

CORONA

←27.56 FT→

←165.34375 FT→

UPDATED DIAGRAM OF VORTEX

"Watch me very closely," I told her. "I'm going to back up slowly toward the house. Keep your eyes on my body as I go back."

As I stepped backward over the line in the dirt, I saw two things happen at once. First, she quite suddenly seemed to get just a little farther away, and second, her eyes widened every so slightly in surprise. She was an old vortex hand, tough to surprise, so I knew she had never seen this before.

The effect is reciprocal. When, to me, she appeared to get smaller, or lose distance in a way that normal perspective could not account for, I knew that she saw the same thing happen to me from her perspective.

"When the world changes its view of us," I told her, "we change our view of the world."

I then led her through the house toward the backyard. "The reason some people feel a little queasy, in here," I said, as we moved along, "is that inside this primary vortex the continuum is more dense, and reality is spinning faster. That line of demarcation outside is why some feel dizzy even before getting inside."

About four feet outside the building, and running parallel with the face of the structure is that 30-inch, by ten-foot wooden platform that yields those amazing results I first saw in 1970. Early, in all the tours, we point out that the demonstrations work only because the platforms are running along Litster's north/south Terralines, then when we get to the backyard of the house, someone invariably notices that this platform runs east and west. During our early education, Maria, told Bryton and me that these east/west height changes were possible because of being so close to the center of the vortex. For some time this had been an incomplete explanation, and now the student told the teacher that she was wrong.

"We're not really all that close to the center," I pointed out. "The true center of our sphere of energy, since we're uphill, is about forty-five or fifty feet straight down. What we're close to is the axis. But that isn't even what causes the effect here. What causes the effect is that new line of demarcation I showed you in the front yard. It completely circles the house, and is now running at about sixty degrees across the west end of this platform".

I punctuated my words by slowly and deliberately stepping across that invisible line while looking her in the eye. I could, by the raised eyebrows, tell that she saw me instantly pop up about two inches. I knew that it looked as if I had suddenly stepped on a two-by-four.

"This east/west platform works because of this line of demarcation." I pointed down to my foot. "It has nothing directly to do with the close proximity to the axis."

Maria had grown up a vortex brat, and had seen a lot, but all this one was new. "Do you suppose,

Litster knew about this?" she asked, her tone flat and matter-of-fact.

"He spent thirty years working in here," I answered, "How could he not know?"

She nodded thoughtfully. "He was no dummy, that's for sure. So why didn't he point this out?"

In 1960, Maria's parents bought the place from Litster's widow. Maria was getting up in her elderly teens when Litster died the year before. She had known the man when he was alive. I, in 1959, was busy being underwhelmed by The Miner's Haunted Shack, and had never met him. I treated her question as rhetorical.

"Maybe this is one of those things he didn't think the world was ready for?"

I wondered if this might be one of those more-truth-than-poetry statements? If Litster really was, "no dummy," why did he hide this aspect of the vortex? I could feel things coming together. I had knowledge that Litster, because of the time in which he lived, probably didn't have. I felt that the coming together of these two sets of knowledge would unlock whatever it was that he thought might so damage the poor unwary, and unsteady population of the world.

For one thing, I suspected that an aspect of the vortex that Litster might have worried about, and maybe even pried open, was a temporal overlap.

Perfunctory time studies have been done in the vortex with varying results. Maria and I, for

#3

Local map of the Oregon Vortex

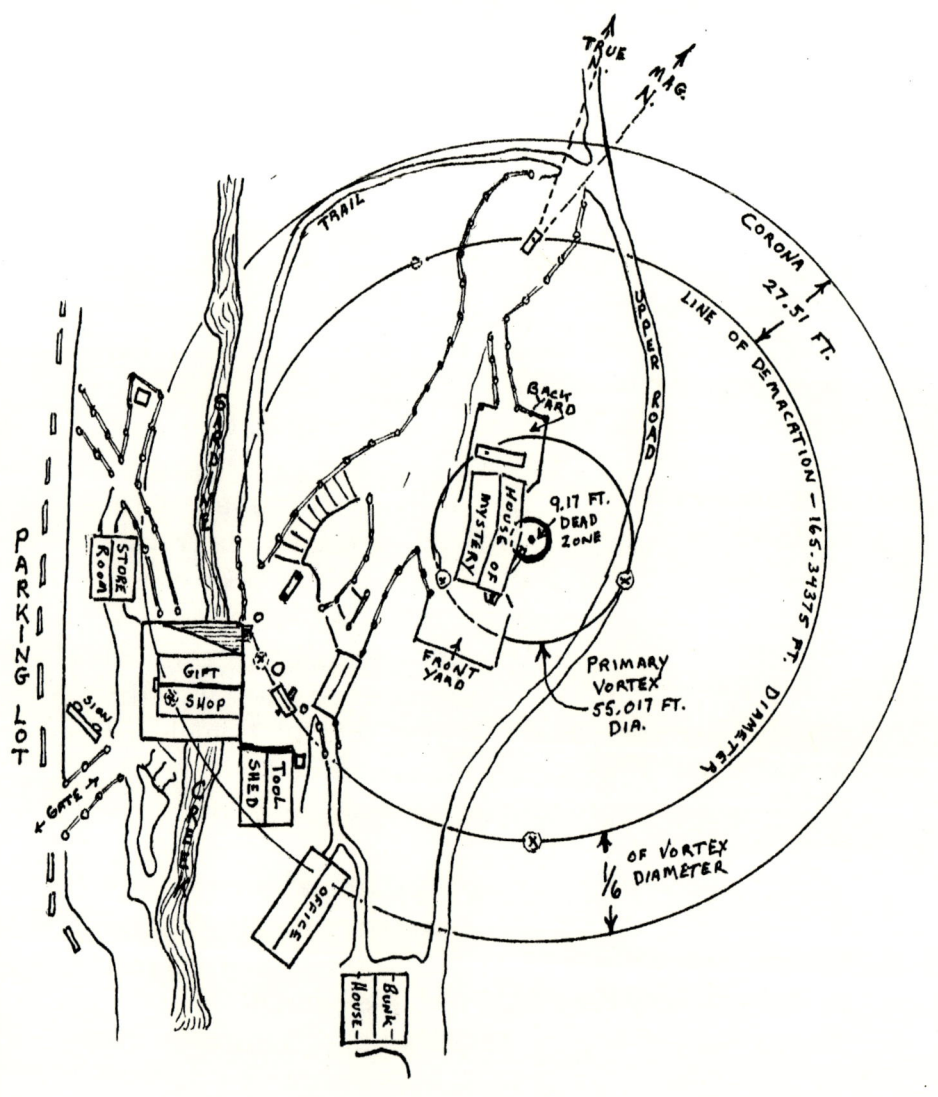

46

instance, spent the entire summer running a simple time test. This involved synchronizing four identical quartz watches, then placing three of them at different positions inside the vortex, while the fourth was kept outside.

After several months, we compared the second hands. If the fruit of this endeavor means anything, then time seems to run about a quarter of a second per day slower in the vortex than outside. Should I decide to accept this unscientific result, then my 1999 is about ten seconds shorter than everybody else's' 1999. I am the first, though, to discount this rather clumsy experiment. Like us, without the use of million-dollar atomic clocks, others haven't fared much better.

In 1996, another researcher wandered into the vortex with the desire to see if time was affected by the field. He brought with him a resonating quartz crystal device of his own invention, put it out in the yard, and ran a cable up to the parking lot to power his "clock" with a car battery. For an hour or two his oscilloscope registered a lot of disappointing normal ups and downs, but, as any experimenter knows, results quite often don't follow the rules of expectation.

He was about to give up the vigil when a large family showed up at the ticket window. Among this group were two or three boisterous and undisciplined children. They ran, whooping and hollering, into the yard and across the line of demarcation, and even though these kids were nowhere near the experimenter's device, the scope went nuts. Electronic spikes nearly jumped off the screen.

The researcher didn't reach a conclusion about the movement of time, but he did document that the vortex does not like loud and unruly children.

The Oregon Vortex reacts to people, just as people react to it, and that brings about an interesting paradox. Even though the vortex's existence is dependent on a magnetic field, the magnet of the Planet Earth, it is not a magnetic field. A compass, for instance, functions just fine almost anywhere inside the area. If the vortex was itself a big magnetic field, a compass would not relate to the Earth, which it does. The vortex obstructs those magnetic Terralines that Lister discovered, bending them as they pass through the energy sphere, which in turn, many think, causes the warped optical effects seen on the north/south demonstration platforms.

The vortex is made of something we can't yet hang our hats on, and I don't think this something is a tangible substance. I simply refer to this something as a "line". When *lines* cross and interact with each other in an electromagnet field, perceived reality occurs. Like the tree that falls in the forest without being heard, reality means nothing if no one is there to witness it.

The vortex is an entity that is the product of an electromagnetic field, and it is surrounded by a corona that is not electric. A living being is an electromagnetic entity that produces a surrounding field that is not quite electric. Human beings, horses, and loud unruly children act as obstructions in the electron flow of reality. Just as a rock in a streambed causes an eddy to form in the moving water, we make waves in the electron flow. If the vortex is anything, it is a very simple, though elegantly intricate, electron flow, and nature may contain only one basic vortex form.

One of the things we do at the House of Mystery is let ordinary folks find out for themselves that dowsing rods really work. The scientific name for water witching, or dowsing, is radiesthesia, but no matter what it's called, it is a way to interact with those *lines* of mine. A lot of *lines* cut through the vortex. Most people who take a pair of L shaped copper rods in hand, and walk around the yard, will find them seemingly moving on their own. Outside the area they might not function for the same people.

To set up the demonstration, I point out that copper rods are used because they are non magnetic, which allows us to avoid the charge of having buried electromagnets in the ground. The rods are about 18 inches long, with a ninety-degree bend that forms a six-inch handle to hold in the fist. They are then held firmly, parallel with one another and out from the body. When they turn in the hands, they may go either clockwise or counterclockwise. Direction does not matter, only movement.

One day I was showing a group how the rods would react over the bricks marking the line of demarcation. Instead of doing what they had always done for me, which was cross one another, they forcefully twisted around and instantly stopped, pointing in unison to my right. I was more than surprised, I was dumbfounded. Frankly, I half believed that the rods movement was the result of an unconscious tilt of the hands. This particular movement was overtly dramatic. The metal wires felt as if they had been grabbed and yanked. Showing up for work in this place means that the unexpected should always be expected.

I turned my head and looked where the rods were pointing. Some of the things Litster left were three small, round cement platforms where he said north/south Terralines crossed east/west lines. On these spots, inside the vortex, these lines oscillate causing some people to sway, or circle with the movement. I was looking toward my favorite concrete circle where, if my trick back was acting up, I could stand and get some relief.

On my favorite circle a young girl of 14 or 15 was standing, swaying gently, her eyes closed, and smiling. When I aimed my body away from her position, the rods moved, staying locked on her as if physically connected. I was about eight feet from where she was, and as I began walking around, the rods followed her, not losing adherence to that position until I was at least 12 feet away. I again moved in the direction of the platform, but an angle, and the rods leaped back toward her. I turned my back on her, and those fool rods whipped around and pointed right at me. Right *through* me?

I was oblivious to the tour group that had just formed. They must have thought I'd lost my mind.

After that, I always had someone stand on the circle while I dowsed him or her. I found other strong reactions, out to four or five feet, but never anything like that first time. The usual distance from which I can "find" a person, is about a foot, but sometimes I need to get within a couple of inches. I think the vortex is showing the sensitivity of people. I believe that in one respect, I'm measuring auras.

In the early summer, I was leading twelve people around, and it wasn't too long after starting that I realized I had a hardcore skeptic on board. I don't mind skeptics, even the hardcore variety, because they usually come out the other side cured. This one, however, was a determined skeptic, the kind that doesn't utter a word, just camps in the back of the crowd and nods knowingly. Skeptics come in all ages and sexes. Kids around twelve or thirteen are the worst. When backed into a corner, kids usually fight. It's either fight or listen. Most skeptics are men, but this one was a woman. She was in her mid-thirties, tall, so she stuck right up there in the back row. It's amazing how people can get in your face from as far away as possible.

We had gotten through the house and were just about to leave the back yard, and my skeptic was as determined as ever. She was into the arms-crossed stance, and every once in a while her head and eyes would roll skyward. I could almost hear the inner voice, saying "Oh boy, what a crock."

I was about to classify her as a debunker. Debunkers are those who walk in knowing everything, and walk out the same way. I used to talk to debunkers, but stopped when I realized they were void of realistic arguments. Happily, there aren't many of them.

At the top of the hill where the last platform is, I was harboring fading hope. Why these people fascinate me, I don't know. Maybe it's the challenge. The last demonstration is usually the kicker. I get them there, or never, and it was beginning to look like never.

I had gone through all the demonstrations accompanied by the usual gasps from the crowd, and her arms were still crossed. This sale was not going to get closed.

It was a slow morning. I looked down the hill, and noticed no other group was waiting in the yard, we had lots of time; so I let everyone who wanted to walk the platform do so. Many times a person walking this short four-foot piece of cement will feel themselves grow and shrink. It's also possible for the spectators to see the instant a person makes a change, and I was hoping my skeptic would see it and catch on.

So it was that I was looking right at her when she became an ex-skeptic. Her arms flew apart, her eyes snapped wide open, and her jaw dropped. She stood shaking, and pointing with a near spastic arm and forefinger toward the platform. I also noticed that she could talk— yell, actually.

"That guy...that guy...that guy!"

It was such a startling sight, that I didn't look where she was pointing. Some one else had to ask her, "what guy? What about him?"

"He...he's...vibrating!" she screamed.

I looked. A middle-aged man was on the platform staring bemusedly back at her. I think *my* jaw must have dropped. About a foot out, and all around his body, he was outlined by what appeared to be wavering heat lines such as are seen above pavement on a hot day. The background behind these lines was obscured by a faint whiteness that wrapped his entire body. He appeared slightly out of focus, and looked to be vibrating.

This was a starkly real sight, and one that everyone on the tour saw. I know, because after he stepped off the platform, and became normal, quieting the excitement, I asked everyone what he or she witnessed.

Later, in conversation with the man, I learned he made his living giving psychic readings. He was interested that everyone saw his aura, but didn't think it was all that big of a deal. After all, it was something he saw any time he wanted, and what he saw was always in living color. The peons were still using their black and white sets.

Auras are something I've had some minor experience with, but I'd always chalked it up to a visual trick. If one looks just to the side of a person who is in front of the right background, usually green or blue with the light behind them, the difficult task of focusing on nothing will reveal these wavering lines, or some other faint outline. I liken this to peering at those computer-generated pictures of dots and nonsense swirls that was a brief fad a while back. Focus behind the picture, and a 3-D image pops out. Cross the eyes, focus in front of the picture, and the same image emerges, but smaller and in reverse relief.

I had performed this very trick on the young girl who had made my dowsing rods take on a life of their own, and was rewarded with a fairly good "black and white" image of those familiar wavy lines. It was nothing in relation to the psychic on the platform, though. That was so apparent and real, that it is difficult, in retrospect to accept the product of my own eyes.

Human reason will work hard to forget something that has forced itself into Reason's construct of reality. Reason jealously guards its view of life, and is always just a glitch away from having its absolute interpretation vanish back into the quantum soup. Reason needs to run the show, and if actors appear that don't belong, it turns into a quaking bundle of fear. Witness the nearly complete unreasonable outlook of debunkers. I have seen stark fear in the eyes of those 12 and 13-year-old kids who fight so hard to retain the solidity of a world that a recent revelation told them was solid. First Santa Claus, and now this?

Psychics have told me that the vortex has an aura not unlike those of cats, dogs, and human beings. On a near-freezing morning in October, I unwittingly tested that assertion. I was sweeping up in the assay shack, while mulling over deep thoughts. In this small trance, my gaze was out the glassless window, and down toward the horizontal logs that make up the gift shop building. Slowly, I realized that the gift shop seemed to be wavering. By holding my focus on this effect, the whole landscape, as outlined by the window, took on a grayish tint that was decidedly shimmering.

When I came down off the hill, I asked Bryton to go up, look out the window and stare at the gift shop. We had been together long enough to know that if one asked the other to do something odd, that the question, why, would not yield an answer.

We didn't want to color the results of an experiment by an expectation.

Five minutes later, she was back, slowly shaking her head. "It's like looking through a rainy mist," she said. Case closed.

Subsequently, we learned that cold air allows this sight to solidify. After the day warms up, the effect disappears. On another cold morning, we stood side by side in the assay shack's back yard at a position that had our noses practically touching the edge of the primary vortex. Together, we blew warm breath steam toward the windows of the old house, projecting a small, momentary cloud against the blackened interior. After several puffs, I took out a notebook, and wrote two words.

"See any thing?" I asked Bryton.

"Well," she hesitated, and exhaled some more breath. "It does look like some square shadowy stuff." She huffed more warm air. "You'll think I'm nuts, but…it looks like a big gear. You know…just a shadow, but gear teeth."

"No, not nuts," I said, and held up my notebook. In big block letters, I'd written: GEAR TEETH.

What did we see, not necessarily *in* the house, but probably projected *on* that shimmering curtain of the vortex's edge? The past? The future? Somebody else's universe? We don't know, but we both saw the same thing.

It's almost as if the vortex goes out of its way to pull in and reveal the extremes of human sensitivity. It outlines some, like the psychic on the hill, and it shuts down in the presence of those it seems not to like. Those in the middle can only stand around in awe, or simply try to have a good time. Psychics and shamans are the most obvious entities the vortex points out, and because they tend to be the most serious, they tend to not be as sporting as some others.

I was beginning a tour, one busy Saturday afternoon, when I looked up toward the parking lot. A big van was dispensing a mob of people. Ten men, all middle-aged, swarmed the yard as I was relating the history of the House of Mystery to about 15 others who had gotten there ahead of them. For the next two hours, these guys took over the joint, and I felt like I'd stepped into a Marx Brothers' movie.

They called themselves a discussion group, and they brought along an array of tools, like levels, tape measures, and really big laser pointers. They were underfoot, almost literally, jumping right into demonstrations to measure people, and asking questions that would stump most fourth-year physics students. I swear, one of these men looked exactly like Albert Einstein, with his wild, graying hair, round, red nose, and bulging eyes. While I was trying to show something to the regular folks, he got right up on the platform with me, and with a four-foot level, began to measure the angle of a demonstrator's arms,

"Al," I pleaded to him, "I thought you died in 1955?"

I was beginning to sound like Don Rickles.

It turned out the discussion group began their discussion of the Oregon Vortex that morning, 450 miles to the north on Vashon Island in Puget Sound. One of them evidently asked the others how they could discuss something none of them knew anything about? Good question, and at that point, normal people would have changed the subject. These guys chartered a plane, and rented a big van.

The group contained one or two research scientists from the University of Washington, a few Boeing engineers, some lawyers, doctors, writers, and an artist. After the dust settled, I had to admit that it had been great fun.

Even Maria, who would rather have things orderly, had a good time. Never the less, she still wouldn't let them fire a rifle through the place so they could check the bullet's trajectory. It's been done, she told them. Nothing happens to the bullet's path, but you have to use incredible Kentucky windage, because you can't hit what you aim directly at.

The vortex seemed to like this bunch, and really showed its stuff, but one day it came upon someone that was too much for it.

A normal tour starts with a quick history in the yard near the canopy where the sign used to hang, then I set up the first demonstration by picking someone shorter than me, usually a woman. Since this is the first demonstration, I want it to work, and this arrangement shows off a height difference to the best effect. As usual, on this day, the lady victim was placed on the small platform outside the demarcation line, and I was on mine inside the line.

"As we change places," I told the newly assembled gathering, "watch closely and see if something peculiar happens."

The lady and I passed on the line of demarcation, mounted the opposite platforms, and turned to face one another. I looked at her, and my worst fear materialized!

The short person is supposed to get even shorter, and the tall person taller. The group gasps, snorts, and otherwise expresses wonder. That's not what happened. I saw a lady who was the same size as when she started, and heard a deafeningly silent crowd.

"I walk out the door everyday, asking myself, 'is this the day it all goes away'?" I told them with a gulp. "Well...what do you say we try this again?"

We traded places again, then again, and once more. My audience seemed a bit restive.

Luckily, I had a few months experience, and one similar occurrence to draw from. I remembered three couples on a tour months before. The vortex that day was absolutely rejoicing. The top platform in particular was yielding monstrous height changes. One by one, each of the six people walked the platform and felt themselves growing and shrinking. The rest of us watching could see them almost literally bounce and drop.

It was marvelous, until the sixth person, a man, strolled along the concrete slab. He walked, stopped, looked over at us and said, "I didn't feel anything."

It was no wonder he didn't feel anything, the rest of us didn't see anything. There are some people the vortex just won't accommodate.

For some reason, I don't know why, I didn't think my problem was the young lady's fault. I scanned the crowd, and my eyes settled on a tall man in a straw hat. He had the look of a troublemaker skeptic, and he was straddling the line of demarcation. Whenever I've put one leg on either side of the line while trying to talk, my words and mouth don't seem to fit. The best way, it seems, to get on the wrong side of the vortex is to get on both sides of the vortex.

"Ah, sir," I asked a bit tentatively, "I'd like to try something. I wonder if I could have you step a foot or so to one side or the other?"

He shrugged, then raised one foot to move. I turned my head to the woman just in time to see her flicker. Like an image on a TV during a power surge, the entire scene flickered! Then, instantly, she lost three or four inches.

A voice came from the audience. "Oh, now I see it."

The lady across from me owned eyes as big as full moons.

After the tour, she sought me out, and asked, "Did you see what I saw back there?"

I asked her what it was she saw.

"It was so weird. I mean, there you were, then all of a sudden it was like, well a movie film skipped a frame. There was a jerk of some kind. In...in reality? Does that sound funny? Then, well, you shot up like a rocket. This isn't special effects, is it? I mean, darnnit, this is broad daylight. How'd you do that?"

I commiserated with her, related the story of the three couples, and pointed out that I was just as puzzled as she.

Reality blinked. I think the vortex sort of pushed its own reset button to regain its balance. The tall fellow in the straw hat evidently acted like a battleship in a magnetic field. Some lines of force were sucked into the "battleship", while the rest of them flowed around.

If I hadn't come so close to losing my wits, I might have thought to ask him to stay for a while so I could have tried some experiments that seem obvious now. Would the hill seem taller at one end than the other if he had been straddling the line of demarcation? Did the whole place shut down?

On rare occasions at this position another anomaly occurs that defies explanation. One day

Bryton rushed into the gift shop abandoning her just formed tour group. She was waving her arms and shouting.

"Get outside, quick! You gotta see this!"

"What's the matter?" I asked.

"That thing!" she yelled. "You know, that roof over the platforms. It's shaking!"

By the time I got outside the old canopy she was referring to was perfectly still, but Bryton made her group attest to me that it indeed had been shaking.

A month or so later, I was just beginning a tour while standing beneath the canopy, when a lady interrupted me.

"Pardon me," she said, "but could you tell me why that building is moving?"

I looked up to see the edge of the roofline gently swaying back and forth. The canopy was obviously one of Litster's installations, and is little more than a roof built on four two-inch steel pipes. Two of the pipe legs are inside the line of demarcation, and the other two are outside the line of bricks marking the edge of the Vortex. As I looked, the canopy picked up speed and began a violent shaking. For perhaps thirty seconds, it rattled the signs and the demonstration level hanging from it, then it quieted, and stopped.

There was no earthquake. No other building shook, and no one felt the ground move. The next time I saw Bryton, I told her I now believed her.

Maria knows this sort of thing happens, but her interest is more on the business side, and her instincts in this regard are very good. I'm the goofy, pretend scientist. One of her better instincts involves picking candidates for temporary summer help. She goes to the speech teacher at the local high school and asks for the cream of the crop.

One her champion picks was, Clare, a young woman of sixteen, going on thirty-five, who, since this was her second season, had seniority over both Bryton and me. I listened in once when someone asked Clare where the center of the vortex was, and what went on there.

"Well," she began studiously, "the center is actually underground. We can't get to it, but the axis is just on the backside of the house, and it's a dead zone of sorts. It's like the eye of a hurricane, calm, and nothing happens there."

Like the eye of a hurricane! Why didn't I think of that? I went up to her and asked if I could use the metaphor. My faith in America's youth soared. If I can last 19 years longer, I might vote, Clare for President.

Of all the fascinating people the vortex has lured in, one amazing encounter I had was the least dramatic, and was provided by Clare. On a very busy day, she came toward me in the gift shop after one of her tours. A smallish senior citizen male tagged along behind her.

She introduced her charge as Harold, and said that Harold had some questions that maybe only I could answer. I took Harold's limp and tentative hand, asked what I might do, then waved to Clare as she moved off to sell someone a candy bar.

Harold was in his early seventy's, short, with wavy graying hair, and he seemed nervous and jumpy. He stood there, licking his lips obviously not knowing how to start.

"If your problem is weird," I said as an icebreaker, "you've come to the right place."

"Well, yes," he stammered. "Something the young lady said made me think of asking. Anyway, it was during the war." He stopped and looked around furtively.

"The Second World War?"

"Well, yes. No. Actually it was a little after. The War was over by then." More silence, as he looked at the door, I thought, longingly.

I waited, then asked, "What happened?"

He jumped. "Oh, yes. Certainly. I'm sorry. It's just that it's been so long ago. Yes, ok. I was a radar operator. A trainee, actually." He stopped. I wasn't surprised. It had been a big speech.

"Where were you stationed?" I prompted.

"Florida," he said so low I nearly missed it. "It was a B-seventeen." More silence.

I looked at my watch. It was just about time to take a new group on tour. I was about to excuse myself when the dam exploded.

"I was training as radar operator on this B-seventeen. The regular guy got sick that morning. Look, I was only eighteen. I didn't know what I was looking at. For a while, there were these planes out there in formation, and some really strange radio traffic. I mean these guys said they were lost, but it was a one-sided conversation. It sounded like they were talking to someone, but nobody answered. It was nuts. They weren't any more than five miles away. If I'd looked out the window, maybe I could have even seen them. How could they be lost?"

This time I was glad he fell silent. It gave me time to stop hyperventilating. I took a couple of breaths, then asked, "Where were you, exactly?"

"About, I don't know, about one, maybe two-hundred miles east of Boca Raton. The crazy thing is, I was looking at the scope. The sweep goes around, lights up the planes. They fade, like normal, right? The sweep comes back around…they ain't there." He paused to look me over. My mouth must have been open wide enough to fly that B-17 right into.

"I mean, listen, if those guys had fallen out of the sky, I coulda followed them all the way down to the sea. They just weren't there, and the radio traffic stops right in the middle of this guy saying he's takin' over the squadron. Right in the middle of a word…bloop, he's gone."

I realized I was holding my breath, and I let it out in a whoosh. "Were there five planes?" I asked.

"Yeah…"

"Were they Grumman Avenger Torpedo Bombers?'

"Say, do you know something about this?"

"Was this December the fifth, nineteen-forty-five?"

"How do you know these things?"

"Was the original flight leader, the first guy on the radio…was his name Charles Taylor?"

Now, Harold was really nervous, and it was a contest to see which of us had the larger eyes. I found it impossible that a find like this could just come out of a nice sunny day and land in my lap like a great big lottery prize. I wondered how he could be honestly ignorant of any public knowledge about the incident he was describing.

"Are you aware, Harold, that you could not only be the only surviving witness to the disappearance of Flight 19, you could be *the only witness that ever existed?*"

Poor Harold was like a cat on a frying pan. I took his arm to keep him from fleeing. Maria called to me to say I had a tour waiting. I managed a pleading look at Clare across the room, and asked if she could go out and stall them for me. Please.

Clare nodded knowingly, and headed for the door. No problem. I promise, in the 2020 Presidential Election she's going to get at least one vote.

2

PORTALS TO ANYWHERE

A few months after the trauma of World War II a tragedy occurred off the coast of Florida. In the early afternoon of December 5, 1945, ten men and five airplanes left a Navy base near Fort Lauderdale, flew east out over the Atlantic, and never came back. That evening, a search plane with a crew of 13 flew toward their suspected last position, and it never came back. For the next few days, the Navy mounted a vast, but totally unsuccessful search and rescue mission for six planes and 23 men. These are simple undisputed facts, but agreement stops here.

This incident was not a secret, especially to the families of those lost, but it didn't become widespread public knowledge until twenty years later. Why the story didn't receive greater press coverage at the time is a bit of a mystery, but probably goes no deeper than that CNN didn't exist in 1945.

The five planes were Grumman Avenger torpedo dive-bombers. Each carried two men, a pilot, and a navigator/weapons operator. All but the commander, Lt. Charles Taylor were novices. Their assigned Flight number was 19. Considering the unknown means to their end, some researchers have dubbed Flight 19 as The Lost Patrol.

This was a training flight, and Lt. Taylor was the teacher. Those who choose to see no mystery in this disappearance point out that war-veteran Taylor was not familiar with the Florida area. Even so, the mission was simple - fly east over water until out of sight of land, then see if the new guys could find their way home. Every plane had radios and the navigation equipment of the day. This was just a chance for flight hours, and experience in reading compasses. As long as they stayed north of Miami, land was always due west.

The flight was a routine training mission and no big deal, until of course, they got hopelessly lost. Even if the five planes had just gone out and were never heard from again, that would be a mystery in itself, but this disappearance became a huge mystery, because they *were* heard from.

Lt. Taylor tried to contact his base, but for some reason couldn't talk to them directly. Another pilot in a plane many miles away heard him clearly, and acted as a radio link relay. Controversy erupted later when amateur ham radio operators told what they heard while listening to Taylor complain of being lost. About the only thing the Navy, and non-Navy witnesses agreed on, was that Taylor said his compass was malfunctioning.

Evidently, another eavesdropper, a young radar operator on a B-17 by the name of Harold, was also listening in five miles from where the Flight was "lost". At the time, Harold made sure he didn't get on the official record, but more than half a century later, when he walked into The House of Mystery, his back was bowed by an old load of guilt that made it almost impossible to get a word out of him.

"This radio traffic?" I asked reluctant Harold. "Did you hear someone say he didn't know which way is west? Did he say, the ocean looked strange...not as it should look?"

These are not statements from the Navy's official documents, but from civilians who claimed to have heard the drama as it unfolded.

Harold's answer to me wasn't exactly a sterling confirmation.

"Somethin' like that...I guess."

"What was your altitude in the B-17?"

"I don't know."

"Well, were you wearing an oxygen mask?"

"No."

"So, you must have been at or near ten thousand feet."

"Yeah, must have been."

"The flight on your scope, how high were they?"

"Maybe a little lower."

"How about the weather? How was the weather?"

"Not good. Not bad."

Frustration was crowding my curiosity. "Did anyone ever interview you at the time? Did the military debrief you?"

He shrank away from me. "No."

I had a sudden insight and pursued it.

"At the time, did you tell anybody what you witnessed? Did you at least tell your pilot?"

Harold was immediately on the defensive.

"No. I didn't know this was serious. Look, I was only eighteen...a kid. I was just a trainee, I told you that. I was all alone."

It seemed apparent what this man's dilemma was, and it looked like the only help he might get would be from a good therapist. I didn't think he was crazy. I believed him. It just looked to me that he had been keeping his head down for an incredibly long time, worried that any minute the Government would crash through the door and take him away. From his viewpoint, if he had just had the courage as a young trainee to say something, the Navy would have known exactly where to concentrate its search, rather than randomly combing hundreds of miles of ocean.

Harold must have wondered later what might have happened had he provided the exact longitude and latitude of his sighting, thus speeding up the search. The horrible thought that his inaction may have contributed to the death of ten men had relentlessly tormented him across the span of 54 years.

In spite of this revelation, I'm afraid my next question wouldn't qualify me for the diplomatic service.

"Did you know about the Martin Mariner flying boat that went after them and didn't come back?"

"Oh, my God. No." Harold suddenly looked like an air mattress dropped on a tack, and I'm afraid I did nothing to patch the leak.

"Why, through all this time, didn't you at least follow the story?"

A naked self-justification that had been guiding his thoughts for more than five decades surfaced instantly.

His back straightened, he glared at me, and snapped. "Look, this was a Navy problem. I was Army-Air Force."

He turned and headed for the door.

I chased after him and for the second time, grabbed his arm. He looked down at my hand, and so did I. This was not like me. I let go.

"Look, if you'd said something back in forty-five, it's possible more search planes would have flown into limbo with them. Maybe your silence saved lives." My lame attempt to help prop up his old rationalization got about as far as the end of his nose.

"I'm sorry, if I seem judgmental. I realize you're just looking for an answer to the fate of those planes. If you leave your address I'll send some information."

"No," he said flatly.

"Ok." I jammed a House of Mystery brochure into this hand. "You can find me here if you need to talk. I promise not to use your name."

He took the brochure, but I never heard from him, and I'm sure I never will. I watched him climb up to the parking lot, and turn to an elderly lady waiting for him. Together, they walked out of sight toward their car. For a brief moment, I thought of sneaking up for a look at his license plate as they drove by the gate.

Then I asked myself, *What if I find him? Do I stake out his house? Turn myself into a stalker?* With great sadness, I went out into the yard and took over my tour from Clare.

The search for Flight 19 and the missing flying boat was enormous. It's been portrayed as the largest sea search ever conducted. Hundreds of planes and ships turned over every piece of kelp across a wide span of the Atlantic, and didn't find so much as an oil slick. The Navy's final report ran 400 pages, and boiled down to no more than the fact that six planes were gone. Twenty-three men were assumed dead.

Although no trace of the search and rescue plane was found, its vanishing may have a conventional explanation. Observers aboard a steamship, the Gaines Mills, reported a midair explosion at about 8:00 PM that night. The Martin Mariner flying boats had a reputation as accidents waiting to happen among crews who called them "flying gas tanks". The stink of fuel within the fuselage of these aircraft discouraged the most ardent smoker from firing up a Chesterfield, and engendered real worries of electric sparks, that could cause the very thing reported by the Gaines Mills. The report from the ship pinpointed the explosion within a few minutes of arc, yet the Lost Patrol mystery also swirls about the rescue plane's disappearance, since not even a seat cushion was found floating where a huge debris field should have been.

The disappearance of Flight 19 is but one report of many incidents regarded as being beyond the normal in this area of ocean. This story though, is the defining tale that has made the name, Bermuda Triangle a part of our modern lexicon. The area itself stretches from the islands of Bermuda, to Miami, then to just southeast of Puerto Rico. From there the line returns to Bermuda to complete the triangle. Within this area come hundreds of claims of strange, mysterious incidents. Others look at the same stories, and claim nothing unexplained has happened.

I didn't ask Harold if he ever heard the name, Bermuda Triangle, but I think most of us have, so

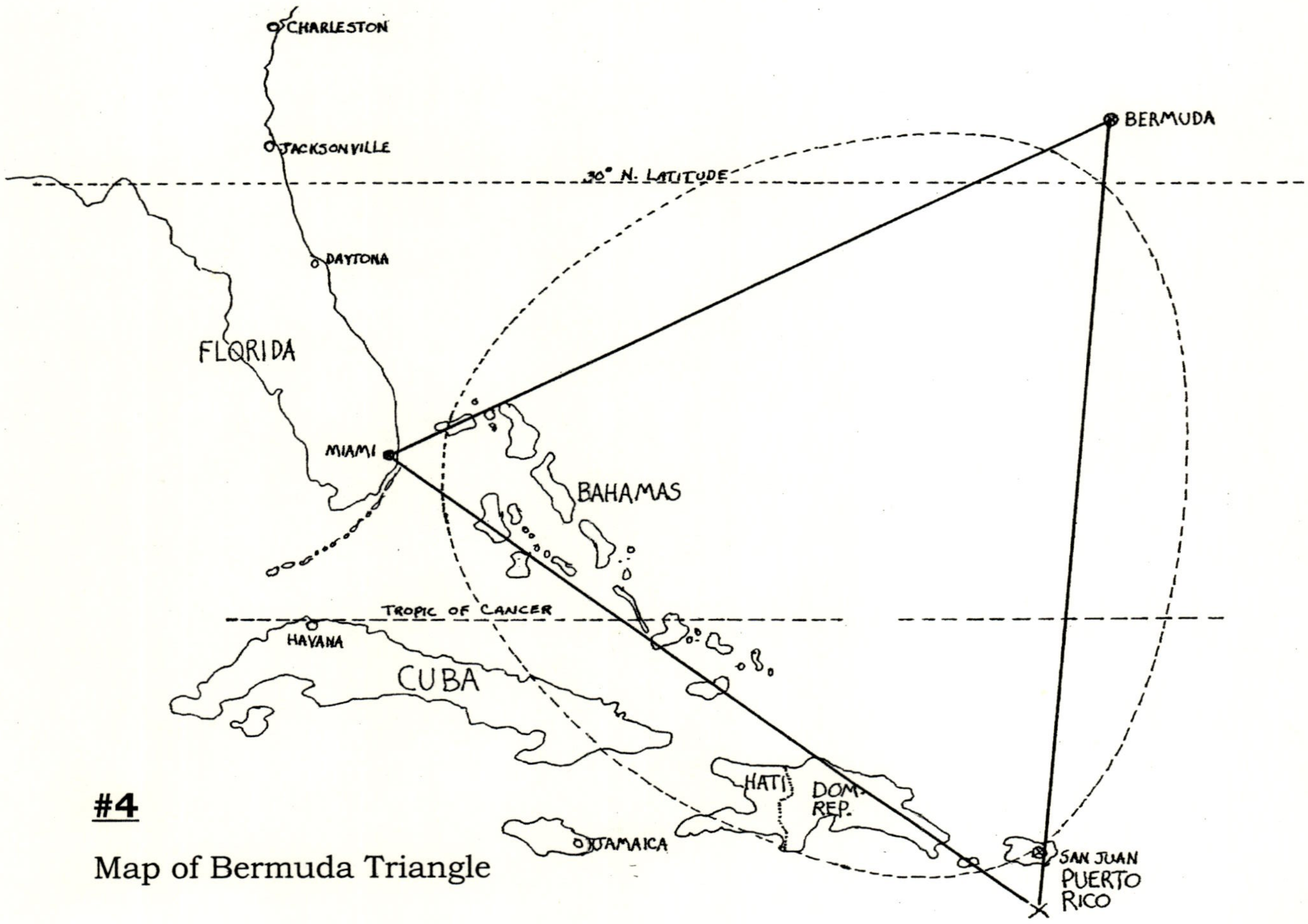

#4
Map of Bermuda Triangle

it isn't my intention to detail more incidents. Suffice it to say that examples range from unexplained disappearances, to overt impingements on reality, such as an airliner vanishing off radar only to reappear, and then after it lands, timepieces on the plane disagree with those on the ground by ten minutes or so.

The first public knowledge of these odd occurrences was reported in an article published in a 1964 Argosy Magazine, by a writer named Vincent H. Gaddis. Hot on the trail of the Gaddis piece came another, better known writer, Ivan T. Sanderson. In other magazine articles, he affirmed that the Bermuda anomaly was but one of ten such places spaced regularly about the Planet. Sanderson called these places, "vile vortices", and because of the nature of his discoveries, I developed my theory.

There is no lack of theories. In 1973 even the Encyclopedia Britannica made note of this wedge-shaped spot. In the same year, John Wallace Spencer published the book, *The Limbo of the Lost*. In 1974 Charles Berlitz climbed on Spencer's efforts with his huge best seller, *The Bermuda Triangle*. In 1975 the inevitable debunking occurred in the form of Lawrence D. Kusche's book, *The Bermuda Triangle Mystery Solved*.

Some are fascinated by the mystery, which leads others to become fascinated by the fascination of what they consider no mystery.

If a plane crashes off the coast of California, or if a ship wrecks near Maine, pieces of the wrecks frequently are found which explain the fates of the people and machines involved. When a boat struggles into port after a storm, its mast broken and its hull damaged, it's easy to see that wind and sea, acting with predicable violence, caused the damage. We expect these things as a consequence of living in a real stub-your-toe universe. However, when there are no clues, or if the clues provided make no sense, what can be done? Some look deeper, and some do not.

It's hard to avoid rock-solid reality which states that since missing ships sink and missing planes crash, all missing ships sink and all missing planes crash.

On the other hand, it's fun to wander off into an area that doesn't always correspond to standard concepts of what looks to be rock-solid reality. Think of a chair from a physicist's outlook— a bunch of whirling atoms with immense distances between them. How solid a barrier can such an obstruction be between a person's backside and the floor?

Many nonstandard solutions have been offered to explain the mystifying aspects of the Bermuda Triangle. Some surmise that the lost continent of Atlantis lies beneath those waters, and that functioning esoteric machinery, or that even living inhabitants of the sunken civilization are responsible for the disappearances. Another theory claims UFOs from other worlds use the area as a hunting ground for human specimens. Others hypothesize a time or interdimensional warp, cosmic rays, some sort of antigravitation effect tossing selected things into outer space. Or giant firestorms of ball lightning which incinerate everything into dust, whirlpools, really bad clear air turbulence, sea serpents, huge tidal waves, waterspouts, earthquakes, seaquakes, localized nasty weather, modern pirates active in the drug traffic, even a mind over matter psychokinesis effect.

By now, the reader may have deduced that I am going to introduce the concept of a vortex to explain the Bermuda Triangle. Well, 25 plus years ago, I believed the vortex concept nicely explained this view of the unexplainable. I don't believe that any more. Belief isn't necessary. I like my theory best, not because it's mine, but because in light of the unfolding discovery of the unconventional way this world is made up, it just makes sense.

In the time of Copernicus and Galileo the notion of a round world no longer at the center of the Universe was rabidly resisted. The conclusions drawn by this work will be similarly resisted. There will be those who will not accept a notion of world structure other than that with which they feel comfortable. Like Harold's pervasive fear of authority, some in the presence of unconventional ideas, will fear infinity closing in about them, robbing them of a hard place to stamp their feet.

To dull the edge of this fear, the physicist's view of a wispy, infinite chair of whirling atoms can again be consulted. Having found one's self living in an infinity where atoms have to align immense distances between them to keep one's rear end off the floor, one's place is found to always be at the center of the Universe. A hard place to stamp a foot will be there for as long as it's needed.

There are several pieces of observational evidence to fit into the mosaic of the Triangle mystery. As first pointed out by Ivan Sanderson, the Bermuda Triangle zone is but one of several such areas located about the globe. The second best known spot where disappearances take place is located just east of the East China Sea, and south of Japan. This area is almost as infamous as the Bermuda Triangle, and offers a small clue when seen on a map. Both mystery zones lay between the same lines of latitude, varying between seventeen degrees north latitude, and thirty-three degrees north latitude.

At times both areas share the same alternate names, the Devil's Triangle, or the Devil's sea. Since these areas are probably part of the original glue that holds the whole production together, we may wish to reassess who gets the blame.

There is another area of similar mystery in a little traveled part of Afghanistan. During World War II this area became much traveled by pilots flying supplies into China "over the hump" of the Himalayas. Out of that adventure came the usual stories of disappearing airplanes, fouled up instruments, and even a sighting of a giant white pyramid in a hidden valley. Sanderson noticed that this area is on nearly the same northern latitudes as the Bermuda, and Devil's sea anomalies.

He also dug up reports of disappearances from an area slightly northeast of Hawaii, and from another spot located near Morocco. Both of these places also rest near the same lines of latitude as the Bermuda Triangle. Thus there are five similar zones lying east and west in the northern hemisphere of the planet Earth where the known laws of reality are now and then knocked out of kilter. These spots are equidistant from each other at about forty-seven hundred miles as the crow flies.

These five Triangle zones are not alone. Off the coast of Chile, with Easter Island slightly southwest of its center is another area of strangeness. Proceeding west, there are stories of strange disappearances from an area north of New Zealand. More stories come from west of Australia and south of Indonesia. Most of the already strange island of Madagascar uses up the area within one of these Triangle zones. In the empty ocean east of Rio de Janeiro provides word of the last spot that finishes Sanderson's list of ten vile vortices.

Each of these Triangles are also on the same exact south latitudinal lines, between seventeen degrees south latitude and thirty-three degrees south latitude, and, as with their northern counterparts, also forty-seven hundred miles apart. Each southern area rests on lines of longitude halfway between their northern hemisphere neighbors, and the distance between any southern Triangle to the nearest northern Triangle is about forty-eight hundred miles.

If the Planet didn't bulge at the equator because of centrifugal spin, these larger areas would be equilateral triangles in the same fashion that each one of the smaller Triangle zones is a sixty-degree equilateral triangle. Twenty years ago the idea of the equator bulge distorting the greater triangles was of only minor interest to me. This bulge shows up now in an astounding string of recently discovered facts that will be covered in a later chapter. Looking back, I wonder how I was able to key into these things without even knowing what I was doing?

Almost certainly the greater notoriety of the Bermuda Triangle is because it is located in one of the most heavily traveled waterways in the world. Think of it as a crapshoot. The heaviest traveled areas of the ten Triangles would naturally generate the greatest number of sevens, because more dice are thrown in these areas than in the others.

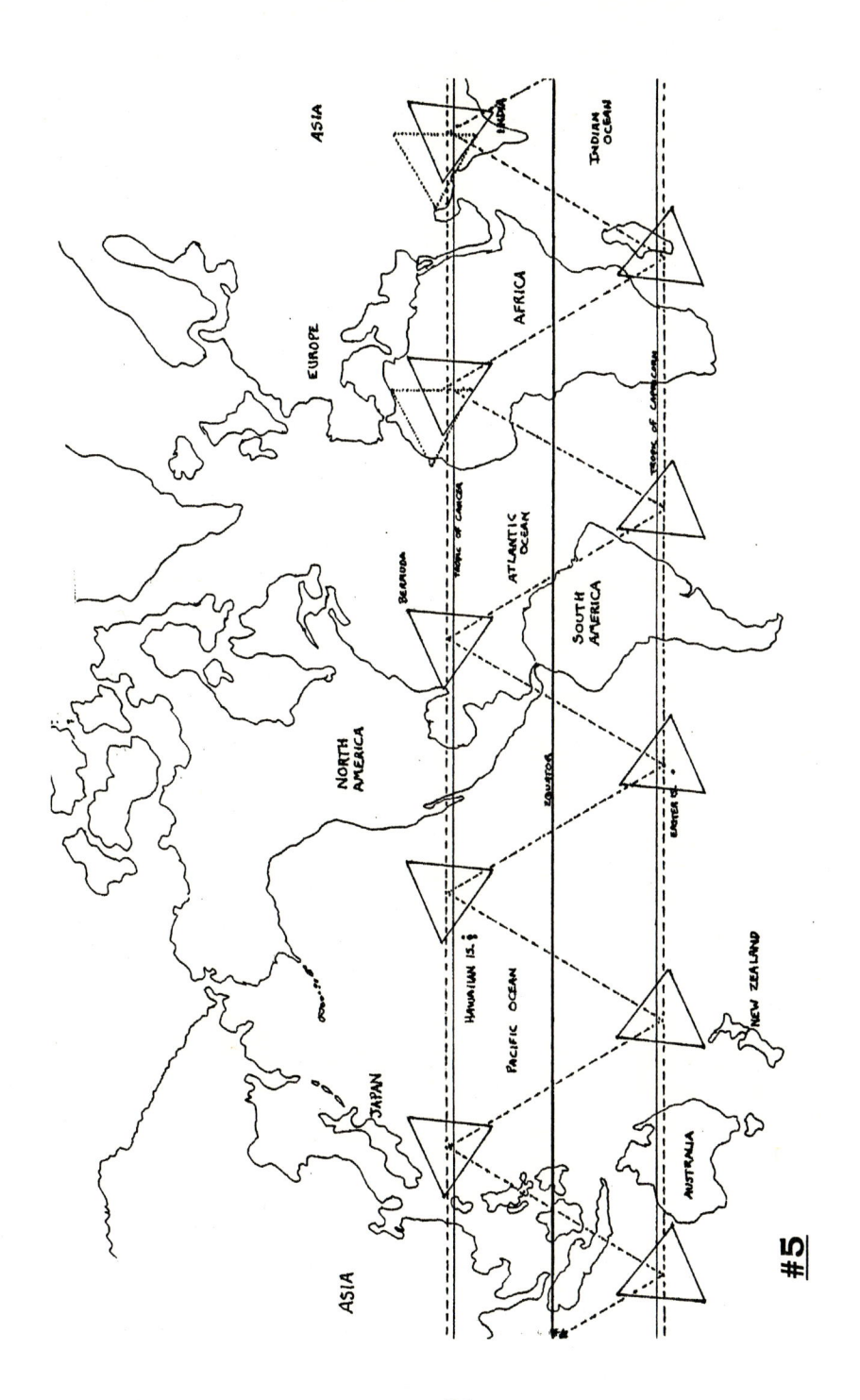

#5

Each of these ten spots is responsible for haunted sea stories of disappearing ships, planes, and people. All but two of them are located over water, with the exceptions being the Morocco and Afghanistan areas. These are also the only areas that do not fit precisely into the forty-seven to forty-eight hundred mile radiuses. The Morocco phenomena is actually found covering most of Algeria, and the Afghanistan effects are talked about as really being in India and Tibet. So the stories that give rise to their suspected existence are really situated northeast of their geometric centers. The probable reason for this is that each of these two areas is located over landmasses, thus causing some sort of geometric, rather than geologic shift.

Even the Oregon Vortex has about it this same kind of built-in *unbalanced* character that seems necessary to keep reality's show on the road. Anyone seeking true perfection, should consider what might happen if a balanced perfection ever was attained. A reality not seeking balance, *is* balance. Friction would no longer exist. With no differing points of view, there would be no view. When the infinity snake grabs its own tail, perfection starts, and everything else stops. As they say south of the border, *nada.*

We're lucky that infinity makes us contend with things like friction. Friction made us invent grease.

To be sure, infinity is the great unbalancer that gives us all this grief, but it also makes everything work.

Some of the strangest facts I deal with in this book are the semantic relationships found in the very language used to name these areas. The term Bermuda Triangle is actually a misnomer, because when the disappearances and strange events are plotted on a map they extend beyond the sides of the triangle. In terms of the plotted events, the Triangle is actually a circle or a lozenge shape, yet the language turns around and describes beautifully the relationship of all ten areas to each other. The term triangle seems to be the unconscious application of an apt description, which could not be known on a conscious level when the thing was named. This is a human phenomena verging on mass telepathy, and it will visit us again in a rather spectacular fashion.

These Triangles present a picture of a wide angular belt around the fat part of the Earth. Spread along both Tropic lines and across the equator, they leave us with a world that is split in thirds. The picture of the planet presented by Sanderson seemed awkward. It appeared as neither a sphere nor a pyramid of triangles. Something was missing, and that's why I looked north and south.

The Earth's axis poles are about the same distance from these Triangle areas as the areas are from each other. Why should the poles be left out of the equation? It seemed to me they should be an integral part of the whole strange picture.

Toss in the Planet's poles and Sanderson's discoveries make the Earth resemble a geometric solid called an icosahedron, or because all the Triangle points are plotted on a sphere, an icosahedral. The Greek name, icosahedron, refers to an object with twelve points and twenty sides made up of equilateral triangles.

The poles are not without a few odd stories of their own. Some of the irregularities reported about the Poles, especially the North Pole, involve the migration of bears, caribou, musk ox, and other birds, animals and insects to the north as winter approaches. Some explorers have said that above eighty degrees latitude the weather seems to get warmer, and the closer one approaches the North Pole the warmer it becomes. A tale is told of a ship that attempted to sail to the North Pole and was driven back by a dust storm. In the very far north, areas of colored snow have been examined, and the strange coloration was caused by vast amounts of pollen evidently blown in by a north wind. When the Eskimos were first asked where they came from, they pointed north and related a story of their ancestors arriving by large birds.

United States Navy Rear Admiral Richard E. Byrd, after his 1947 fight over the North Pole spoke almost mystically of the "...land beyond the Pole.

REGULAR ICOSAHEDRON

EARTH ICOSAHEDRAL

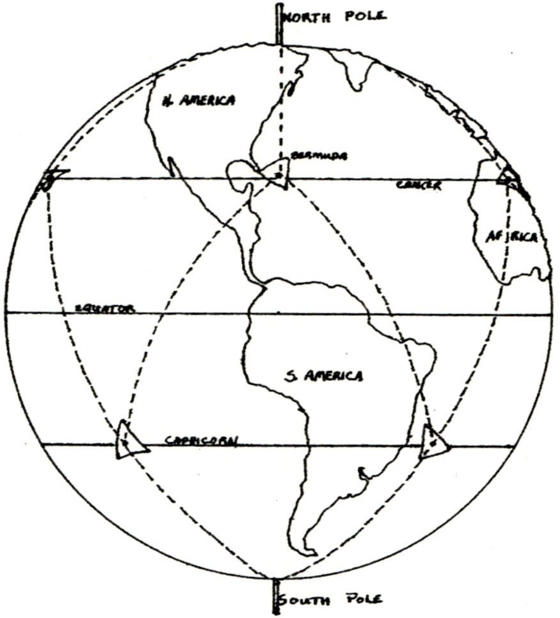

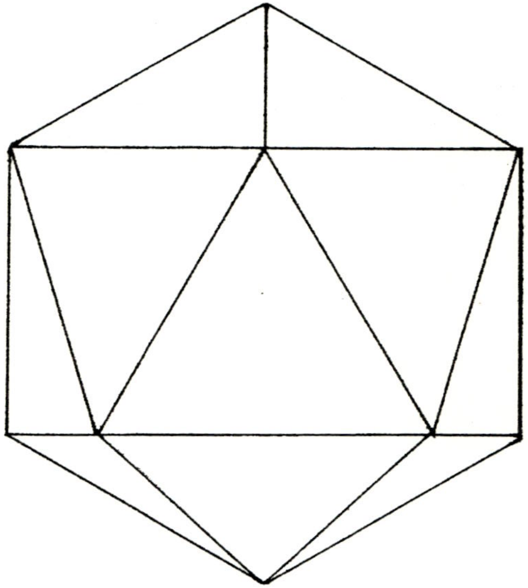

#6

That area beyond the Pole is the center of the great unknown." These are decidedly enigmatic statements when it's realized that no land exists

Where Admiral Byrd spoke of seeing land. It's all water and ice. Intercepted radio messages, reported in the newspapers of the time, told of green mountains and even a large animal resembling a hairy mammoth crashing through the brush beneath the plane. According to maps, beneath the supposed position of Byrd's airplane there was no place for brush to grow through which a mammoth might crash.

The above odd facts have been responsible for a theory that views this planet, and maybe all planets, to be hollow. In this construct, the Earth has a central sun keeping things inside nice and cozy. It has inhabitants who fly out of fourteen-hundred-mile wide holes at the poles in flying saucers to make sure the untrustworthy outer-worlders aren't about to blow everything to smithereens with atom bombs.

Well, think about it. How could the Great Ice Barrier be formed unless interior rivers flowing to the outside provide freezable fresh water? And how do those bits of gravel and rocks end up in the ice pack, if not from the riverbeds of the interior? The Hollow Earth Theory was formulated before satellites began taking long range pictures of Earth, and since those fourteen hundred mile holes don't seem to photograph well, it probably no longer has many proponents.

But, what about all those just mentioned aberrations of nature? What about polar bears heading north to get warmer in the winter? And what about Admiral Byrd? What the heck happened to him?

Briefly, Admiral Byrd loaded up his plane with gas as close to the North Pole as he could get a fuel dump. He then flew the plane grid north, straight at the spinning axis of the planet. Ostensibly, he flew over the North Pole, and then beyond some seventeen hundred miles, turned around, and retraced his route back to the base.

In 1956, the Navy and Admiral Byrd did the same thing in the Antarctic. Presumably with better equipment, he flew some twenty-three hundred miles beyond the South Pole. In the words of Admiral Byrd, "The present expedition has opened up a vast new territory." It seemed to some that this new territory might have been better opened up by coming in from the edge of the continent rather than crossing the pole and going clear across it. Byrd referred to the land beyond the South Pole as, "...that enchanted continent in the sky, land of everlasting mystery!" A strange statement to describe a twenty-three hundred mile vista of snow and ice.

Allow me to oversimplify, and bend Physics just a bit. As we reckon the passage of time, the Earth spins its near 24,000-mile circumference about its axis once every twenty-four hours. Therefore we can say that a person standing on the equator is traveling almost one thousand miles per hour in reference to an arbitrarily fixed point in space. We'll put another person in this mental experiment one foot away from the exact center of the North Pole. This fellow is only one short step from the other side of the Earth, but we want the planet to carry him all the way around to where he and the other experimenter at the equator started. For our guy at the Pole, it's going to be a short, excruciatingly slow ride of twenty-four hours. His circle will be six feet, and his velocity will be three inches per hour. The demonstrator on the equator will get back to the starting point in the same 24 hours, but he must travel some 21 million times farther than the man at the top of the world, even though they're both riding the same body. The equator racer has to clip right along to keep up to the slowpoke at the pole.

I wonder if Aesop had this in mind when he spoke of hares and tortoises?

This simplistic mental experiment might shed a little light on what may have happened to Admiral Byrd. By aiming his airplane directly at the spinning axis of the Earth, Byrd's motion was at 90-degrees to the movement of the planet. The velocity of the plane was orthogonal, or at a right angle to the velocity of the Earth's spin. At some point long before he reached the pole, his plane exceeded the speed of the planet below him. As a consequence it may be that Byrd never even got to the physical pole, much less flew beyond it. As the plane maintained a constant speed, the space, or the continuum around it slowed, but from a mechanical viewpoint, not the ground below. The crew, from their position, didn't even notice the moment something stopped, and maybe even backed up. Like the miners who worked in the Oregon Vortex without paying attention to their surroundings, Byrd, without even noticing it, may have veered off toward somewhere else. If the Earth itself is seen as a vortex, then the only difference between the Oregon anomaly and the Planet is one of size and intensity.

    The reader shouldn't condemn my little mental experiment to quickly. Einstein came to relativity via what were once considered some pretty weird thought experiments. When he noticed his train, for instance, was traveling against the Earth's rotation, instead of wondering how soon the train would get to the station, he considered the amount of time the station would need to get to the train.

    Einstein theorized that clocks at the rim of a spinning disk run slower than clocks at the axis. We are all a second or two older than an astronaut who has been zinging around the Earth at 18,000 miles per hour, because of his or her greater speed and the lack of gravity. One shouldn't forget those ten seconds a year I have on everyone else because I hang around inside a whirling energy sphere.

Travel far enough, fast enough in a straight line, Einstein theorized, and we'll end up right back where we started.

Let's say that Byrd's 1947 airplane was tooling along at 180 knots per hour. At the position where his speed matched the spin velocity of the ground below, the plane's motion began to skid in relation to the right angle of the Earth's motion. So long as his direction remained grid north, every foot beyond would see the relative speed of the plane increasing exponentially from the viewpoint of those of us who just sort of putt along further down the body of the Planet. If someone in Seattle had been watching Byrd with a magic telescope, he would have seen the plane moving increasingly faster until its motion became only a blur. Onboard, however, the pilot would always read his air speed indicator as 180 knots.

We now have Byrd traveling across a rapidly narrowing space that is adjusting to Einstein's relativistic idea of time dilation. Perhaps, the faster he went from our point of view, the further he had to go from his. Theoretically, the exact center of a spinning disk, or sphere, does not move at all because it reaches a point where the smallest particle of the quantum finally gives way to infinity.

Byrd and his crew were flying into the eye of a huge vortex, and the only way they could have crossed the actual North Pole while caught in this strict orthogonal motion between planet and plane would have been to reach the local relative speed of light. If he had done that, he would have breached infinity and we would have no more than a few radio broadcasts to cause a greater mystery to his having vanished forever.

The plane and its crew would not have dissipated into their constituent atoms, or turned into energy as would happen if a physical entity actually achieved relativistic light speed of 186,281 miles per second. From Byrd's point of view they would be just as alive as ever. They would not, however, still be on the planet Earth. A person in such a situation, if he knew what to do, might still turn around and come back. This severe event did not occur to Byrd, but if it had, we wouldn't even have realized he'd been gone. Whatever the length of time away, it would be but an instant to the person in Seattle with the magic telescope.

Unhappily, those poor guys on Flight 19 do not have a realistic option of coming home. No, I didn't mix my tenses, and I deliberately used the phrase "realistic option" in juxtaposition to the phrase "of coming home". The Earth is now too far away for their equipment to reach, and even if they had enough fuel to make it happen, 1945 is hopelessly beyond attainment.

There are lots of vortex energy whirls and the big ones, if their structure is fiddled with, can provide some surprising, mostly unwanted results. The vortexes themselves, whether we consider them big or small, are not in themselves pathways to other realities. But when one gets crosswise of their special physics, by accident or on purpose, they can open portals right on the edge of their connections with other realities. One of the things Litster did write in *Notes and Data*, is that "...the energy-wave involved in both the Vortex and the Terralines is transverse." We regular folks should read the word transverse as, *crosswise.*

Can these vortexes really open such portals and cause grief to us poor mortals who are otherwise just minding our own business? If the literature on odd occurrences is even only half truthful, the answer is a resounding Yes.

Consider the story of a Midwestern farmer disappearing into thin air in front of his wife, children, and the family doctor. In illustration #7 consider that all the participants exist in the same universe labeled, B. In panel 1, the farmer is out in the pasture with his horse. He sees the doctor coming down the hill in a buckboard, and turns to walk over to where his wife and kids wait in the yard.

In panel 2, the farmer steps into the unseen line of demarcation of a vortex that has long been benign, but unknown circumstances, for a very brief moment have caused it to rotate open a portal. The poor farmer steps into a trillion to one shot, and his family and doctor see him vanish. From his point of view he sees his family disappear. He

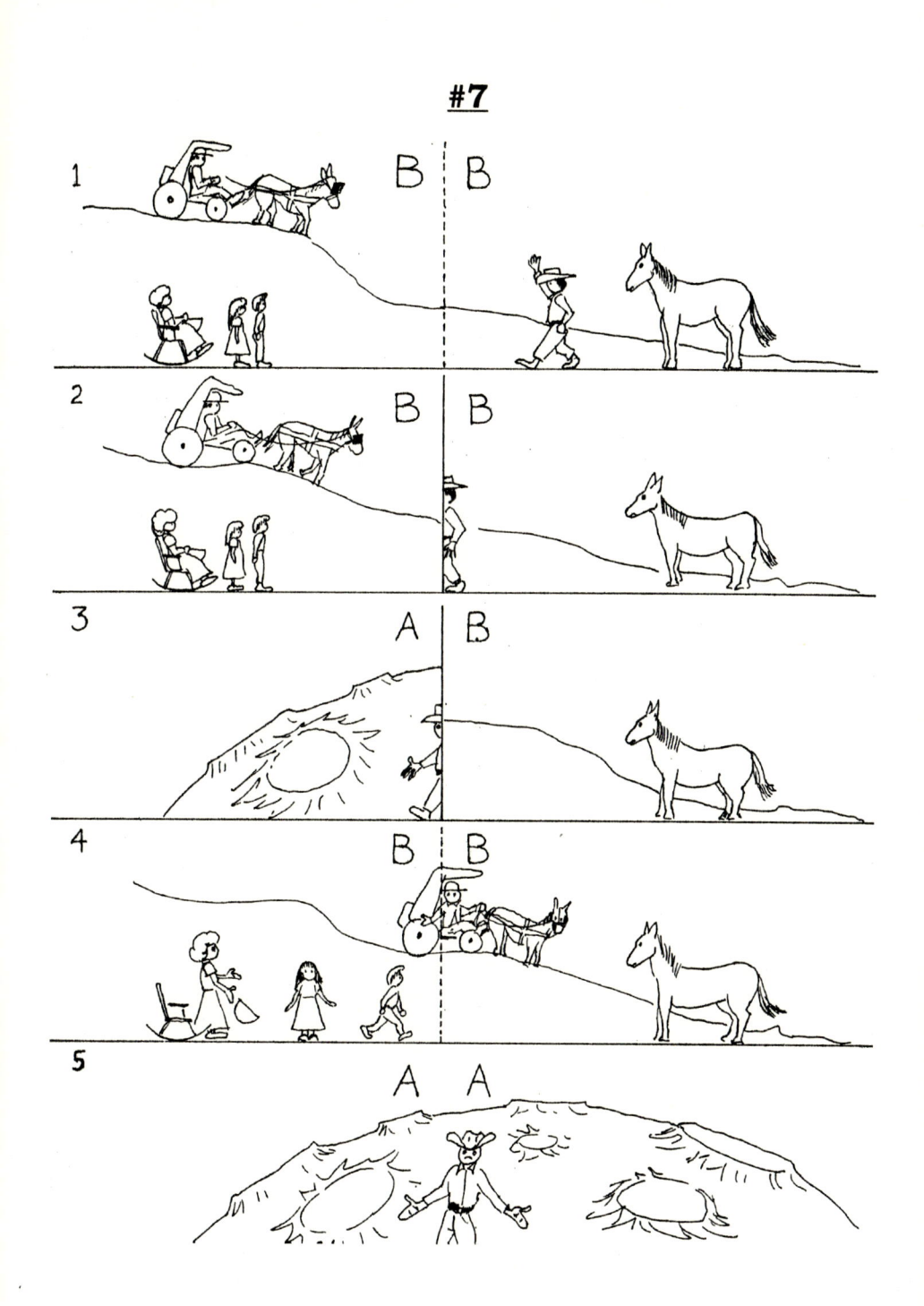

#7

runs forward to save them and seals his own fate by rushing into Universe A, panel 3.

In panel 4, he is gone much to the horror of the onlookers, and the vortex closes the portal. The farmer is forever lost to his family and becomes the unwilling resident of another world. If this world represents a lunar type of environment, it's certain he didn't survive.

This fate supposedly happened in 1880 to a Tennessee farmer by the name of David Lang. There is no documentation to prove that any of the participants ever existed, yet this is a story whose elements force it to be looked at as if it actually occurred. For instance, the last part of the tale involves the children hearing their father calling them in the vicinity of his last sighting about a month after the incident. Whether the entire story is true or not, this aspect of it has a strikingly similar ending as the Flight 19 incident. Quite some time after every plane in Flight 19 had to have run out of gas, a radio operator swears he heard the Flight's call sign being given and then nothing more.

I need here to digress to black holes. A black hole is considered the remnants of a giant star that has used up its fuel and collapsed in on itself. The material of such a thing would weigh so much, and be so dense that a spoonful of it would weigh many tons and sink in a concrete slab like a rock in water. It would actually pull the slab into itself, but that's another story. A black hole doesn't just sit around grabbing anything that comes near; it is rotating around an axis just like more normal celestial bodies. It is so dense that nothing can escape its gravitational field, and this field forms an outer boundary called an event horizon. The event horizon can be thought of as a knife-edge line across which no event can be witnessed because even light cannot escape.

At the Oregon Vortex such a line isn't nearly as extreme and is called the line of demarcation, because the events across it can be witnessed. They just appear a little strange to someone expecting the continuance of normality.

There are respectable scientific theories that black holes, under certain circumstances, can create the popular idea of wormholes in space. Thus science signs on, if only gingerly, to the science fiction writer's idea of hyperspace, whereby the writer has his characters travel immense, light-year distances in a very short time.

If something akin to a black hole's event horizon is in operation in the Bermuda Triangle, the reported radio transmission an hour after the planes would have run out of gas makes sense. One of the planes, just as it straddles the knife-edge event horizon at a slight angle sends a message. Because the demarcation line is receding almost as fast as the radio waves only a fraction of the transmission gets out, and that part takes hours to battle past the line before the event horizon and radio waves reach the same velocity.

The farmer's voice is heard calling his kids names a month after he disappeared. Perhaps, as he rushed toward them he was calling their names thinking something was happening to them rather than himself. If a radio wave takes hours to get out from the demarcation/event horizon line, it shouldn't seem strange that a voice would take a month. If there were an atmosphere between here and the Moon, a month at the speed of sound would be just about right.

There is another story which is probably fiction but illustrative of this same thing. A New York man of the 1890's takes a stroll to enjoy an after dinner cigar which his wife won't let him have in the house. On the street, he steps into a vortex just like the one that ate the farmer. Unlike the farmer who ran forward when he noticed something wrong, this man stops exactly on the line of demarcation, turns around and rushes back. If a radio wave takes a few hours, and a voice takes a month, a man walking or running might take years to get back.

According to the story, 60 years.

He supposedly appeared on the streets of 1950 New York, where he panicked, ran into the street, and got run down by a taxi. Supposedly this discovery came by comparing an 1890's missing persons report to the 1950 accidental death report.

#8

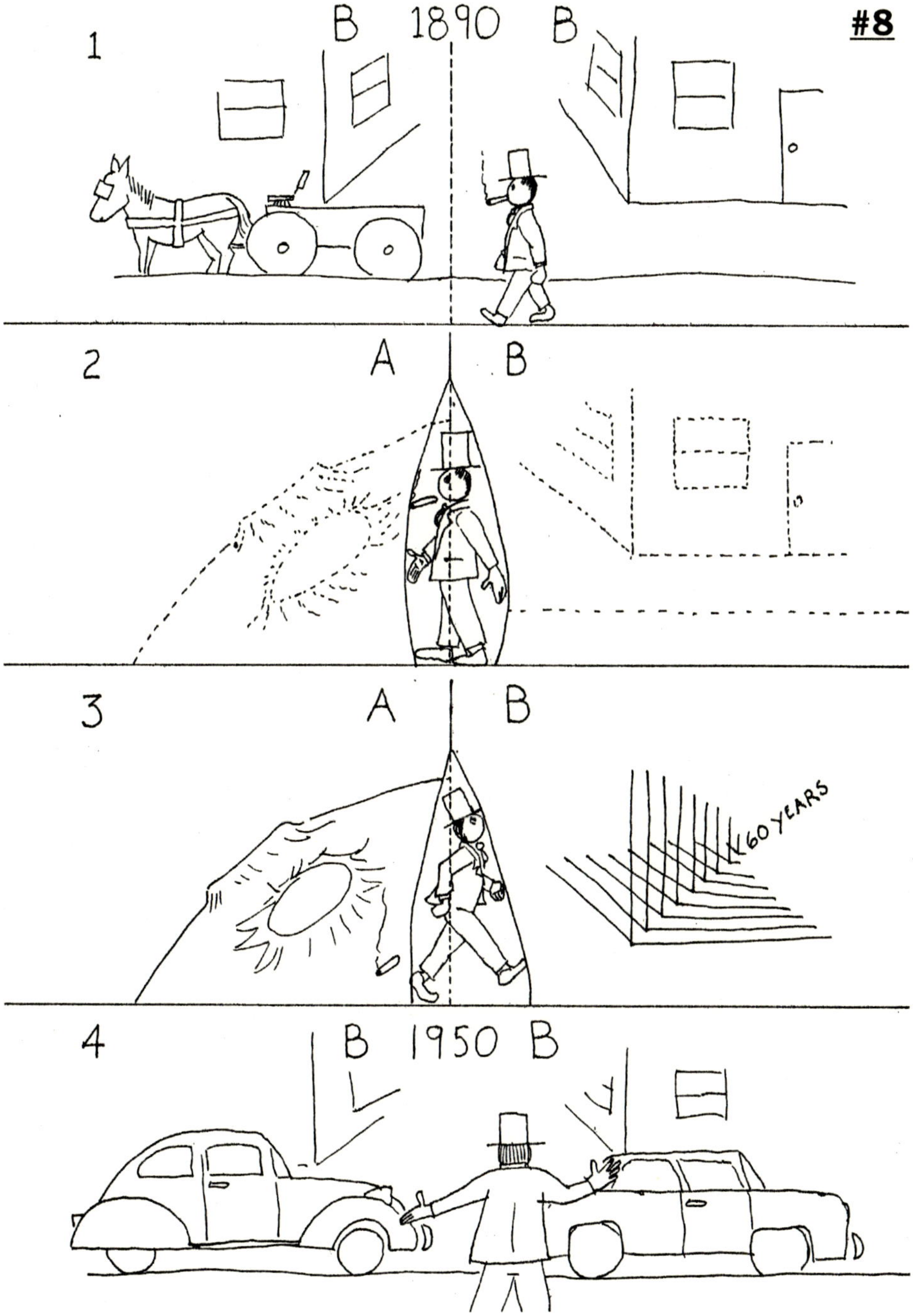

The victim carried some rather unorthodox identification claiming he was one Rudolph Fentz and lived on 50th Avenue in New York. The story is reportedly told by a retired police captain, Hubert V. Rihm, and certainly has the ring of a story that could be true.

Other than stories about disappearances, and even appearances, a wonderful example of two entities from different worlds occupying the same space exists. In a sense, they waved at each other. Supposedly, in Ohio in the early 1960's, a pilot was in his private plane flying alongside a low cloud, when out of the cloud comes a pre-World War One flying machine. They dodge each other but not before the wing tip of the modern plane grazes the side of the antique. The pilot loses sight of the biplane, which flees back into the cloud. He turns for home, and after landing, files an angry report with the FAA. The authorities look, but are unable to find the old airplane and its reckless pilot.

Months later, under a pile of rotting hay, an old relic of a flying machine is found in a barn being torn down. An aged logbook is still in the cockpit, and its last entry records a near miss with a strange silver flying machine. The entry is dated, 1911, and there is a long rip in the fuselage fabric in which is contained tiny flakes of silver paint.

These are interesting stories, and if true, confirmatory evidence. If they are not true the very manner of the telling is strange, because they ought to be true considering the descriptive detail with which they are told. Again, the language use seems to provide unconscious knowledge that cannot be known on a conscious level. These stories make sense even if they are fabrication, because they relate exactly what might be expected if a human being is at the wrong place when vortexes collide.

As a model, studying the benign Gold Hill Vortex can tell us a great deal about what happened to those who fell victim to the more "vile" vortexes. The men and machines of Flight 19 were composed of solid matter, and though matter can be altered, it cannot be destroyed. Therefore they did not vanish into nothingness, but had to conform to the universally accepted laws of relativity, even if it took a slight detour around them. Flight 19 went on in reality, but obviously not our reality. Where did they go?

It is not enough to say they fell into the fourth, fifth, sixth, or any dimension the reality of which we can't recognize or logically number. I could be evasive and say they were squeezed through a time warp, but I don't know what a time warp is, even if the language is properly describing such a thing.

I do have a fair idea what a vortex whirl is though, and I assume they got crosswise of a really big one. By comparing the Gold Hill Vortex to the much larger vortex of the Earth, and the mechanics of what did, and could have happened to Admiral Byrd, it should be possible to deduce at least a partial fate for Flight 19. I think I know *what* they ended up in, but I can only surmise a recognizable *where*.

The Gold Hill vortex is measurable and fixed at one geographic location, and from our local point of view, so are the axes of the entire planet. The Bermuda phenomenon, however, seems to be mobile within an area taking up several hundred square miles, but never fixed at a precise and constant point to which anyone might return with accuracy. Even if we wanted to find the darn thing, it won't sit still. The analogy of a vortex being like water going down a bathtub drain still holds up, but in the case of the Bermuda Triangle, the drain hole moves around the bottom of the tub. Also, why are events here selective? Why does just one plane or boat disappear down the drain when others a few miles away remain untouched? Harold claimed his B-17 was only five miles from the flight that vanished from his radarscope.

Gold Hill is fixed on the map, and so far as the Poles are concerned the globe is the map. Consider a thought experiment: A hypothetical person is at a fixed point in space above the North Pole. This person is two-dimensional and can't see three-dimensional objects. Since the Earth cannot be seen by this mythical person, he would only know it exists by noticing the effects of our North Pole as it draws a magnetic image on the face of his flat space map. Because of the Earth's axis tilt of twenty-three degrees, twenty-seven minutes of arc relative to his flat universe, the spinning axis of our planet would trace a circle or lozenge shape; not a static pinpoint, but a moving pinpoint.

One vortex, when aligned at ninety degrees to another vortex, is unapparent unless measured by the proximity of a third vortex at ninety degrees to it. Let's switch from the analogy of a two-dimensional space dweller above the North Pole to the idea of an imperceptible fourth-dimensional planet aligned at ninety degrees to our reality. Two-dimensional people can't see three-dimensional stuff, so three-dimensional people can't see this really, really big four-dimensional planet connected at ninety-degrees to the Earth. Some might think of these twisted, ninety-degree connections as wormholes. I prefer the term, portals. Admiral Byrd, until he turned around and came back, was close to passing through his portal.

From here on, for the purpose of identification, I will call this invisible sphere The Planet Byrd.

Now, let's look at those ten Triangles, one of which is the Bermuda Triangle. Considering that they are also aligned at ninety degrees to the Earth, we can't see what's going on there any more than we can see Planet Byrd. I suggest the moving vortex within the Bermuda Triangle is an unseen, much,

much smaller planet spinning and tilting on a polar axis in the same fashion that the Earth does on its axis.

Since Flight 19, commanded by Lt. Taylor, was more successful in getting through this portal than Byrd was through his, I christen *the cause* of the Bermuda Triangle, Planet Taylor.

Planet Taylor's angular motion may or may not have a more complex relationship to the Earth than its orbit being the circumference of our world, but its axis wobble traces an erratic path of strange disappearances on and above the Atlantic Ocean east of Miami.

This explanation is a bit simplistic, yet it describes a very complex set of universes acting with each other under the direction of forces outside our understanding. Unhappily, there is little in the language other than analogy and metaphor that can be used to discuss this phenomenon. We can babble on about parallel universes, time warps, and other dimensions that are outside our ability to comprehend, but these things are not part of our everyday, observable world. So, until we can reach out and take a handful of this stuff, simplistic metaphors will have to function as intellectual roadmaps.

My basic problem is the need to describe something that cannot be seen, and only measured in a subjective way. Forgive me, Albert, while I impose on the folks a short description of Relativity.

There is no fixed point, Einstein told us, from which to view the Universe, or any event in the Universe. Two different observers cannot see and report in exactly the same way an observation of the same event. All observers, no matter how close together, have their own angle from which to watch the chorus line kick. The very telling of my tale is a colossal anisotropic grappling with an intangible as I try to point out what I think is obvious. When I measure an angle in one direction, the danger is that someone else is measuring the same angle from a different direction.

For instance, when I say the vortex at the North Pole (Planet Byrd) is tremendously large, the vortex in the Bermuda Triangle small (Planet Taylor), and the Oregon Vortex tiny, I am defining a problem from our local frame of reference. I think of that moving portal within the Bermuda Triangle as the entryway to a microcosm, and the North Pole portal as the entryway to a macrocosm. If the Earth could be seen from Planet Byrd, its inhabitants would need a really big microscope to bring in the picture. Someone looking up from Planet Taylor on a clear night might see nothing but trillions of spots before his or her eyes.

No matter where the observer is standing, though, the size of everything in the local neighborhood is going to look just right.

So far the data forces our nice round planet into an unseen geometric icosahedron with twenty triangular sides and twelve points of shared five-sided pyramids. From the point of view of our senses and measuring devices that have been constructed from using these senses, this observation seems ridiculous.

It also seems ridiculous that reality within the Oregon Vortex does not always correspond with normality. The Vortex field, and its eerie perception shifts, are not wholly classifiable by familiar labels like gravity or magnetism.

In *Notes and Data*, Litster pointed out that the Vortex is not electromagnetic in nature, and the proof of this contention is that a regular magnetic compass functions just fine inside the area. We are, however, able to demonstrate one overt exception to this rule.

When a compass is brought close to the surface of any of those small round platforms where Litster claimed Terralines cross, and where I dowse for auras, the instrument drastically moves away from north. This is probably a form of what is called a ground effect. For instance, when searching for treasure, a metal detector must be adjusted to screen out natural minerals in the local ground; otherwise the background signal can mask a treasure signal. A simple compass is not delicate enough to be affected by these minerals, so something powerful is going on at these ground positions.

Since the land in the Vortex is on a rising slope, the exact center of its spherical field is perhaps 45 feet underground. Using a variety of methods, it took me quite a while to locate on the ground the exact axis, or that spot where the center is exactly beneath the feet, or 180 degrees in line with a standing body. Once I found this position, several more unknowns that Litster probably knew about, but didn't reveal, fell into place.

After I discovered that smaller, 55-foot primary vortex surrounding the old assay shack, I went looking for its corona. Following the one-sixth rule, I expected the primary vortex would have a corona of a little more than nine feet, but no detection method showed such a second demarcation line. This lack of a corona was a real frustration, until I located the exact axis of the Vortex.

At the axis is yet another vortex, and it measures just a tad more than *nine* feet across its diameter.

As Clare had correctly pointed out, this inner circle is a dead zone like the eye of a hurricane. It does have a distinct line of demarcation, but it is a line being constantly drawn by a small, rapidly spinning force, which has a diameter of about 38 inches, and is in orbit about the perpendicular axis of the larger vortex. The orbit of this whirling force has a circumference of a little more than 27 feet. The radius of the 55-foot primary vortex is a little more than 27 feet. Litster measured the corona of the larger vortex at one-sixth its diameter, or 27 and a half feet. The assay shack was built

#9

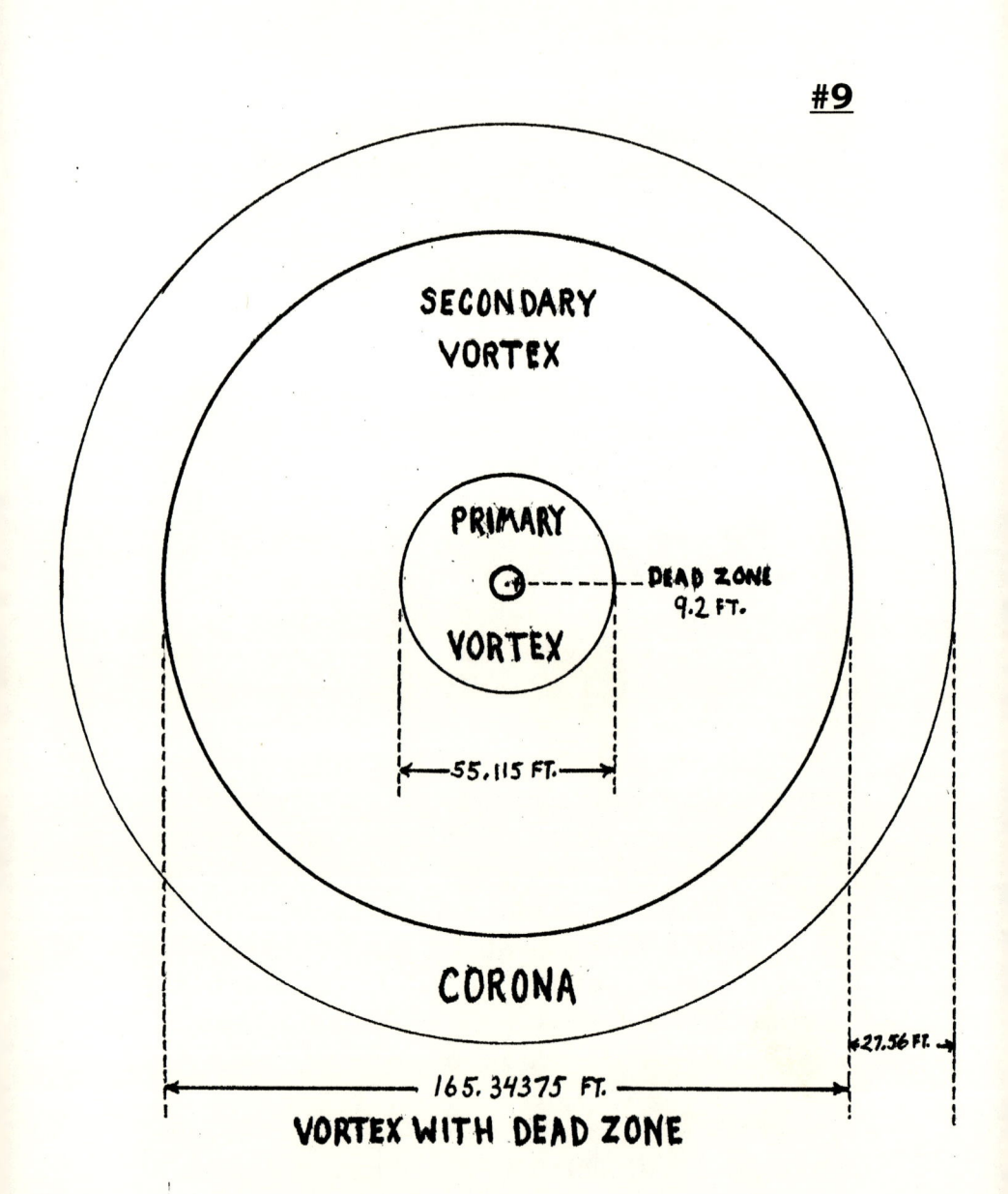

SECONDARY VORTEX

PRIMARY VORTEX

DEAD ZONE 9.2 FT.

←— 55.115 FT. —→

CORONA

←27.56 FT.→

←——— 165.34375 FT. ———→

VORTEX WITH DEAD ZONE

more than 20 years before Litster did any measuring, but since the Vortex seems to affect the human unconscious, perhaps it should not be surprising to learn the Old Gray Eagle Mining Company constructed the building, which later became the House of Mystery, with a floor length of 27 and a half feet.

I do not know how fast this 38-inch entity is spinning, but it is completing the 27-foot orbit in a tiny bit less than two hours. Two hours is one-twelfth of our day of 24 hours, which equals one-sixth of the Earth's half-spin radius. If we consider the 27-foot orbit to equal an Earth year, a mathematical guess would be that the spin rate is about 3 revolutions per minute. Since this thing, from our point of view, is comprised of nothing but whirling electrons, or a little vortex, the half-spin rate would double to six revolutions per minute. At the site, though, the spin rate seems much, much faster.

Because the orbit rate is easily timed, it provides a benchmark tool that allows a more thorough investigation of other abnormalities within the Vortex. One of these probes appears to show that over the course of that two-hour orbit the entire place shifts about 12 degrees of arc left and right. Up and down, as seen by the difference in the hill slope, seems permanently deviated by the same 12 degrees when observed from a north to south angle.

A person can wander around for days, months, or years inside the Vortex and not notice this shifting because he or she is part of the movement. However, by standing still for a period of time, under certain circumstances, and in certain places, the phenomenon becomes starkly obvious. It's not a circumstance that hits one between the eyes, but is evident as a slow folding and unfolding, accompanied by a chill creeping up the spine.

The continuum inside the Gold Hill, or Oregon Vortex can actually be seen to undulate to the rhythm of the planet, if not the Universe.

If there is a portal to anywhere within this special area, it opens and closes in a little less than four minutes, and takes up twelve degrees of arc. The timing would be longer in the Bermuda Triangle, much longer at the Poles, but the same twelve degrees of arc is a universal constant for all vortexes everywhere.

Time, in this equation, equals Pi.

3

PORTALS TO ANYWHEN

Consider the relatively uncomplicated job of determining boundaries from known values.

A surveyor, asked to find a straight line across the Earth's surface, sets up a tripod holding a little telescope with crosshairs called a surveyor's level, or theodolite. He or she aligns and levels the instrument over a longitude and latitude mark, allows for the local compass declination, then sights the scope on a tall, marked stick held at a known distance by a member of the surveyor's crew. The holder of the stick moves side to side at the direction of the person peering through the instrument, until told to stop when the stick and the crosshair match up.

At that point, the stick holder pounds a stake in the ground, then walks ahead, stick and all, to a new position.

The surveyor picks up the surveyor's level, hikes up to the stake, and resets the instrument to take a new setting on the stick holder's stick. This process continues until the straight line is marked for as long as is needed. It's a nice outdoor job, but after one gets on to the mechanics, it can get a little boring.

Now, let's complicate their job.

The survey crew takes a sighting, and then goes to lunch, leaving the equipment right where it is. They return after a half-hour break, and the surveyor resights the last stake just to make sure everything is okay before moving on. A problem is noticed immediately. The stake is now three degrees off. The crew was hungry. Things happen. They take a couple of minutes to realign, and pound in a new stake.

As soon as the stake is in, the surveyor's cell phone rings. It's the home office. The crew waits twenty minutes until the conversation is finished, and the surveyor takes one more look before moving on. The new stake is now two more degrees off. Accusations fly. The crew argues among themselves about who's playing unfunny jokes, and finally decides to bring up the spare theodolite.

They take a sighting with the new instrument, and it's about half a degree off the last sighting. The first level must have gone bad. It takes twenty minutes to pack up the old equipment, and then, to satisfy an itch in the surveyor's belly, one more sighting is taken. The itch is replaced by a feeling of falling. The last stake is two degrees off, but this reading is marching off in the opposite direction. They have five or six stakes out there, and not one of them can be trusted.

This is a scenario that has probably never occurred to 99.999 per cent of surveyors, and that .001 per cent wouldn't admit the experience if it did happen.

This is, however, exactly the kind of thing that occurs within the Oregon Vortex on a continuous basis.

I have made several attempts to draw scale maps of the platforms and buildings in the 165-foot circle, and not one of them is exactly the same as the other. Either my measurements changed each time I took them, or I'm not as good at reading a tape and compass as I thought I was.

The House of Mystery employs a jack-of-all-trades handyman who answers generally to one of three names, Art, Ort, or Heyyou. Art is an older fellow, but don't tell him, it'll hurt his self-image. Among his many talents, is that he is the best storyteller the place ever had, and his best story is the one about measuring boards that don't fit the hole after they are cut.

Art is not one that can be easily led. He and I have a standing disagreement about whether the hill really does look steeper from one end to the other. He's an old logger, and road grader. Hills, he will tell you, always look steeper from the top than from the bottom. Maybe so, but this much?

Another discussion we've had involves something that seems to be happening with Litster's old cement platform on top of the hill. The platform is a foot wide and four feet long. It is aligned on its long axis magnetic north and south, and is also laid perpendicular across the Vortex's main line of demarcation.

Once I had found the center axis of the Vortex, and timed its orbit, I was able to use the platform to experiment on the assumption that the field does not affect compasses. When I stand facing north on any part of the platform holding a compass, nothing is out of the ordinary. No matter how long I stand with the compass needle parallel with the long lines of the platform, or how much time has passed between sightings, the compass needle always points to zero degrees, and directly at the same tree, which is more than eighty feet out of the vortex field.

Art finds nothing wrong with this. It's just what a compass did in the good old days.

The discussion gets more interesting when I turn and face south. With the compass needle still parallel with the sides of the platform, the south, 180-degree end of the instrument, points toward the gift shop more than a hundred feet down the hill. A problem shows up when I walk down to the indicated spot in front of the gift shop, and sight back to where I just came from. If I'm on a north/south line, the arrow should point right at the platform, but it rarely does. In some cases, it deviates by quite a bit. Art says we need something better than a hand-held compass, even if it is a good quality Lensmatic.

After a half an hour, when I return to the platform and resight the compass on the gift shop, it points a few degrees to one side or the other of the first sighting. It's almost like looking down from the fulcrum point at a slow-moving pendulum swinging in a very narrow arc. In the middle of a swing a half hour absence produces a three-degree deviation, but on either end of the swing, sometimes it appears that no movement at all occurred.

Art still wants an instrument that can be locked down. He doesn't trust a shaking hand. I don't disagree, but point out to him that the complete difference when checked through a whole two-hour orbit of that tiny vortex at the axis, is six to eight degrees of arc, back and forth. I don't think my hand shakes that badly.

He concedes this point, and allows that maybe the Vortex does affect the operation of a compass. Then I point out that the compass needle is always parallel to the platform sides, which means that it does not move relative to the Earth's Magnetic Pole. So, I ask, does that mean the solid cement platform pivots, and then swings back as soon as I turn around and face the other way?

We agree this is a silly question. The trouble is…if the experiment is being done correctly…*the only other answer is that the scenery moves!*

If the scenery doesn't stay still, that means that The House of Mystery Vortex distorts its own image. It's really worse than this. If the image is reality, then this movement doesn't relate anything positive about the solid corporeality of good old Planet Earth.

Art wondered what Litster might have had to say about this revolting state of affairs?

Surprisingly, we may know the answer to this question. Litster theorized in Notes and Data that atoms in the Vortex might show aberrations along their axes, which, "…will result in a corresponding change in the physical structure of any object within the field of the Vortex." He also wrote that this sort of blasphemous physics might, "…involve the larger sphere of astronomy."

Evidently, Litster thought this stuff really happens, as opposed to simply being a refracted light show. Had he been around when NASA was at first unable to hit the Moon with its rocket arrows, I wonder if he would have blamed the bad aim on a target that was outside its own image by as much as twelve degrees of arc?

It doesn't take much to jiggle reality.

Back in my Reno chasing days, I was renting a house that came with a monstrous living room table. After the first year, the tabletop was covered with cardboard models of geometric objects, some of which seemed to tinker with the continuum in a subjective fashion. These were the days when pyramid power was in vogue, and I tried all the recommended experiments. My pyramids didn't sharpen razor blades, or even dehydrate organic matter, and I sure didn't notice a pyramid shape produce anything that resembled the normal concept of "power". However, possibilities opened up with the pyramid's ability to make dowsing implements function dramatically well.

When a four-sided pyramid is aligned with one of its flat sides ninety-degrees to magnetic north, the dowsing rods cross themselves when maneuvered over the object's point, or apex. Turn the pyramid ninety-degrees so that a corner points north, and the rods lay in the hands without so much as a wiggle. Whenever someone visited me, I stuck my bent clothes hangers in their hands, and asked them to walk them over the pyramid. I have yet to find the person who does not get a reaction, but from watching people at the Vortex, one day I will.

For a while, I was stuck in the fascination of simply watching the wires cross over pyramids, and then an old friend, named Fred had one rod swing away while the other stayed above the object. After experimenting with this new development, I was forced to the conclusion that different people get different reactions. When Fred walked up to the pyramid from the south or north, the rods did this new trick, but from the east or west direction, something I hadn't tried, his rods crossed. When I approached the pyramid from the east or west, I got Fred's north and south effect. The only discernible difference between us is that Fred is left-handed, and I am right-handed

I pulled my foot out of the mud and began trying different things. I learned that when the pyramid's corners are aligned north and south, that the rods would still react if a magnet was placed inside the hollow shape. Since I was at the beginning of formulating my Bermuda Triangle theory, I made a small icosahedron, stuck it on a pedestal and dowsed it expecting nothing. What I got was one rod moving over the object, and the other swinging away to hit me on the arm. This was my east and west Pyramid reaction. With a bar magnet inside the object, the rods crossed regardless of my direction of approach.

The tabletop soon began to overflow with a variety of cardboard geometric objects, but only the pyramid and icosahedron shapes caused the radiesthesia effect, regardless of whether a magnet was added to the experiment.

Fred walked in the door one day while I was plotting Sanderson's vile vortices on a little six-inch globe. Out of recent habit, he wandered over to the littered tabletop, picked up the bent coat hangers and began dowsing objects. He had become adept at this new addition in his life, and in later years used his ability to locate water and sewer lines for the maintenance department of the town in which he lived.

For a few minutes he played with the "sticks", as he called them, then walked them over the globe in my hand.

I had already tried this experiment. "Spheres won't work," I told him.

He shrugged and held them over the globe anyway. I slowly spun the orb to admire all the little penciled triangles I had just applied.

"Hey!" he exclaimed. "Did you see that?"

"See what?"

"Spin the globe again," Fred commanded.

I gave it a good shove around its axes pivots, and looked up at the rods held close to my face. They instantly crossed over the *spinning* axis of the sphere. Serendipity does visit, but you have to be trying when it comes.

When I held the rods and Fred spun the globe, my result was opposite from his, naturally.

This accidental observation put the final nail into the Bermuda Triangle theory, but that "nail" also ended the experimentation. It would be years, and a lot of gray hairs later, before I learned that things other than geometric objects change, and manipulate magnetic fields.

Never the less, I was on to many things. A spinning sphere, with forward velocity applied at ninety degrees to its axis, curves in midair. Anyone who ever stood at home plate with a bat can testify to the paradox of that statement. So does something peculiar happen to a spinning sphere in midspace, which also has forward velocity along its orbit around a star?

The Earth is a spinning sphere, and it is also in other terms an icosahedron, with Planet Byrd attached to one of its twelve points, and Planet Taylor stuck to another. These positions seem to act, in a sense, like event horizons of black holes in that they can swallow some fairly substantial hard objects. The idea of black holes goes back to a contemporary of Einstein, named Schwarzschild, who formulated what became known as the Schwarzschild Radius Theory. By using some fairly esoteric thought experiments, he decided that odd things would occur if a gravity field got really, really dense.

If one of two people on the edge of a black hole falls into the field, a time paradox seems to take place. The poor fellow who fell in wouldn't know what hit him. He'd be instantly stretched out like a string, and then slammed into infinity as a piece of matter smaller than a dust mite. His partner, on the other hand, would see him frozen at the edge of the event horizon as a kind of holographic light image. It's pointless to wonder what the guy who fell in sees.

Some of these scientists sure get weird ideas. I wonder if I would get any scientific traction if I postulate that ghost ships reported in the Bermuda Triangle might be a light image imposed on a kind of event horizon the moment the ship passed over?

When NASA makes one of it's horse-and-buggy space shots, it relies on trajectory to get from here to there, and as a consequence has to wait for "windows" to open in the sky. Are there other kinds of windows travelers might use to good advantage, rather than getting swallowed up like a black hole?

A common reported event in all these Triangle spots are sightings of UFO's. The most common argument that flying saucers from other stars can't be visiting Earth is that those other stars are so far away it would take lifetimes to get here. Even if aliens could make a machine that could travel at the speed of light, a star a hundred, or a thousand light years away, is still a hundred or a thousand years away. Einstein's concept of time dilation would make such a trip irrelevant in terms of the civilization from which they came, even if the travelers put themselves in deep freeze. The travelers, upon returning to the home planet, would find that everyone they ever knew were hundreds or thousands of years dead and gone.

This is an argument that in essence only considers a walk across the street, and has ignored the Schwarzschild Radius. Rigid adherence to ideas can even cause science to bury itself in dogma, and forget that things like wormholes, which provide possibilities of light year jumps, was conjured up by itself. Science has also tinkered with a theory that a particle called a tachyon can whip along faster than light. Einstein was once heard speaking of particles that pass through solids as having gone through the fifth dimension.

Even science can camp on a ledge only partway up to the mountain's summit, and shout, "I'm safe...I'm safe!"

A large amount of scientific opinion is that UFO's can't get here, because we can't get there.

Yet.

Science fiction writers aren't bothered by dogma, and they dispense with the problem of immense distances without much thought. Just give the Enterprise a warp drive and away they go. To move the plot along, these writers long ago coined the word, hyperspace, which allows their characters to dash from star to star by using another kind of space, which "warps" space, and contracts distance.

Science fiction is famous for predicting science fact. Does hyperspace exist? And, if it does exist, what is hyperspace?

The above questions spark an obvious assumption: *If hyperspace exists, it must belong to someone else.*

Buried deeper in the assumption is another question that might answer the second part of the first question: *Does this mean our normal space is someone else's hyperspace?*

If there are aliens piloting flying saucers around the Earth, it's safe to say they didn't waste colossal chucks of time putting along at the speed of light to get here. With technology far beyond ours, they just opened portals, or used portals such as nature provided at the poles, and like the one east of Miami. If there are aliens around, it's not likely they mean us any harm. Like my dance with Annette Funicello, they just tolerate their thirty seconds with us. To a few of them, we might have an anthropological academic value, but I can't think of anything such advanced creatures would need to steal from a backwater joint like this. A few might pull over for a rest stop, or as a joke, make a crop circle to confuse the local yokels. It isn't likely they want to conquer, and rule us. If that was the case, it seems it would have already happened. If it has happened, considering the political direction of this planet, it doesn't say much for the intelligence of our conquerors.

An alien tourist might snap a picture of the Grand Canyon to show the folks back home, but if UFO's aren't something the CIA is flying around, then most of them are using the Earth in the same fashion I used the State of Oregon on my way to Nevada. Before I lived here, I used the State as a highway.

We could be a hyperspace highway to half the Galaxy.

The fate of Flight 19 seems evident. The planes arrived at the edge of the Vortex's line of demarcation, and were flying alongside as the one in a billion opening of the portal occurred nearby. They did not immediately go "down the drain" though, and were able, via radio to convey their confusion and instrument failure to the outside world. Maybe it was not yet possible to pass through. Perhaps the portal needs to open wider, even to the full 12-degree yawn to be dangerous.

It might be the Flight needed to be moving at a slightly different angle to the line of demarcation to be accepted. All disappearance accounts have the victims in motion, and stories from survivors talk of severe disorientation and malfunctioning instruments. I think it's safe to say that while they were being heard on the radio there was still a chance to turn left, so to speak, and get out of there. They were told to turn west, and it was almost certainly good advice, but according to some radio witnesses, they didn't know which way was west.

Finally, either the portal opened enough to welcome them to Planet Taylor, or they turned east, at which point they blinked off Harold's radarscope.

It's my belief that once they crossed over, becoming "The Lost Patrol", the landscape changed drastically. One moment they were flying over a semitropical sea, and the next instant a polar vista of ice and snow was below. How far south, or down the planet from Planet Taylor's axis they emerged probably depended on air speed, and the relative ground velocity of the new planet. A boat would emerge much closer to the axis than a plane.

Considering that Flight 19 took off from south Florida, it's not likely they carried arctic survival gear.

A traveler crossing into Planet Byrd would experience a gradual transition from an arctic condition into a much warmer one. From our point of view, this traveler would go "up a drain" rather then down. By now some readers have asked how that base at the South Pole got established if it's so dangerous to travel toward the Poles? The disappearances in the Bermuda Triangle are rare, but they are far more rare at the Poles. There is no concern about that 12-degree portal opening, since at the poles the traveler is going toward the center rather that around it. Byrd actually flew over the South Pole in 1929, but made no cryptic statements about that flight.

I know of no untoward problems, or danger associated with commercial flights "over the pole", as they used to be billed. None of them actually pass over the axis, but cut across the arctic on what are called, great circle routes. Flights into the South Pole base, for ease of navigation and to conserve fuel, are almost certainly done as great circle routes. Nobody lines up directly with the axis, either because they've been told not to, or more likely because it's just the best way to get from here to there. Obviously, the Poles can be reached, and even if a problem does develop on the way there, it's much easier to turn aside, or turn around and come back, as Admiral Byrd demonstrated.

No matter which planet a traveler ends up on, he or she is going to have a time problem, but it won't be a noticeable problem as reckoned by a clock carried with the traveler. It's just that the new local time cannot be matched with the time of the environment from which the departure was made.

Consider a scenario for Flight 19. What if the five airplanes landed on a nice flat spot on Planet Taylor, and aboard one of the planes is a genius who figures out correctly what has happened? Suppose they then transferred fuel from three of the planes into two of the others, and sitting on each other's laps, five men to a plane, they took off for Planet Taylor's axis? Our genius knows where the axis is, of course. Had they done such a thing, then from our point of view they are still flying. If they get back, they won't be home though, because everyone they left behind will probably have been dead for a hundred years.

Most probably, if they survived the hostile alien environment of Planet Taylor, they took as their own the local time, and have all died of old age by *our* time calculation.

The question is: If they lived on Planet Taylor and died of old age years ago, why haven't they died of old age no matter what they did? Reason doesn't care for conundrums like this, yet there is no other way to resolve the problem. If they didn't get killed immediately, then they either died of old age on Planet Taylor, or they will arrive in our future still young men.

I am reminded of the New Yorker stretching the line of demarcation of his private little vortex, and perhaps hesitating before turning around to run away. The hesitation may have caused him to lose a few decades of our time. From our viewpoint he was frozen in time, yet simultaneously, from his perspective he only paused a moment to make a decision. Even if his decision was instantaneous, he would still have lost the ability to return to 1890.

No matter what Flight 19 did do, or does do, they cannot go home. On the other hand, a traveler across Planet Byrd can go home or anywhere he or she wants, but not strictly, anywhen.

If someone escapes from the Bermuda Triangle, the world to which they return is older, and they are the same age. Travelers who come back from Planet Byrd return the same instant they left, but they are older. Are both these places to be avoided, or are there advantages to using them?

Scale references in terms of size, and time are useful for visualization, but probably have no value as definitive measurements. For the moment I'll put aside this assumption, and take a stab at a measurement anyway.

Assume that Planet Taylor is more or less a twin of the Earth, and that its orbit is the surface of the Earth. Of course, this isn't true because it's Taylor's axis that's going around on our sphere, and not its equator. Planet Taylor's sun has to be set at a right angle to our Universe. Still, we are making assumptions, so let's assume a time scale ratio of 365.25 days to one between Earth and Taylor. Physically, this four to one model can't work, but the metaphor might tell us something. Taylor has an axis tilt similar to Earth's, and the area of Atlantic Ocean where the disappearances take place is about 800 miles in diameter, so a little mathematical juggling gives us a measurement of Taylor as about six thousand miles in circumference. This doesn't work either, since our measuring device taken onto Taylor would probably show a planet 24,000 miles around. This is a problem similar to weighing a 200-pound man in the Oregon Vortex, and expecting him to weigh 220 outside. It doesn't work like that. The scale is relative to whatever its environment, and so is the man.

It doesn't look like we're getting to far, but let's see what happens by turning the math around and measuring Planet Byrd.

Earth is Byrd's Bermuda Triangle.

If one of our days is equal to one of Byrd's years, then our North Pole moves through all the tilts of its axis in twenty-four of their hours in the same way Planet Taylor's pole rushes through the Bermuda Triangle area in one of our days. This description isn't perfect either, for there are times when the effects of the Bermuda vortex seem to be fixed. Those moments when the vortex seems fixed occur only to someone in motion near the line of demarcation, and then the apparent static position is only the illusion created by the time differentials. It's no wonder we can't pinpoint the exact location of the vortex in the Bermuda Triangle.

Let's conjure up a jet plane that has a cruising speed of one thousand miles per hour. On Earth, our mythical jet can travel between Triangle points in four hours and forty-two minutes using a great circle route. So, in 4.7 hours it travels forty-seven hundred miles from Triangle point to Triangle point. Now, let's throw out normal mathematics and mentally move this rate of speed into Byrd's environment without fooling with the laws of relativity. From the pilot's point of view his speed would still be a thousand miles per hour, but from our reference the plane would disappear. The jet, having crossed the line of demarcation or event horizon, is now invisible to us, but at what rate of speed would the plane's thousand miles per hour be through Byrd's atmosphere, if we could measure it from Seattle with that magic telescope?

It stands to reason that if Byrd has one Bermuda type triangle, it probably has at least nine others. So once past the first line of demarcation, we direct our jet to fly to the next closest Triangle point on Byrd's surface, or forty-seven hundred of its miles. We expect the trip will take four hours and forty-two minutes Byrd time. In Earth time and in Earth miles per hour, it might work out something like this:

Our year has 365.25 days, or 8,766 hours, therefore a time scale ratio of 365.25 to one yields 3,201,781.5 of our hours for one of its days. Divide this by the relative time in flight of four hours, forty-two minutes, times the actual air speed of one thousand miles per hour and the relative speed across the surface of Planet Byrd, as seen from our point of reference, gives a relative speed of 681,320,106.3 miles per hour. As we measure it, the speed of light is right in the neighborhood of 670 million miles per hour. So the answer to this crude mathematical finagling tells us immediately why the plane disappears to us.

Physics tells us that anything that exceeds, or matches the speed of light, must do so at the expense of losing every single molecule of its matter to achieve that velocity. From our point of view, the jet plane obliterated itself, but from the pilot's frame of reference, he still exists. The scattered energy we think he has become is simply the form of matter the pilot is now experiencing.

The pilot in this scenario might consider tightening his seat belt, because for every one of his hours, he's traveling one of our light years. When he arrives at Byrd's next Triangle point forty-seven hundred miles away, he will have traversed a little more than four of our light years.

Well, golly. An astronomical fact up and slaps us across the face. Here in the Milky Way, our nearest solar neighbor is a dual star system, catalogued as Alpha and Proxima Centauri. From there light takes 4.3 light years to get to the Earth.

Here comes the criticism, faster than a speeding photon. There will be those who won't accept any of this number juggling, and will say something like, "numbers can't lie, but liars can use numbers."

Sometimes how the question is phrased, can determine the answer.

Numbers can do all sorts of things. They can even lie.

Not that mine do, but since more numbers are going to be encountered on this literary trip, perhaps the following old story should be held in mind as a future reference:

Three salesmen check into a hotel, one at a time. They are each charged ten dollars for a room. (I said this was an old story) After the men are up in their rooms, the clerk realizes he overcharged them. He calls over the bellhop, hands over five one-dollar bills and tells him to refund this money to the salesmen. On the way up in the elevator, the bellhop grapples with how to evenly split five things among three people? The problem seems insurmountable, but in flash of inspiration the solution becomes clear. He gives each man one dollar, and pockets two dollars as a hidden tip. Problem solved.

Or is it?

The three guests, after the one-dollar refund, have each paid nine dollars for their rooms. Anyone who passed the fourth grade knows that three times nine is twenty-seven. The bellhop pilfered two dollars. Thirty dollars was spent, but anyone who passed the second grade knows that two added to twenty-seven is twenty-nine.

Does reality suffer because we can't find that last dollar?

Not really, because by restating the solution, not the question, the dollar shows up intact. The hotel collected twenty-five dollars, the bellhop stole two dollars, and the three guests each got one dollar. Twenty-five, plus two, plus one, plus one, plus one, equals thirty.

How does three times nine, plus two go awry? Three, six and nine can be tricky numbers, and they will be encountered later, but here, perhaps we have no more than a problem of interpretation. It's a canon that the Theory of Relativity says faster than light speed is impossible. This is an interpretation. Albert Einstein did not rule out faster than light speeds. He simply ruled out the ability to physically move faster than light *in this universe.*

What happens to my questionable math if the jet plane on Byrd is only going 500 hundred miles per hour? In this case, by using my numbers, it is only going half the speed of light and shouldn't be able to disappear from our sight. But, wait, since Byrd's universe is operative already at our speed of light, the question is moot. The only thing we may know for sure is that our jet plane can fly from here to Alpha Centauri in a little under five hours, plus the distance from the starting point to the Pole, and then the distance from Alpha Centauri's pole to the landing point.

Remember, this is time spent by the pilot. From where we stand, the flight time over Byrd's surface registers as zero. Let's put two magic telescopes in Seattle, hook them up to video cameras, and then feed the real time images to a split TV screen. The first magic scope shows the plane disappear on the left screen, and the second one, focused on Alpha Centauri, shows them appear on the right screen at the same instant.

Well, the jet plane departs and arrives at *almost* the same instant. Actually, if one travels a given distance without a clock being able to measure departure and arrival, then we have to come to grips with the unsettling notion that time ran *backwards*. As viewed from local Earth time, it cannot be proved that the plane arrived before it left, but the instantaneous arrival represents distance reduced to nothing, and the only way to do this is by going backwards in time while going forward through space. The Mad Hater would understand this perfectly.

Back in Seattle no one has aged a second, but the pilot of our jet is four and a half hours older. This is not a bad a price to pay, especially when considering what a trip across Planet Taylor might cost.

A similar trip on Taylor would take four and a half relative hours from the pilot, and if he didn't dawdle to make a crop circle, a minimum of four and a half years would be lost from the home universe. Probably more, considering my math, but even losing the minimum amount, would make it tough to run a business.

Planet Taylor may be referred to as a "time machine", whereas Planet Byrd can be called a "space machine." Both planets affect the time-space continuum, but unless one wants to escape civilization, Byrd represents the route of greatest benefit. However, it should only be used as a highway. If one liked it there, and didn't come home for fifty years, friends and relatives might not recognize the person who knocks on their doors. Not only would they not know that wrinkled old face, they wouldn't even know it had been gone.

In terms of space travel, or travel to the vicinity of other stars, this discovery if correct, could speed things up by centuries over the estimates of those who look toward galactic travel in terms of unconventional still to be invented technology. All we really might need to get to our nearest star system is an existing airplane with a really big fuel tank. There's no reason to think that Byrd doesn't have a breathable atmosphere, or Taylor for that matter. Air, along with things like pollen blown on the wind, is probably being exchanged all the time. Great chunks of light year distances of empty space may be traversed without ever leaving a planetary atmosphere.

A simple alien navigation route might work something like this: Planet Taylor, causing our Bermuda Triangle exists in Universe A. Planet Taylor #2 causes our Devil's Triangle in the South China Sea, which is also in Universe A. The distance between Taylor #1 and Taylor #2 across the expanse of Universe A is about nine light years as the photon crow flies. A resident of Taylor #1 has business on Taylor #2, so he climbs in this flying saucer, points it at the pole of his Planet, and darts through the event horizon into Universe B. Universe B is the Planet Earth. The businessman then uses our air space (without permission) and flies 9,400 miles across the Earth. This takes him half and hour (remember, he has a flying saucer). He has a schedule of when the

Devil's Triangle portal opens, and he has a detection device to show him exactly where it is. He plunges through the vortex, emerges near the pole of Taylor #2, and then flies from there to his business meeting.

This commute took less than an hour, and was instantaneous from the view of either Taylor #1 or Taylor #2.

Longer trips would take a more time. Let's say the business meeting was on a planet a really long way across Universe A First our Taylor businessman crosses the Earth (Universe B), and then passes beyond our North Pole and into Planet Byrd (Universe C). He directs his flying saucer north on Byrd to its pole, and flies beyond that into Universe D (there's bound to be one). On this Universe D planet, he goes down the drain of one of its triangle points back to Universe C, which is Byrd's domain, but not the same planet. On this planet, he flies to another triangle point, and goes through to Universe B, but not the Planet Earth. One more triangle transition later, and after about two hours, he lands for the business meeting more than a hundred and ten light years from home. There was no reason to call ahead. The trip from Universe A's perspective was instantaneous.

I'm not trying to prove the existence of UFO's. I shouldn't have to even try to do this. There is a mountain of empirical evidence to confirm the existence of something flitting around up there. If

#10

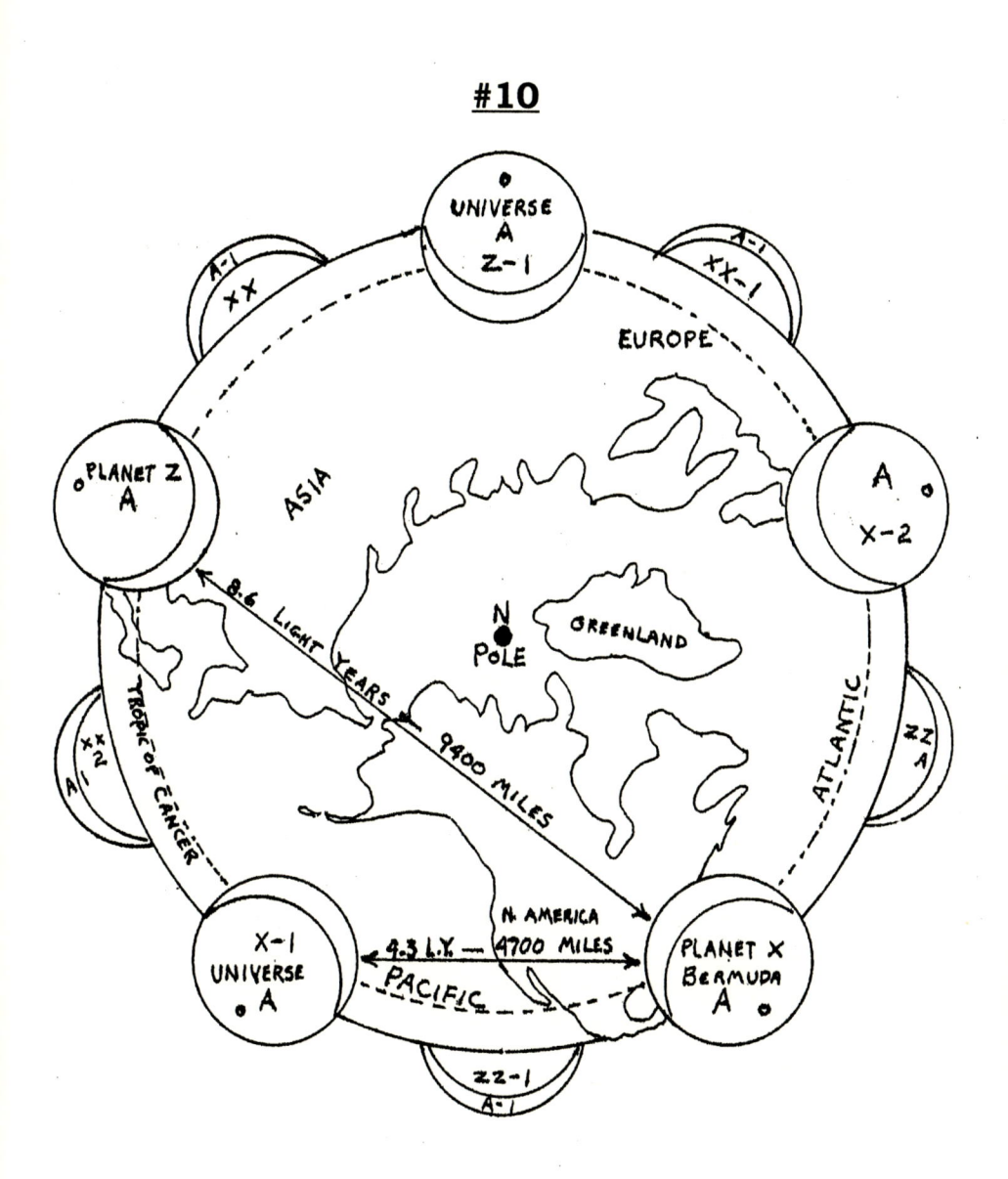

the rules used in courts of law were applied to this evidence the controversy would long have been over.

Aliens don't stop for pie and coffee, because there's probably a Galactic law against messing with developing tribes. We should also realize that any time "they" stop anywhere but in their own universe, they rob themselves of time from their own culture. One little crop circle to jerk the distant backwater cousins awake, then it's off to Sagittarius for the class reunion.

Considering evidence already presented, and the blockbuster stuff yet to come, I don't think all this is to far fetched. Science tells us that space is warped; that each mass taking up space is curving space, and that time is warped or curved right along with space. The closer one is to the center of a gravity field, the slower he or she experiences the passing of time as opposed to those who were left behind. The continuum is one thing made up of two things, time and space, and if some mainstream scientists are consulted, it looks like they might agree with me when I say that this whole menagerie is splitting off into a myriad of universes.

A few years back a quantum physicist, J. B. Hasted of Birkbeck College, University of London, formulated a many universe theory based on the wave function of an atomic transition. According to his theory, the wave function splits into an infinite number of universes. Hasted didn't think

#11

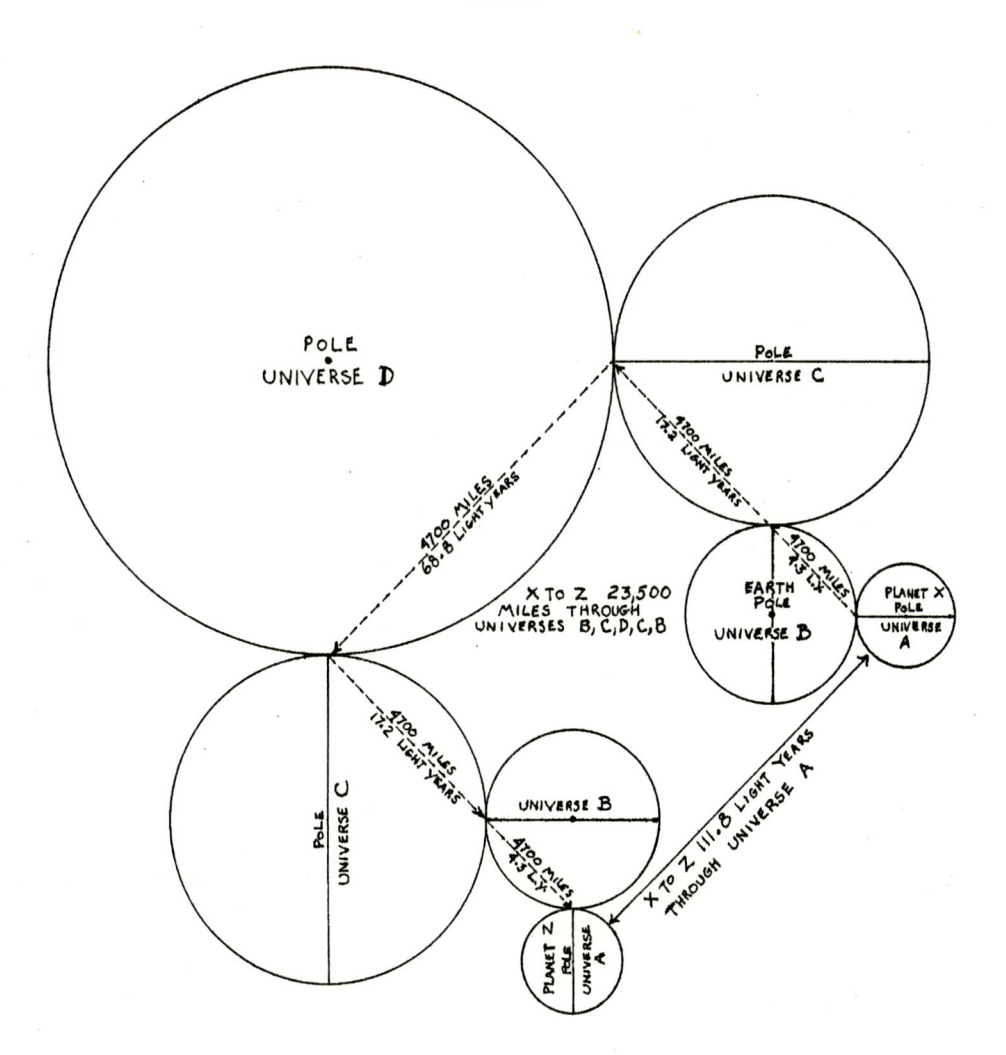

Diagram labels:

- POLE UNIVERSE D
- POLE UNIVERSE C
- 4700 MILES 68.8 LIGHT YEARS
- 4700 MILES 17.2 LIGHT YEARS
- 4700 MILES 4.3 L.Y.
- EARTH POLE UNIVERSE B
- PLANET X POLE UNIVERSE A
- X TO Z 23,500 MILES THROUGH UNIVERSES B,C,D,C,B
- POLE UNIVERSE C
- 4700 MILES 17.2 LIGHT YEARS
- UNIVERSE B
- 4700 MILES 4.3 L.Y.
- PLANET Z POLE UNIVERSE A
- X TO Z 111.8 LIGHT YEARS THROUGH UNIVERSE A

that spatial boundaries exist between these infinite number of universes, or at least he could not identify them. To bad Dr. Hasted couldn't have hung around the Oregon Vortex. Spatial boundaries are abundant here, not to mention the severe boundaries found in the Bermuda Triangle.

Waves are interesting stuff whether they are sound waves or quantum waves of intention. Quantum waves are probably the direct cause for the Oregon Vortex. It's as though Jack's giant dropped a rock off the bean stock into the quantum pool near Gold Hill, and the waves are still spreading out in concentric rings.

A fellow came to the Vortex one day and walked around blowing a tuning pipe. He tweeted and tooted for about ten minutes, and then announced that B-sharp cannot be attained within the line of demarcation. He produced a so-called B-sharp for me, and then we went up to the parking lot where he blew another B-sharp for comparison. Being tone deaf, I took his word for it that the two sounds were different. Sound is a wave function. If the Vortex doesn't like loud children, maybe it also can't stand a B-sharp?

In the evening in certain places around the Vortex I can hear my own voice being echoed back to me as if the source, or object it is bouncing off is six inches from my ears. There is also a spot where all tour guides learn not to stand and try to talk. About the time one gets to the second sentence the Vortex makes an effort to strangle the speaker. The larynx freezes right up and words become gasps and raspy squawks.

Waves, say waves in a bathtub, or waves stirred up in a lake by a speedboat, and even sound waves decrease the amplitude of each other when they compete for the same space. Wave fronts meet and pass through each other, but when they come out the other side each appears to be the same wave, yet qualitatively they are less of a wave. Quantum waves are different. When they meet, they add to their amplitudes. Professor Hasted evidently decided that addition didn't mean they get bigger like regular waves get smaller, but that they become more in a quantitative sense.

A vortex, a creature of the quantum, cuts across a second vortex and another vortex is born. Multiply this event by an infinity of vortexes splitting like amoebas at the same microsecond, and we've got a mess of universes constantly heading out into the great unknown. To a finite mind this is an abominable idea. Take this sort of nonsense serious, and right away a person has to contend with the possibility of an infinity of duplicates all eventually going their own way and thinking their own thoughts. People have to watch their thoughts more carefully. Sooner or later, that threat about shooting the neighbor because his dog barks is going to become an intent, and then...it's anyone's guess.

Who's responsible? Your Honor, duplicate number 18,639,405 made me do it. He had the thought first.

This splitting of universes and addition of vortexes affects time as well as space. Space is split outward. Time is split inward. Or the other way around, depending on the observer's vantage point. The quantum vortexes, no matter the size we perceive them to be, use each other as frames of reference. Its either that or they compare themselves with the void, and when something is compared to nothing, the result is the same as any whole number being multiplied by zero.

I've played with trying to diagram this idea of splitting universes without a great deal of success. Two-dimensional drawings make poor charts of four or five-dimensional realities, but they do allude to a couple of things. A top view drawing showing Earth at the center of a five-way split shows the small circles labeled X (Taylor planets) not to be touching the other E (Earth planets) depicted as splitting outward. This seems to be a picture of what happens beyond three-dimensional reality when the X circles tilt to the limit of their *ecliptics.* Apparently a new planet/vortex is the product of the splitting of two larger spheres. E splits in five directions and X-6 through X-10 are cut loose on their own. Then the whole thing begins anew.

Consider the top view as space.

#12

Top view of universe splitting

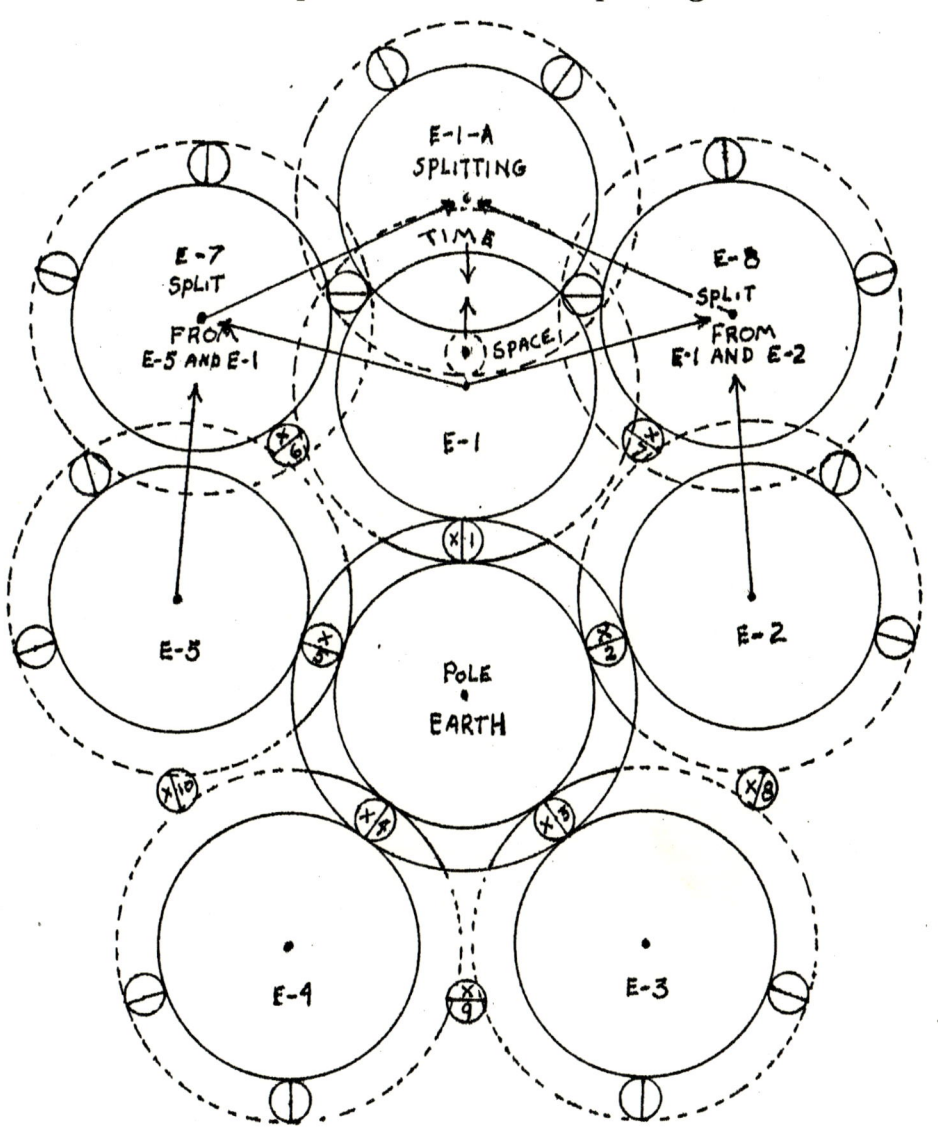

In the side view the X planets exhibit a back and forth motion that three dimensions would interpret as the X planet's axis tilt. Note that the splitting occurs at the limit of the lines labeled 51 degrees 51 minutes of arc from the equator line (X-5). This tilt angle is what some researchers have regarded as the Great Pyramid's inclination from its base to its apex. It seems no one has been able to agree on an exact inclination in terms of minutes of arc, but most do not argue with 51 degrees. This is a right angle drawing to the top view, and I regard it as a depiction of a time split.

A highly relevant aspect of both these drawings is that the coronas of the E circles appear to create the X circles, and these coronas are exactly one-sixth the diameter of the E circles. Litster measured the Gold Hill anomaly with a corona that is one-sixth the diameter of the Vortex. Somewhere buried in this function might be a restrictive form of time machine, but more on that later.

The wave of the split rolls outward and inward adding in both directions to the quantity of the building material that forms the continuum. Since our bodies are made from this same stuff, we surf the wave at the same moment we are the wave. Whatever *is...is.* We are *it*, and *it* couldn't care less how we look at *it*. *It* shoehorns its infinite self into a finite space for the comfort of having walls, and then pulls an endless cascade of time into the same box, which then shoves *it* out the other end of the box.

#13

Side view of universe splitting

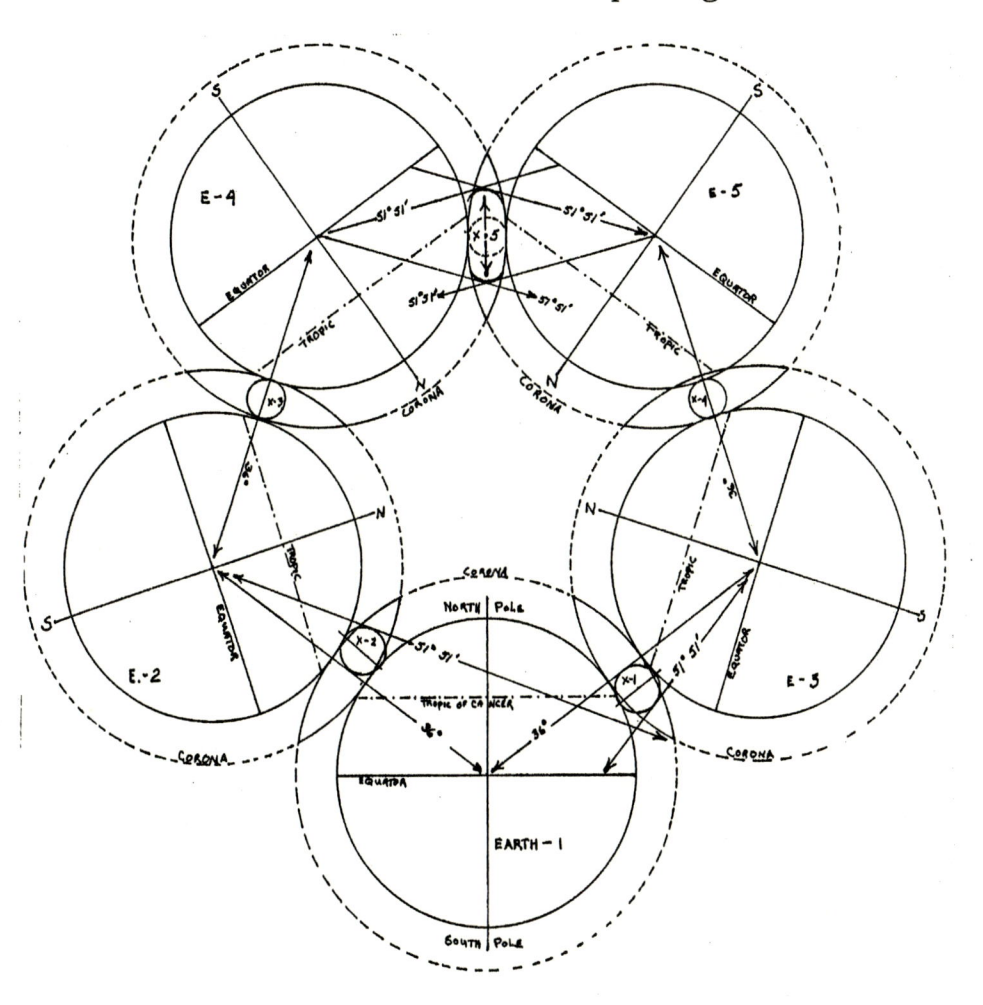

It is *us*. You'd think we'd have more fun, but as Pogo knew, the enemy is *us*.

Time and space intertwine, then either create, or just depend on built-in imperfections for existence. We might have to face up to the possibility that we exist as the subjects of mathematical irrationalities. A sphere when spinning, and moving transversely against the direction of its own spin exhibits two aspects, and both are irrational.

The first aspect is orbit: The orbit of a sphere about another sphere can be expressed as the ratio of the circumference of a circle to its diameter; *pi,* an irrational number, or a transcendental equation that cannot be satisfied. If Earth's orbit were to justify itself to a string of unending zeroes, the planet would fly off into the Galaxy to find a better neighborhood.

Time, is the icosahedron.

The second aspect is spin. Spin is made visual by another transcendental equation, which describes another, more compact geometric object. This is an equation that, unlike *pi,* produces expected, predictable numbers, yet it too cannot be satisfied. It's a venerable old number, and one that has suffered horrible misinterpretation. In the next chapter we'll visit this number, which when divided into the *result of pi,* produces:

Space, the pyramid.

Time and space change places in a fifth dimensional twist that occurs at the center of a vortex. On becomes off, then off becomes on. South becomes north, and clockwise becomes counterclockwise.

Time and space are parts of the thing they add up to. Time plus space equals reality, or the continuum, or just plain, *it.*

It can be interchanged with another badly misinterpreted word, *trinity.*

There's a very old philosophical concept called *The One and the Many*, which asks the question: Why does it take at least two of something to make one of something else? And then: Why does it take two more of those newly created ones to make another one thing?

The idea of *The One and the Many* shouldn't be a brain-buster, but the volume of illogical blather on this subject has fogged the atmosphere so badly that all that's left is the fog.

Science comes close to a common sense description of a trinity construction, but then wanders off into its own dogmatic Wonderland. Science breaks matter down into molecules, and molecules are broken down into atoms. Atoms have a nucleus and at least one electron, and inside these things are still more particles that science calls quarks, which make up the atom. Inside quarks is supposed to be stuff called tops and bottoms and colors, and somewhere along about here science nods off into Quantum Theory where it seems all that's left are a bunch of madhouse electrons.

In the Quantum, all bets are off. No local accurate predictions can be made, yet statistical predictions are right on the money, and yield items like cathode ray tubes (TV). Quantum predictions are like weather prognostications going wrong when they should be no-brainers. The analogy would be to look up at an ugly black cloud coming our way, say, "it's going to rain," and then have the cloud, at our utterance, perversely head the other way. A quantum prediction that it will "rain" today doesn't happen because the predictor predicted it. A quantum prediction that it will "rain" someday is dead-on.

Einstein understood how quantum theory fathered television sets; after all, his study of the photoelectric effect fathered Relativity, which helped Max Planck flesh out the Quantum Theory. But Einstein hated the ludicrous idea that the Quantum Theory placed his Relativity events at the mercy of the *intent* of researchers who were mucking about at the atomic level. Researchers learned that the act of simply looking at the quantum changed the quantum. Since the quantum can be thought of as our foundation, he spent much of his life trying unsuccessfully to formulate a Unified Field Theory that would avoid throwing the relativity baby out with the quantum bathwater nonsense.

It's well known that Einstein didn't believe that God played "...dice with the Universe."

Ah, Albert, you should have investigated the *trinity*. No, not the fog of the Father, Son, Holy Ghost religious confusion, but *The One and the Many*. This old concept doesn't unify the fields of Gravitation and electromagnetism, it *is* the field. And this weak force, strong force stuff is just one part of a one. Simplistic? To be sure, but the first things troubleshooters look for are simple things, and often the trouble is that a nut just fell off a bolt.

A common bar magnet is a perfect analogy for an example of a simple trinity construction. When we consider the magnet, we think of the object that the word magnet describes: *The One.* The poles of the magnet are parts of the whole object: *The Many.*

We can't speak of a magnet as just a negative, or just a positive. To do so would put us in the untenable position of defending the existence of a singularity. As straightforward things, singularities are thought to be impossible. Science hates a singularity, even though the scientific discovery of black holes seems to rub their noses in just such a thing. Sometimes even science doesn't know whether to come or go.

Singularities cannot exist. Magnets can't have just one pole. Think of a coin with only a head, or just a tail? Such a thing wouldn't fit in a pocket or a purse, and it would really confuse a vending machine.

So what's at the core of a black hole? A white hole? And what's a white hole? A star in another universe? What is a dead star? A white hole that finally gobbled up all the matter in its alternate, black hole universe?

A friend once said, "You know, with the Sun blasting all that matter off into space, you'd think it should be getting smaller."

Well, think about it. After three or four billion years of sucking out of the old hydrogen fuel tank, you'd think it should have trimmed down just a little.

Nah, too simplistic.

Cut a magnet in half, and two magnets are the result, each with it's own negative and positive poles. Out of one magnet comes two. Out of two magnets can come four, and four yields eight. We have to stop all this dividing when the saw blade becomes wider than the pieces of magnet, but on paper we can keep cutting forever. A straight forward forever, on a saw blade and magnet level, presents a problem. Infinity does not allow singularities even though it allows forevers, and before we know it our paper saw blade gets down to the same size as atoms, quarks, and colors and here comes the quantum that is a little less than an objective sliceable medium. We can't cut any

148

more, and if something doesn't twist the whole thing back in the other direction pretty soon, we're going to run smack into ourselves. Antimatter and matter, being of a mutual exploding nature, we can't afford to run into ourselves or we're back to nothing, and nothing is a singularity, and singularities can't exist.

On paper, if a person leaves work and decides to go home half the way at a time, he or she will never get home. Einstein knew this. He was the one who said the Universe is a finite thing that contains an infinite number of other things. The new "science" of Chaos explains how this can be done, and provides a fantastically beautiful visual example built from a mathematical equation called a Mandelbrot Set. The bathtub drain hole and water are the finite things from which the vortex springs as an infinite structure, and then somewhere along this swirling path another drain hole appears.

Chaos Theory tells us that eventually the disorder of chaos will produce order, and that symmetry carries within it the seeds of shapelessness. The pendulum of creation swings first to balance, and then to unbalance, and on its way back we notice that *the ecliptic has developed an obliquity.*

Any concept to which we can apply words must end up as a pendulum swing, because whatever may be beyond the extension of its swing can't be named. Pendulum motion is harmonic motion, and everything contained within the displacement of either side of its balance point is amplitude, which can be described as a form of a *wave*. But we're okay. Reality is a perpetual motion pendulum.

Don't blame me for all this confusion. I just report it.

I don't know why, twenty years ago, I thought I'd solved the mystery of the Universe by taking a round trip through the Bermuda Triangle. All I did then was wash the scum of ignorance off one window, peer through, and then be satisfied at telling what my limited view revealed. As it turns out, there are lots of scummy windows, and John Litster scrapped the crud off a few of them before I got there.

Even though I can't make a map of the Oregon Vortex that will stay put, I can get close enough. My map shows that Litster outlined another, more universal map on the ground inside the vortex. The locations of the demonstration platforms are set at precise angles in relation to true north, magnetic north, and the center axis. Lines between the position points mimic exactly the angles embodied in the Great Pyramid of Egypt. I wondered if Litster copied the incline angles and the internal architecture of the Cheops Pyramid on purpose, or if he just found relevant spots inside the Vortex field that the pyramid builders copied from nature?

#14
Oregon Vortex with
elementary Great Pryamid lines

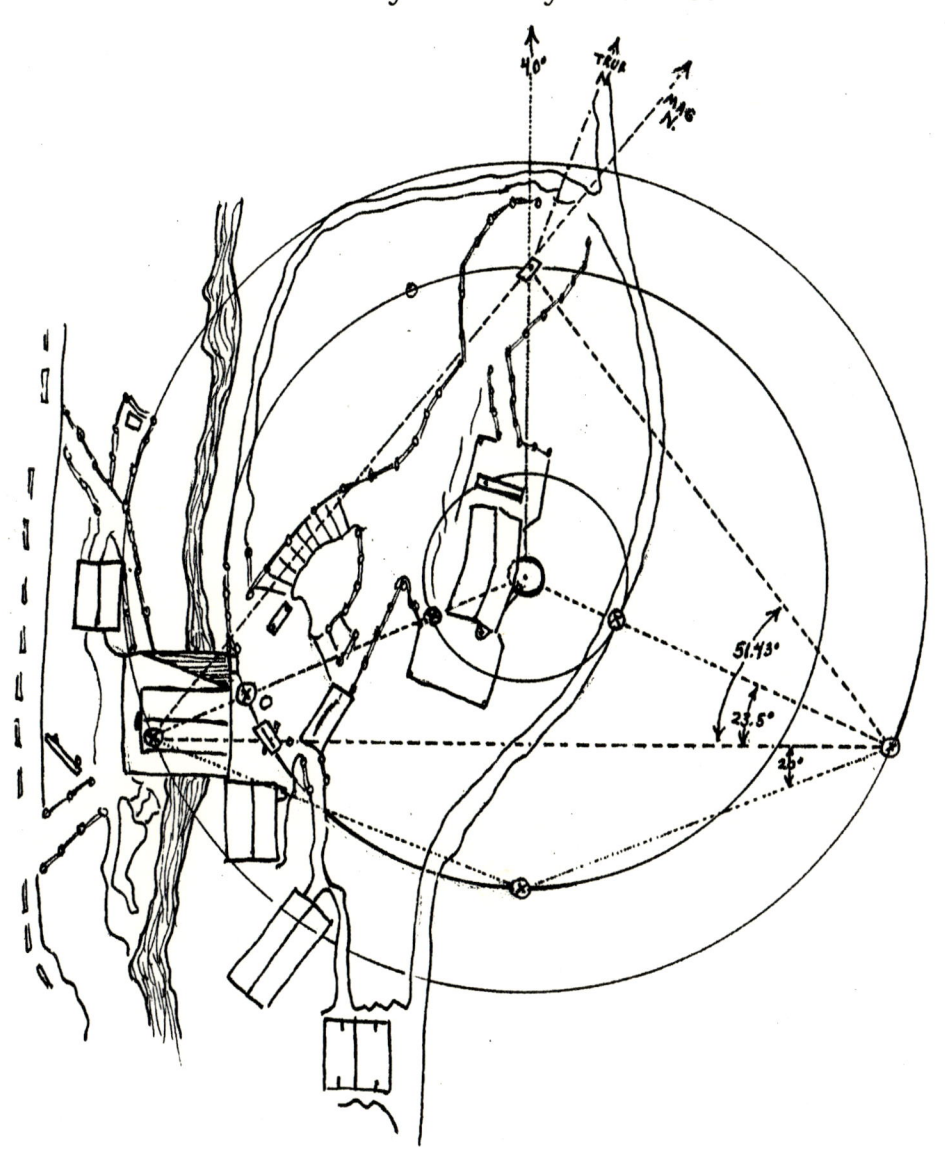

My instincts go with the latter solution. I still wonder, though, if having laid out the Vortex grounds in this manner, if Litster knew they were pyramid angles? After some thought, I believe that he must have known, and my reason for thinking this goes back to the last sentence on that little sign Maria and I took down out in the yard.

The magnetic declination at this point is approximately 20 degrees East.

I fooled around with this proclamation by putting more pencil lines on that same little six-inch globe that I once spun while Fred dowsed. From the vicinity of Gold Hill, Oregon, I drew a straight line at 20 degrees east of a direct line of longitude that terminates at the axis of the Earth. As I expected, my line reaches a spot north of Hudson's Bay close to Baffin Island; a spot that every Boy Scout with a two-dollar compass knows as the position of the North Magnetic Pole. I didn't stop there, but continued the line straight over Greenland, across the lower half of Scandinavia, from where it kept going through Northern Europe coming out near the Balkans to a position between Greece and Turkey, where it continued its linear trip to an encounter with Madagascar, but not before making, as my grandmother used to say, "a beeline" down the Nile valley.

My globe is to small to say for sure that the line cuts exactly across the Giza Plateau, and therefore right by, or through those three big pyramids there, but since it slides just to the west of the Cairo dot, it looks close enough for government work. I'd lay money on it. I'd also bet that Litster knew the exact itinerary of his line of *declination.*

Thousands of years ago, Oregon and Egypt were intrinsically connected by a huge construction project of a civilization that had never heard of Oregon, and presumably, didn't know of the existence of the continent on which Oregon would one day become a part. Or did they know?

Did Litster know the rest of the story?

Did he know that another line drawn at 20 degrees of arc from the first line, and therefore at 40 degrees from a true north longitude line at Giza, runs right down the Mediterranean, across Spain, out over the Atlantic making its first landfall in the Islands of Bermuda, and then on to slice Miami, Florida in half on its way to ending on the fat peninsula of the Yucatan?

From the Egyptian pyramids to the Mayan pyramids, while keeping to an absolute straight path, this line rides on top of the shorter line drawn by Gaddis, and Sanderson from Bermuda to Miami. It would be my guess that it also cuts across an ancient stone circle, which was recently unearthed in downtown Miami.

Did Litster know that yet another 40-degree line heading northwest from the Yucatan pyramids end just about where he hung that little metal sign so many years ago?

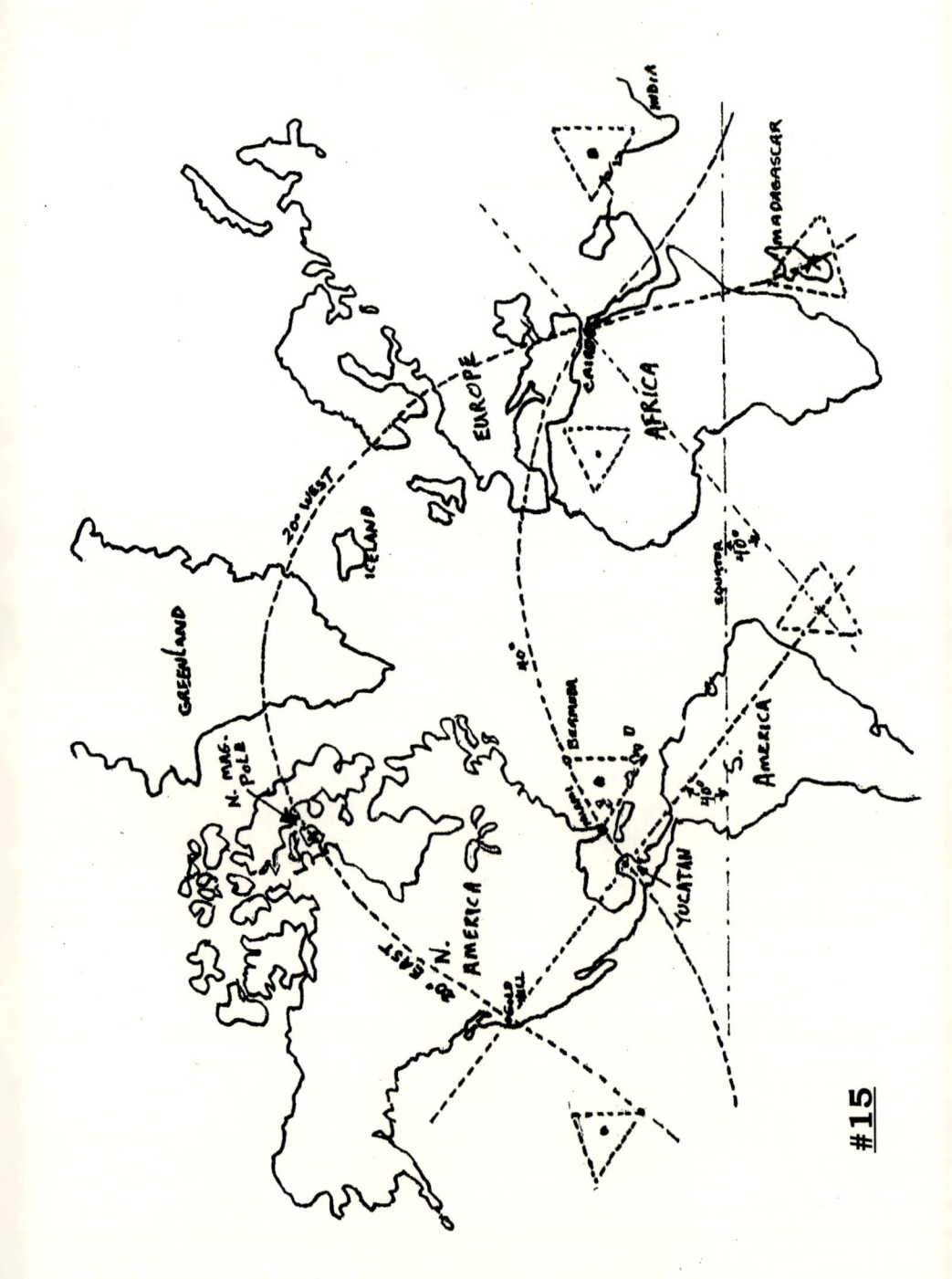

#15

Sanderson in the 1960's didn't know about that Miami stone circle. Litster in the 1950's didn't know about the Bermuda Triangle.

So, gang, take out your vortex insurance, because we are embarking into uncharted waters. Beware, as the mapmakers used to say before Columbus made liars out of them, from here on...there be monsters.

4

THE EGYPTIAN VORTEX

Ernie Cooper said to me more than once that the Great Pyramid was built right on top of a vortex similar to his Gold Hill anomaly. After hearing this statement a couple of times, I asked if he'd ever considered the possibility that the pyramid, rather than being dropped on a natural vortex, might actually cause the phenomenon?

At the time, we were among a group of folks he didn't want to confuse, so his answer wasn't exactly a committal.

"Some people think that," he said, and then went over to stand the broom. From the way he looked at me, though, I understood he was one of those people who thought *that.*

It made sense not to muddy the waters in front of the patrons. Saying that the Egyptians built the Great Pyramid on a vortex lends credibility to the knowledge that such things exist, but a new problem is encountered once the claim is made that the Pyramid makes its own vortex. If this is true, then what makes the Oregon Vortex? The mystery is big enough without complicating it. There's no pyramid in the neighborhood, unless underground, and if underground, how big is it and who put it there?

To be truthful, in those days I thought the idea of an underground pyramid wasn't all that farfetched. I'd done some prospecting and learned nature was capable of manufacturing strange objects. I've broken open rocks, and perfect cubes of iron have fallen out of them. I once took a perfect teardrop of pure silver from a Northern British Columbia river. In the Washington Cascades is a creek with purple sand, and rocks from this stream when cracked open, yield garnets already faceted.

Nature creates geometric shapes. Why not pyramids?

Over time, as I formulated more questions, the hypothesis of the House of Mystery Vortex being caused by a pyramid dissipated. The answers of how it might have gotten there were sounding more and more silly, and the probability of a man-made, or even a natural perfectly shaped mass waned. Just below the horizon of my reason was the errant thought that there could be a bunch of these vortexes, and it seemed they might combine to form their own geometric shape on a grand scale.

Reason sensed this idea building, but still wouldn't let go of the idea of a local cause. For a time, I accepted a compromise between Reason and fact. My idea of the new origin of the Vortex became an undifferentiated mass, which during the volcanic era had pooled in the bedrock and cooled into a lump with no exotic contours. The theory was that nothing more than the density of the mass itself was upsetting the Earth's magnetic field, and playing havoc with local gravity. By 1998, when I made that long delayed trip to Southern Oregon, I was confident this mass was a huge gold nugget weighing two or three tons, and was at the exact center of the energy sphere. The site, after all, was once a successful gold mine, and gold supposedly has an effect on scales inside the Vortex.

I arrived at the House of Mystery with a prepared experiment I hoped might prove my really big gold nugget theory. When I left at the end of the day, however, I was no longer sure. Gold exists on the property, but it's in what is called an auriferous state; tiny grains of the stuff shot through the gravel and not worth mining.

Once I had time to sit down at home and examine the results of my experiment, fact tipped Reason over, and its been lying there ever since kicking its legs like a beetle on its back. The gold nugget theory went the way of the flat-earth.

I had known for a long time that the pyramid shape, dense or not, makes a "dent" in the magnetic field of the Earth, but to find the same dent where there is no such shape, left a mental vacuum. My mind dislikes a vacuum as much as nature abhors one, and something had to fill the hole. Once freed from the misdirection of the gold nugget thesis, my attention left the foreground, looked into the background, and saw a picture that had always been there.

More than twenty years after I posed the pyramid question to Ernie Cooper, I realized there is nothing physical at the site to cause the existence of the Vortex.

Discoveries usually come after plodding over mountains of frustration. It's like waiting for the end of a strip tease. Salome had been dancing in my skull for years, and every now and then she tantalized with a dropped veil. When the long-awaited, mystical seventh veil finally hit the ground, I'd like to say the view was immediately spectacular, but it wasn't even a moderately good revelation. I was still feeling my way through the fog, but once the dance was over, I at least had a map to follow.

It turned out to be a legitimate treasure map, because after following its twists and turns, I crossed the horizon and beheld a stunning panorama. That which Reason once feared as nonsense came to make perfect sense, and I began to look deeply into the Pyramid of Cheops, alias Khufu's Pyramid, and better known as The Great Pyramid.

The conventional wisdom of Egyptologists is that the construction of The Great Pyramid was completed about 2570 B.C., which would make it four thousand, five hundred and seventy years old. This same wisdom contends that King Cheops, or Khufu built it as a final resting place. I don't know why the King has two names unless it's because the pronunciation and spelling exists only in barely translatable picture writing. This pyramid is called Great simply because it's the biggest, and It's considered to be an extravagant tomb, which a King who ruled for twenty-two years, took twenty years to build, and then after completion forgot to hire an interior decorator.

Estimates are that the structure contains between 2.3 and 2.5 million rectangular blocks of limestone, each weighing an average of two and a half tons. In the interior are hewn rocks that run to 60 tons or more. Whatever the exact numbers, this is an edifice that rises more than 40 stories above the eastern edge of the Sahara Desert, and is an astounding accomplishment, especially when measured against the construction abilities of today.

The Great Pyramid has been a source of wonderment to intelligent beings for as long as they have been able to stand in its shadow. In the fifth

Century B.C., the Greek historian Herodotus saw it while still cloaked in white limestone, and estimated that its construction used the services of 100,000 men a year. One theory says conscripted Egyptian citizens provided the construction labor, and another claims slaves were used. The problem is that anything said about this structure is only theory. Even the contention that Egyptologists are all wet, and the pyramid is more than twice as old than is thought, is only conjecture.

Virtually no verifiable early reporting exists about the pyramid's original purpose, and even its method of construction is shrouded in mystery and misinformation. No one really knows how it was put together. One school of thought says the stones were, pushed, pulled, and dragged up ramps, and then slid into place so tightly that a knife blade can't be inserted between the joints. Another idea has it that the Plateau was somehow flooded, and the stones were barged up to each succeeding height as the water level rose. Then there's the school that swears the last populace of Atlantis, about 10,000 years ago, used a form of harmonic resonance to float the stones through the air.

The theories of Egypt's scientists seem to assert that not long after the Stone Age a technologically advanced civilization suddenly bloomed along the Nile, built the Great Pyramid, and then went steadily downhill. Egyptologists are united, have their stories straight among themselves, and they don't tend toward friendliness when other disciplines suggest competing forms of logic.

Recently, a geologist by the name of Schoch noticed obvious water erosion on the sides of the Sphinx, and got himself branded a heretic by saying the statue is older than conventional wisdom dictates. Egyptologists declare that the Sphinx was carved for King Chephren over 4,000 years ago. Many geologists who've seen Schoch's data concur that the monument is at least 7,000 years old, and maybe as much as 12,000. Water erosion, and wind-driven sand erosion make two distinctly different patterns, and it's been a really long time since it rained hard and long in the Sahara. Egypt's scientists have been scrambling ever since, often sounding a little like political spin-doctors after a lost election.

Then there's the problem Egyptologists have regarding the missing bodies. In one size or another, or state of erosion, there are about 35 pyramids in Egypt. If the tiny ones, regarded as queen's tombs, are added into the mix there's about 80. Keepers of the wisdom say all these structures were built as tombs, but not one mummy has ever been extracted from any of them. Grave robbers in antiquity, Egyptologists tell us, looted them. Ancient thieves robbed conventional tombs, and other monuments like the bent pyramid, built for

Chephren's father, Snefru. Underneath this pyramid was an actual tomb, and it was pilfered by ancient thieves. Circular logic demands that since some pyramids were tombs, all pyramids were tombs.

The Great Pyramid was first opened in A.D. 820 by a man named Abdullah Al Mamun. He was not the common run-of-the-mill grave robber. His title was, Caliph, spiritual head of Islam, and the trials and tribulations of his dig into the Great Pyramid are documented with great care. With visions of fabulous treasure, Mamun and his crew chipped into the limestone north face of the edifice. After dangerous and arduous labor, which included tunneling around three enormous granite plugs that blocked the main passageway, nothing but empty rooms was found. Not so much as a gold button glinted in the reflected torchlight off the blank stonewalls.

When they started to dig, they didn't even know who might be in there, and it isn't likely they cared since the Egyptian religion was not their religion. We can only guess at their profound disappointment, and we can't know what value, if any, they placed on the knowledge that no robbers had been there before them.

When Caliph Al Mamun knocked on the door, Khufu wasn't at home. Cheops wasn't there, and neither was his furniture.

The interior rooms of the Great Pyramid are not adorned with colorful paintings of the Pharaoh making his way into the afterlife. The passageways contain no guarding statues. There is no profusion of hieroglyphics painted or cut into the walls like those in genuine tombs of Egyptian Kings, like Tutankhmen, Ramses, or Seti. High above the King's Chamber, modern explorers found on the massive stone blocks the name of Cheops, but by the time they arrived, and the Rosetta Stone hinted how to read the script, the monument had been open for more than a millennium. Much Nineteenth Century graffiti mars this enclosure, and maybe a guy named Cheops got there before Kilroy. Perhaps an early Egyptologist invented a solution to a perplexing mystery.

The explanation that levitation was the construction method of choice is certainly on the fringe, but maybe no more crazy than to think those stones were hauled up 40 stories on the end of a rope by muscle power. The Great Pyramid's age, origin, method of construction, and the location of the mummy of Cheops make for wonderfully fun puzzles, but there are more enigmas that fade all of these others into pale insignificance.

If the Great Pyramid was built as a tomb, why was it sealed up empty? Regardless of who, or what civilization built it, why was it built? Why was it built where it is? Did it have, and does it still have an important purpose? Two other pyramids share the Giza Plateau with the Great Pyramid. Do they share in any larger purpose, or are they placed where we find them because of the expedience of construction?

Mathematicians have had a field day with the Great Pyramid. In 1798, while French soldiers were allegedly shooting off the nose of the Sphinx, Napoleon turned his mathematician, Edme-Francois Jomard, loose on the structure. Jomard concluded that the Pyramid contained within it a record of an ancient system of measures. This is almost certainly a fact, but if Jomard learned anything else, his boss Napoleon, kept it under his vest along with what he learned after spending the night alone inside the so-called King's Chamber.

In 1859 an English mathematician, John Taylor tackled the problem contained in the Pyramid's math. He decided the builders used the same unit of measure Noah used when he hammered together his ark. According to Taylor, Noah launched his project about 300 years before the Great Pyramid was erected. Taylor was sure that both projects relied on the sacred cubit, which has been given an equivalent of 25 inches. The biblical cubit is supposed to be based on the Earth's axis, and if the axis is divided by 400,000, the ancient cubit results.

The number 400,000 seems somewhat arbitrary. I have no idea from where it comes.

Another devoted measurer of the Great Pyramid was Charles Piazzi Smyth who was the Royal Astronomer of Scotland. In 1865, he divided the base of the structure by the width of one of its casing stones and ended up with the number 365, which of course is the number of days in a year. Then he decided that one twenty-fifth of a paving stone equaled a "pyramid inch". One twenty-fifth, of course, brings us back to the cubit, and one pyramid inch is one ten-millionth of the Earth's polar radius.

With this benchmark, Taylor measured the whole Pyramid, and counting each "inch" as one year, reached the fantastic conclusion that he could pinpoint all of the important dates in the Earth's past. With this sort of historical confirmation, it was just a short step to predicting the future via the pyramid inch.

Scholars, after a short study of these calculations, branded Taylor a "pyramidiot".

Those of an apocalyptic state of mind paid no attention to scholars, and went on to use Taylor's pyramid inch for everything from prophesying the second coming of Christ, to the end of the World. Depending on who was doing the calculating, the second coming occurred in 1881, or 1936. The end of the world happened in either 1953, or 1975.

Then there's the astronomy group, who demand that since all the ascending and descending passageways line up with certain constellations, the Great Pyramid was a celestial observatory. The astronomy group hasn't said at what time of day these passageways line up, and is oblivious to what should be a clear fact; from inside the Pyramid a constellation can't be seen no mater the time of day. If it's an observatory, it's a blind observatory, except for one possible exception. The reader might hold in mind, the Constellation Orion.

Finally, in the 1940's, a Czech engineer by the name of Karel Drbal patented a cardboard model of the Cheops Pyramid by claiming it would sharpen razor blades and dehydrate organic matter. In the 1970's, cardboard pyramids became a fast-flaring fad, and the name pyramidologist was coined to denote the more scientific of the faddists.

Scientists, respectable and otherwise, have measured, prodded, poked, and even X-rayed the Pyramid with cosmic rays. It seems doubtful it was meant to be a tomb, and despite theory and speculation, no one has definitively proven what that big implacable stone monster is doing out there in Giza, just in sight of the major city of Cairo, Egypt.

I've never been to Egypt, but I don't think this lack of world travel should disqualify my ideas. In fact, a standoff relationship with the Pyramid should greatly assist my investigation. For instance, when some people hear I have an opinion on The Bermuda Triangle the first question is usually:

"Have you ever been there?"

"No. The place is 800 miles across. What would I see?"

Sometimes it's good to get back far enough from the trees so as to regard the forest. Few of those who have taken a tape measure to the Great Pyramid have been able to get a global view, other than to divide the Earth's axis by the unknown value of 400,000. On the other hand, if I hadn't gotten close to the Gold Hill Vortex, I wouldn't have found that amazing 20-degree magnetic declination line stretching all the way around the Earth.

Whoever built the Great Pyramid took the design from the Earth. The "blueprint" for the Cheops Pyramid can be found woven into nature and, at times, literally etches itself on the terrain that we plow, log, hunt and fish. Vortexes can make hidden pyramid frameworks on reality's fabric, but to find them we must look deep into the background. These frameworks are not fleshed out in stone, but are sometimes represented like a child's drawing on the face of the world. Pyramids can make vortexes, and vortexes sometimes reflect their makers.

In the Thirteenth Century the Giza Pyramids were systematically mined for the fine limestone used to case them in white glory. The city of Cairo was growing and the pyramids were a close, convenient rock quarry. Whatever happened to the Great Pyramid's rumored copper capstone is anyone's guess. Even though undressed, the Great Pyramid still mimics the lines and angles of the planet.

As citizens of the Earth, and not just of Egypt, we should seriously consider restoring it to its original dignity. Time, erosion, and human ignorance are wearing it out, and it may be much more than just a big pile of rocks.

In a sense, it may be ballast.

In preceding pages I described the Pyramid's angle of inclination from base to apex as 51 degrees 51 minutes of arc. I believe this was a view I got from Sanderson, and it served me until that seventh veil hit the stage revealing just what it was the builders were trying to copy. They were shooting for the result of dividing the number 7 into the result of *pi*. They weren't concerned with the numerical result of multiplying the diameter of a circle by 3.1416, they were building to the result of dividing 7 into the *circumference* of a circle as expressed in 360 degrees of arc. By the way, the old Greeks referred to *pi* as three and *one-seventh*. The concept of transcendental numbers goes back aways.

The Egyptians, by some accounts, were considered mathematically challenged. They got along with a clumsy ten-based system, which was devoid of the convenience of division and multiplication. Without this handy short-cut we enjoy, they got where they were going by laboriously adding and subtracting groups of ones to, or from their symbols for 10, 100, 1,000 and so on   As cumbersome as their math was, they were evidently able to square a circle, and they also understood the concept of *pi,* which they rounded off to 3.16.

The Egyptians did consider the number 7 special and had a separate symbol for it. In their symbology, it was written as, 1111111.

A ten-based numbering system can be deceiving. When we look at our own system, there are really only nine whole numbers, and the number 7 is the only number that will not divide equally into 360:

One	divides into 360,	360 times.
Two	divides into 360,	180 times.
Three	divides into 360,	120 times.
Four	divides into 360,	90 times.
Five	divides into 360,	72 times.
Six	divides into 360,	60 times.
Eight	divides into 360,	45 times.
Nine	divides into 360,	40 times.
Seven	divides into 360,	51.4285

142857142857142857142857142857 14
857142857142857142857142857
142857∞ times.

    This is an infinite, irrational answer that repeats the same numbers in the same sequence over and over. It's an infinite sequence in that it doesn't end. Unlike *pi,* which gives no hint as to the next number in its sequence, 142857∞ is predictable, and in an odd way, comforting, because it can be relied on to bring the planet back close to the same spot it was last year. The orbit is off a little, but we can adjust the clocks a second here and a second there. The important thing is that the Sun will come up tomorrow. Reason balks again. It doesn't want to deal with the apparent fact that order flows out of irrationality.

    We round off *pi* to a mere four places, 3.1416, to obtain a number that a machinist can work with, but if the number were rounded once more it would be, 3.142. The Cosmos man, Carl Sagan was fascinated by *pi* to the point where he considered a cosmic message might be found hidden in it if we could just run a string of numbers out far enough, fast enough. Can the *pi* sequence be sucked down to a six-number average of .142857, or would the last number, 7, be unobtainable? Perhaps 7 is not tucked away out there in hyperspace, and will show up. In that case, the same six numbers will continue to fold out of themselves.

    The Great Pyramid is infested with symbolic numbers out of antiquity. The darn thing probably started all that numerology nonsense as people misinterpreted the numbers and couched them in stories. Then once the stories lost their first meaning, ignorance led to superstition. To some the number seven is magic. It is soaked in superstition, and imbued with symbolism. The Bible is awash in sevens. Contemporary gamblers dote on seven. Some notables like Christian Rosenkruez, founder of the Rosicrucians, had seven helpers in train. A square inch equals 0.007 square feet.

Playing with the number 7 on a calculator can be great fun. The six-number string .142857∞ shows up in infinite sequence when dividing 7 into all numbers other than itself and multiples of itself. For example, seven divided into one gives the basic .142857∞, but seven divided into two yields the same sequence that starts with two, .285714∞. Seven into three is, .428571∞, and into Six, .857142∞.

Three numbers are missing from all this fun: *Three, six, nine.* Perhaps if we manage to average *pi* down to the last seven, we'll find them, but if we do, the number three will not start the sequence. Later we'll find those three numbers in a different context, but they won't be found lurking in the pyramid *shape.* Six, three, nine, or nine, three, six lurks in the *field* the pyramid causes.

The rounded-off number for the angle of inclination from the ground to apex of the Great Pyramid is 51.43 degrees. In navigational terms that works out to about 51 degrees 26 minutes of arc. There is nothing esoteric about 360 degrees, though. If the circumference of a circle had been arbitrarily sliced into 180 degrees, 7 divided into it would be, 25.714285714285∞. On protractors representing 180-degree circles, or 360-degrees, the angles of 51.43, or 25.7 would look the same, and be the same

The mathematics that begot the Great Pyramid reveals a natural planetary rule of order. Napoleon's Mathematician, Jomard, was right on when he said that the monument was itself a record of an ancient system of measures. John Taylor's 25-inch cubit, stripped of its nonsense, makes sense, and Charles Smyth's development of a pyramid inch, though a lousy prognosticator, has in it more truth than metaphor.

My personal guess is that the Great Pyramid was built closer to the time when geologists think the Sphinx was carved. It may well be that all three of those pyramids on the Giza Plateau have a similar genesis. I don't have the up-close knowledge to dispute the experts on the details of this issue, but it seems from my distant view that a culture that didn't have the ability to think in the abstract, as the ancient Egyptians are often accused, could have designed the edifice of the Great Pyramid. I hold this view because the Egyptian written record does not mention knowledge of the interior architecture of the Great Pyramid, or hint of an understanding about its greater meaning.

Even though the Egyptians set aside the number seven as special, their cumbersome math used the number ten as a base. Who ever designed the Great Pyramid, knew the Earth was round, and that the universe in which we live is intrinsically based on the number nine. The zero is really little more than a convenience to ease the transition from one group of nine to another group. From 9, we count forward to 10, 11, then 12. But ten less the zero is 1, and 11 added to itself is 2, and 12 added to itself is 3. 19 is a restart since 1 and 9 equals 10, which equals 1, and that means 20 is 2 in the third group of 9.

In his novel, *Ancient Evenings,* Norman Mailer's characters discussed a religious Egyptian symbol for the number seven called a, *Sefekh.* No doubt Mailer is a better researcher than me, because I haven't found any such hieroglyphic symbol. According to Mailer's narration, this symbol is in the form of bow with two little tails hanging down from the middle knot. Yank on the tails and, presto, a straight-line results.

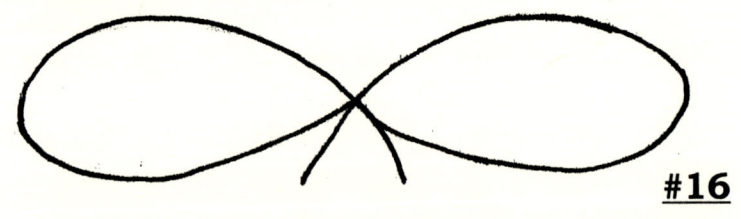

#16

I liked this idea a lot, because by removing the hanging tails we have, ∞, or the modern mathematical symbol for infinity. I asked a person who could stumble through ancient hieroglyphics if she knew anything about this, and she didn't know what Mailer was talking about. She did show me a symbol that looks like this:

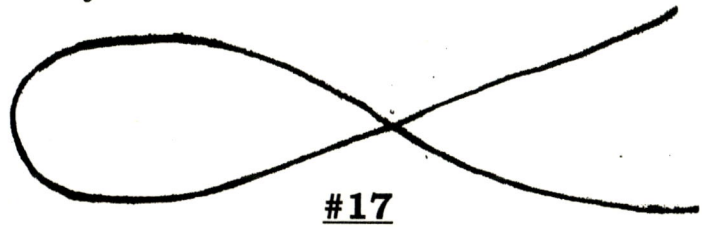

#17

I also liked this symbol a lot because it fit in with my magnetic field research. It also is the same shape as a celebrated UFO photograph of a piece of sky over New Zealand. However it is a symbol of Egyptian writing that supposedly has something to do with ropes, or the coiling of ropes. As translated it has nothing to do with numbers.

There is another symbol not, Egyptian and not written down anywhere, which can be found at the center of an energy vortex: Remove the infinite aspect of the center swirls, and it bears a striking resemblance to Norman Mailer's *Sefekh:*

#18

All three of these symbols will show up again, because rather than just being abstract language characters they depict rather nicely the motion of magnetic, gravity and energy fields. They are almost like little maps of the route those tiny madcap electrons take as they lift out of the quantum on their quest to satisfy the intent of consciousness.

No matter who erected the Great Pyramid, Egyptian, Atlantian, or Martian it could not have been built without the number seven. Seven is important, but there's a second number that rises up through the ancient literature to take on another importance. Messiah types like Quetzalcoatl, Buddha, and Christ gathered this number about them like a cloak. The Great Pyramid could also not have been built without the number twelve.

Open a dictionary to Weights and Measures then duck as twelves roll off the page. 12 inches is a foot. 12 times 12 six times equals a square acre. 12 ounces is 5,760 grains. 12 troy ounces, the measure of gold, is one troy pound. The Great Pyramid can't be measured in tenths without drowning in a flood of numbers after decimal points. It could not have even been conceived in tenths, because the builders first had to think in twelfths. Magnetic fields take on character when the numbers 7 and 12 are applied to them, and without magnetic fields the pyramid would be just another lump of cold matter.

We can't properly measure the Planet in tenths without choking on a profusion of decimal places that make no rational sense. But science does it anyway. Those long-dead French monks who blessed the World with the Metric System are, with the help of science, still trying to suck all of us into the morass of measuring every thing in sight in kilos, and kilometers.

It does not seem likely that the ancient Egyptians, with their unwieldy ten-based math system, could have conceived the Pyramid form. It's more likely that an ancient civilization rose up beside at least three existing pyramids, and then kings called Pharaohs adopted them, copied them, and planted in the sands beside them their cedar boats to the afterlife. But If I'm wrong, it doesn't make a bit of difference regarding the thrust of this book. Being wrong would only mean that the very ancient Egyptians knew about the continent of North America, and were aware of a natural condition there, which we will encounter later as something utterly bizarre. Even though they understood the world to be round, it just seems unlikely they had any grasp of the landmasses upon it.

This was a civilization, after all, that thought the Sun was pulled through the sky behind a chariot driven by the head god, Ra. One would think the technology that constructed such a monument as the Great Pyramid would have had a better understanding of the mechanics of celestial events. Perhaps, they did build the Great Pyramid; their technicians put together other amazing structures. Maybe Ra, while warming his backside with the Sun ball, looked down from his chariot, noticed the world had another side, and whispered this knowledge in a Priest's ear?

The Egyptian symbol for the Sun, as might be expected, was a circle. It was a circle surrounded by a narrow ring that looks to be about one-sixth the diameter of the symbol. It's possible they knew of the corona of a vortex, thus had an understanding on their level that today's science has yet to comprehend. It's also possible they knew how to look at a solar eclipse without going blind. The Sun, as a really big vortex, has a visible corona during an eclipse.

On the other hand, the symbol for Ra was the pyramid, and Ra was the creator. Did the very early Egyptians build the creator on the Giza Plateau, or was Ra waiting for them when they got there?

Whoever built the Great Pyramid had knowledge that is not in our encyclopedias. If we want to learn what they knew, we must examine what has been left without overlaying what we find with our modern prejudices. One way to dig out those ancient, mystic, mysterious, enigmatic, and superstitious numbers is to build a *scale* replica of this grand tomb for Cheops, or Khufu, or no one.

The real McCoy will always be more than any model. Not just because it's bigger, and heavier, but also because it contains within those two and a half million limestone blocks an interior architecture that reflects all those numbers with which we have been becoming familiar. First, though, we'll see how to make a model of the shell, and then we'll get into the complicated stuff.

A pyramid is a three dimensional object, and all I have to work with are flat pages, but oddly, a flat surface functions amazingly well for this purpose.

First, we decide what the baseline of our pyramid should be. The baseline can be any length we wish, but it determines all the other size dimensions. I'll choose a baseline that's large enough to work with, but small enough to fit on a normal sheet of paper; three inches. Should a larger model be desired, all that is needed is a longer line.

To fit this base line into a circle we don't need a protractor. A ruler and a compass will do just fine. A more simple way would utilize only the ruler. We could even dispense with the ruler. A truly primitive effort would make do with nothing more than a straight line, and it could be of a random length; let's say a forefinger. Anyone's forefinger will do.

Let's establish a point somewhere in the middle of a sheet of stiff page and apply a pencil dot.

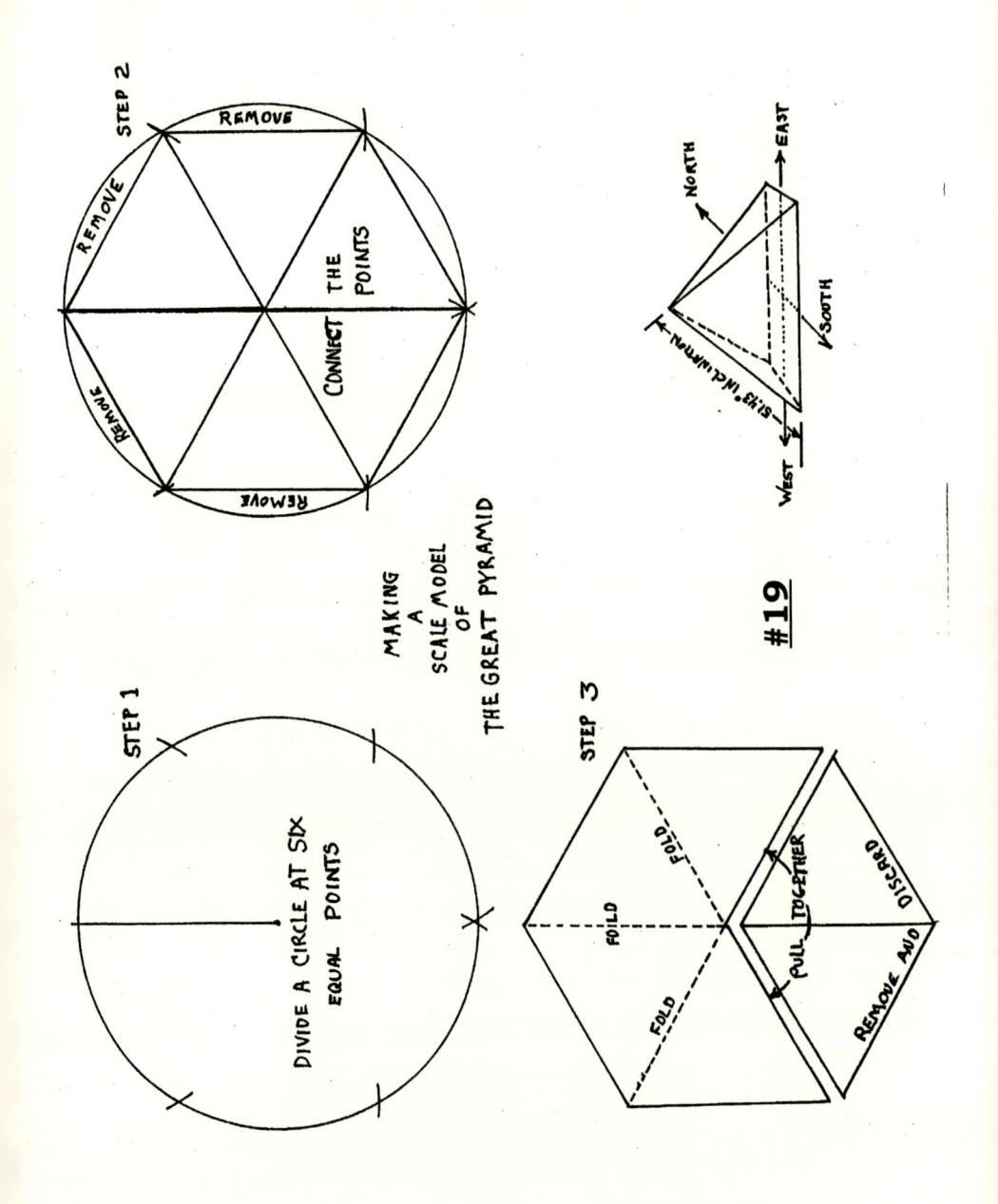

MAKING A SCALE MODEL OF THE GREAT PYRAMID

STEP 1 — Divide a circle at six equal points

STEP 2 — Connect the points. Remove.

STEP 3 — Fold. Pull together. Remove and discard.

#19 — North, East, South, West. 51.43° Inclination

Measure three inches away from this dot in any direction, and make another dot. Draw a straight line between these points.

Insert the sharp end of a compass in the first point. Open the compass so that the graphite, or pen reaches the other end of the line three inches away. Swing a circle, which because it has a three-inch radius, will have a six-inch diameter.

Apply the compass pivot point at the mark on the circle's circumference, and then use the drawing end to mark on the circumference in both directions from the axis of the compass. Repeat this action until the circle has six marks each almost the same distance from the others. Almost the same distance because our friend *pi* will interfere a little bit. Draw five more lines from the center to the circumference marks. We now have a pie, without regard to *pi,* marked into six near equal pieces.

Using the ruler, or any straightedge, "square" off the bases (crust) of each piece of pie. With scissors, cut out two side-by-side pieces of pie, and then cut off the crusts. Fold along the three lines separating the remaining four triangles. Pull the four triangles into the classic pyramid shape, and tape together.

Since the object is to end up with four equilateral sixty-degree triangles, the circle could have been dispensed with. We could measure four triangles using a protractor, cut them out, and lean them together. A sixty-degree equilateral triangle when tilted inward to touch a perpendicular line from the center of a square made from four of its baselines will incline at 51.43 degrees of arc.

I'm incorporating a circle to show how the shapes evolve from the circle, from where the other pyramid angles come, and even how the corona comes into being. We are not done making pyramids, and we'll watch the circles shrink, as the baselines remain the same.

In terms of shape alone, we now have a model to the scale of the Great Pyramid. This is the same model Drbal patented, which he claimed would sharpen razor blades and dehydrate organic matter. Should a reader wish to try these experiments, make a platform one-third of the height of the model, put a freshly used razor blade on it with its long axis aligned east and west, and then put the pyramid over it with a flat side perpendicular to magnetic north. A magnetic compass is necessary. While waiting, make another pyramid; put a dandelion or a bit of hamburger on the platform inside. Align a flat side north. Twiddle thumbs, and don't expect anything.

Few have ever claimed success with these experiments. If an old razor blade seems to remain sharp, or lasts longer than normal, it may be due to the probability that there is some dehydrating action going on. Water may be driven out of the minute pores in the metal, and its just not wearing out as fast from corrosion.

Whatever experiment is tried, it is claimed that one of the flat sides should be aligned to magnetic north. One obvious thing to try has already been mentioned, and that is to walk dowsing rods over it. It's easy to make dowsing rods. With pliers, cut the hooks off two wire coat hangers, straighten them out and bend a six-inch handle at ninety degrees on each wire.

Make sure the model is aligned magnetic north. Hold the rods out from the body parallel to one another in a loose fitting fist, walk them toward the little stack of cardboard, and hold them above it. Let them do what "they" want. They should react to the field by pivoting in the hands. If the reaction is strong, the handles can be felt to twist in the fingers.

A pyramid model with one of its base corners pointed magnetic north, rather than a flat side, should not elicit a response when the rods are brought over it. To further prove magnetic fields and pyramids work together, place a small bar magnet inside the misaligned model, its poles pointed at the flat sides, and the rods will again react. No platform is necessary, and the strength of the magnet need not be great.

The dowser, in an elementary fashion, is locating the vortex field created by the pyramid's reaction to, or effect on a magnetic field. Litster, it may be remembered, made it a point to say that the Gold Hill Vortex is not in and of itself an electromagnetic phenomenon, even though such an influence is present in a larger sense.

The Great Pyramid, and the other two that stand with it on the Giza Plateau, have their flat sides aligned true north. If a cardboard model's flat side is perpendicular to true north, the coat hanger dowser's rods will not be affected. The questions this brings up is, do the pyramids at Giza not create vortexes because of being aligned improperly, or do they have magnets concealed within?

Since Paul Bunyan is not available, we can't walk metal rods over the pyramids to learn the answer to this puzzle. Like other questions I've tackled, the solution came by stumbling around until I barked my shins on the answer.

After watching people in the Vortex wander around with dowsing rods, I rediscovered the difference I once had with my friend, Fred. The problem is with perception. Different people have different reactions. I already knew that vortexes mesh with each other at ninety degrees, and I began to notice that some people detect one vortex in one fashion but not the other. Could it also be that one type of dowsing rod gets a different reaction than another? At the Vortex we use copper wires, so I brought my old and trusted steel wires to work with me.

The answer, I learned almost instantly, is that "misaligned" pyramids like those at Giza still create vortexes, and they do not contain their own magnets. What seems to happen is that by turning the model within a magnetic field, the vortexes show either a vertical or horizontal reaction. An experimenter will get a reaction using copper rods, but not get any reaction when using steel rods, and in other cases the reverse is true.

Once an experimenter makes the steel coat hanger rods, he or she should then make another set from a nonferrous material such as copper, brass, or aluminum. If no reaction is forthcoming from a ferrous, or iron containing material like the steel wires, then the other rods should be tried. Sure enough, when a set of copper rods is used over a pyramid with its corners facing north and south, a reaction is forthcoming.

It has become axiomatic for me to say that a vortex is the combination of many vortexes set on an orthogonal, or at right angles to each other. At the macrocosmic level, a human being experiences one and not the other. In an elementary fashion it can be said that living beings experience what they have become tuned to, and ignore experiences to which others are tuned. On the microcosmic level, this may also explain how some people can walk through a room full of flu virus and not be infected. Life produces people who have different reactions from each other, and in terms of dowsing we can overcome this response, or lack of response by changing the material we dowse with. I've known a few water "witchers", and each had his favorite type of tree from which to cut a dowsing implement. One witcher's tree limb crotch may not work for another witcher.

Dowsing, many will contend, is a subjective experience, and the results therefore suspect. I don't dispute this, and know a dowser can override the subjective aspect and produce false results. I also know it is a practice that works, and one that many scientists begrudgingly accept. In a 1979 *New Scientist* article, writer Anthony Hapgood tested himself and determined that running water causes perturbations in the Earth's electrical field, and it's this disturbance that dowsers detect.

I see patrons in the Vortex tilting their wrists to make the rods turn, but the interesting thing is, most of them aren't aware that they are "cheating". We rely on subjective responses to get us through life all the time. Actions regarded as happening because of skill are hard-won subjective abilities. The reader might try walking up or down a flight of stairs by telling each muscle in each leg every motion to make. A pro in a bowling alley will tell the neophyte to *trust* the ball. On the surface, it seems foolish to trust an inanimate object to do anything, yet when the bowler tries to *steer* the ball, the gutter is far more likely than a strike.

A person who learns to let the rods do what they want to do, and not override the experience by forcing them to do what is expected, can accomplish some amazing things.

Now that we have made and dowsed an empty, hollow Great Pyramid model, it's time to look at the internal structure of the real thing.

One of the unique features of the Great Pyramid is that it has rooms and passageways up inside the structure. Most other pyramids were evidently built on top of chambers and hallways that were first dug out of the ground. The Great Pyramid does have an underground room positioned directly beneath the apex, but it's like a tiny basement, and not adequately explained by Egyptologists. It's just there, empty like the other rooms, and deeper than any other such chamber. It is reached by a steep, 27 or 28-degree passageway, but at a point at ground level, 90-degrees below the north face entrance, the angle of inclination to the chamber floor is an even 20 degrees.

Including the subterranean chamber there are nine relevant points to consider, and four of the nine are not obvious in this diagram.

Just above the underground chamber is the next point I consider relevant. It should be obvious to pyramid measurers, yet it is not. It is simply the center of the ground-level square formed by the Pyramid's sides. This point is directly in line with the underground chamber and the apex. Its angle of inclination from the base is zero-degrees.

#20

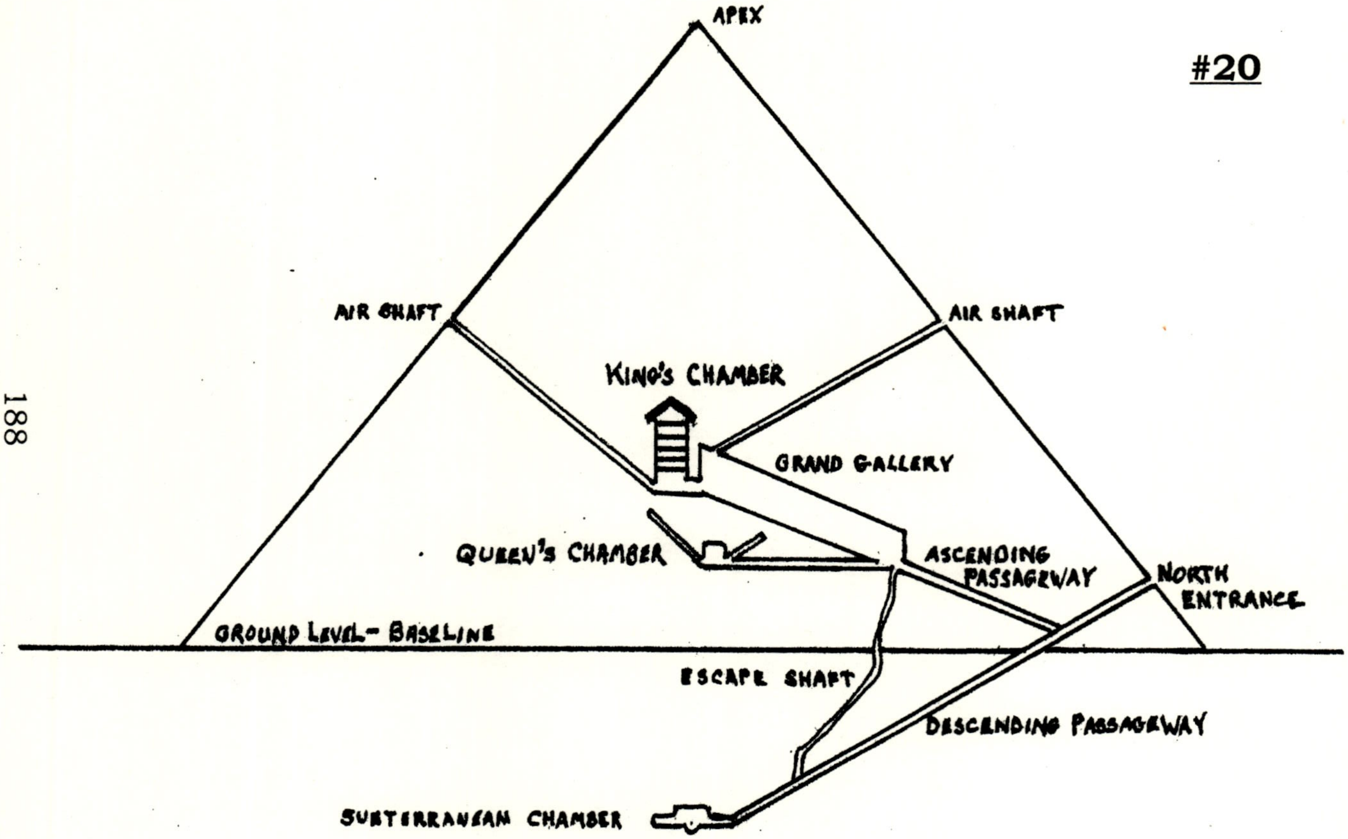

The next point up into the Pyramid is called "the Queen's Chamber". It's not likely any queen, dead or alive, resided here. The room came by its name because the conventional wisdom thought that if Cheops had a favorite wife to take along on the afterlife journey, this would be where he'd have put her.

This is a small, unadorned room, and it is not directly under the apex. A line drawn up from the underground chamber at six degrees north from the perpendicular line to the apex cuts through this chamber, and continues up to the top of the Grand Gallery where it crosses near the opening of a feature called an airshaft. Another line from the outside edge of the base intersects the first line in the middle of the room, and is on an angle of inclination slightly less than 12 degrees of arc.

At a 72-degree angle above the queen's residence is the supposed abode of her husband, the King's Chamber. This room is as bare as the rest, but its shape would make an old Greek mathematician drool. It is a rectangle half as wide as it is long, and its ceiling height is half the distance on a diagonal from one corner to another. At one end is the lidless so-called sarcophagus that no mummy ever went to bed in, and facing across from the low entranceway is the opening for the other airshaft leading to the south. The chamber has five flat ceilings and one pitched ceiling.

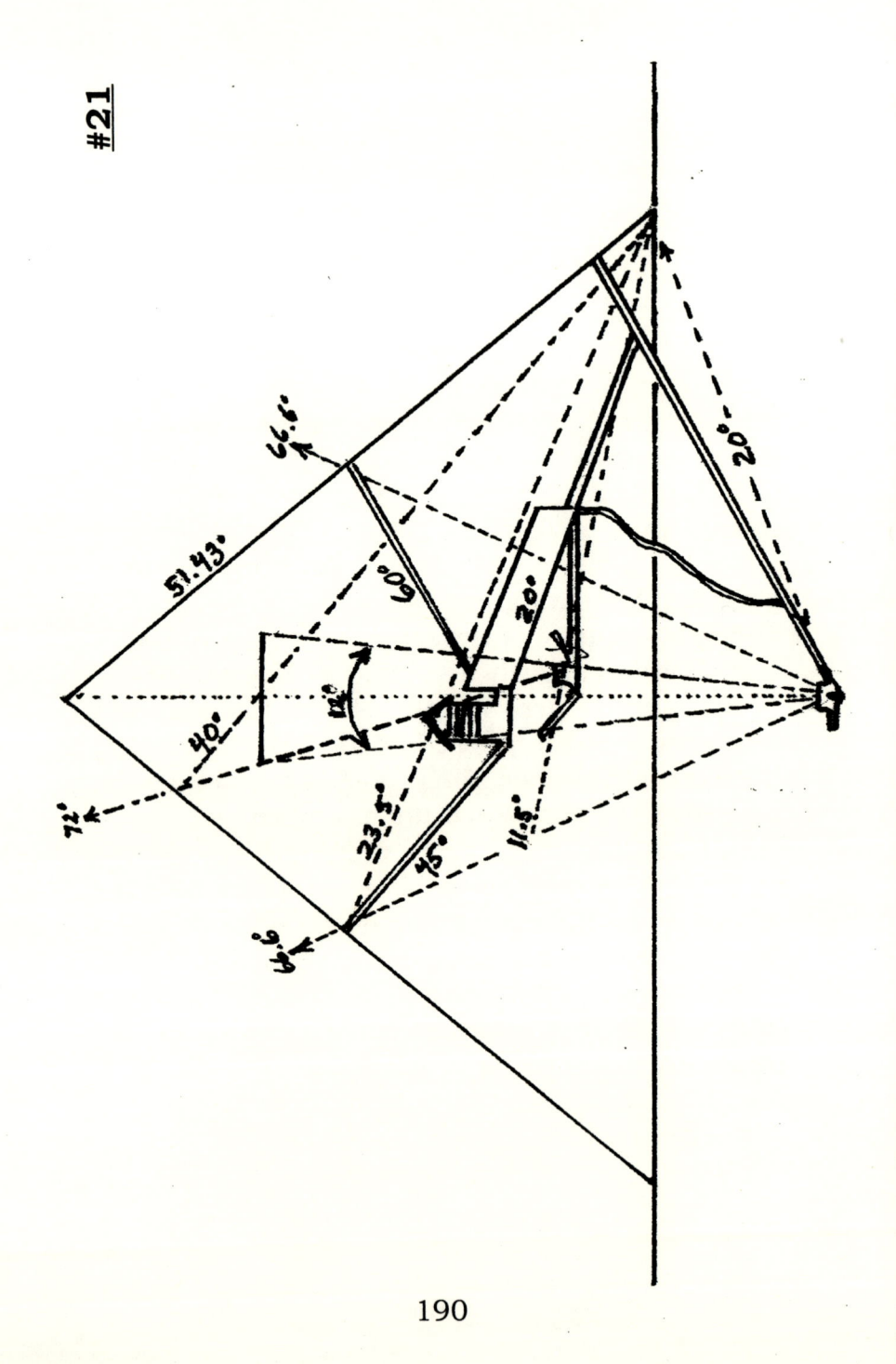

#21

The King's Chamber is also not directly under the apex, but offset at about six-degrees from a south line drawn up from the underground chamber. The several ceilings allow an interesting play of angles on lines inclined up from the base. A line from the outside edge of the base to the chamber entrance is on an incline of 20-degrees. The ascending passageway, and the Grand Gallery slope up to the chamber entrance at 20-degrees. A line from the base to the center of the fifth flat ceiling is 23 and a half degrees and leaves the structure where the south airshaft exists.

Both airshafts exit the pyramid's sides at the same height from the base, but approach at different degrees of angle from their starting points inside. The north airshaft is at 60-degrees to the apex perpendicular, and the south airshaft is at 45-degrees. Though these small passageways act as airshafts, it's unlikely this is their primary purpose. A simple airshaft would undoubtedly have been carved horizontally across one layer of stones. One doesn't have to be a bricklayer to realize the extreme difficulty involved in cutting these shafts on a diagonal, one stone through another, and then have them all line up perfectly.

The combined difference between the Queen's Chamber north offset from the 90-degree apex line, and the King's Chamber south offset is just a hair under 12-degrees.

Two-thirds of the way up from the base along the direct line from the lower chamber to the apex is the first hidden position point. It is at a 40-degree inclination from the outside base, and precisely below the apex. If there are any hidden rooms to find in the Great Pyramid, this is the area where I'd look. If there is no room to find, then perhaps a hollow ring may exist, whose circumference touches both 6-degree lines that rise up from the subterranean chamber. Considering the overall math, it seems unlikely the builders would not place some kind of marker at this point.

The sixth position point is the most obvious; the apex itself at an angle of inclination of 51.43 degrees of arc. It is the top of the four sixty-degree equilateral triangles leaning in to touch points. The difference between the 40-degree line and the 51.43-degree is a shade less than 12 degrees.

As seen in the more comprehensive Illustration, #22 the seventh position is the first truly hidden point, and it is not positioned on the physical pyramid. It is hidden on a continuation of that 6-degree line, which rises up from the basement to touch the Queen's and King's chambers, and the ring around the 40-degree line on the apex perpendicular. A 60-degree line from the south base in this diagram intersects this 6-degree line in space above the structure. Think of this as an ethereal 60-degree pyramid enclosing the physical 51.43 pyramid.

To make a 60-degree pyramid, four triangles are leaned in from the square of their baselines, touching their points to form an apex. These triangles when drawn in two-dimensions have double angles from the baselines of 66.6 degrees of arc.

I know... six, six, six.

The seventh level marks a somewhat esoteric departure from the physical, but it is not impossible to diagram. We now continue the 51.43 line up to intersect the 60-degree line, and at the point of this crossing, our old friend the 6-degree line meets it. A horizontal line drawn to the south from the apex meets the 6-degree line to form a reference point the significance of which will be seen in a moment. On a continuation of this horizontal line, the 72-degree line from the Queen's Chamber, through the King's Chamber, and a 12-degree line from the basement perpendicular both cross at the same distance from the 6-degree line as the 6-degree line is from the apex

At this juncture the essence of the vortex is changing. A new, smaller vortex has begun to twist into existence at 90-degrees to our old one, but at 0-degrees to the original baseline. A top view would show the disk of the new vortex, with the circle being swung from the apex pivot point, but I'm not going to bother, because we still have to plot intersections number eight and nine.

Number eight is a line again outside the physical pyramid. It is inclined at 72-degrees up from the base, with 12 degrees between it and the 60-degree line. Where this line intersects the still rising 51.43-degree line, another line drawn at 90-degrees to the pyramid's baseline intersects the exit hole of an airshaft on its way down. The 72-degree line rises to a point far above the original pyramid, and the 60-degree line terminates at the apex another smaller pyramid above the original. The 72-degree line helps form a tall pyramid built from a flat triangle of about 76.5-degrees, which is 23.5-degrees from 90-degrees.

The horizontal line out from the apex ends being segmented in six exact increments, which form the baseline of the smaller pyramid seen above the apex of our original.

The ninth step in this process is the most simple. It rises up relative to the original base at 90 degrees, and eventually makes a rectangle, the short sides of which are the baselines of two pyramids. One of these pyramids can be thought of as being an inhabitant of our universe, and the other perhaps existing in hyperspace.

Lines drawn from the four airshaft exit points form a rectangle. This rectangle is twice as long as it is wide. Its depth is the height of one of the little pyramids seen inside it, or one-half the distance across the rectangle on a diagonal from corner to corner.

These, it will be remembered, are precisely the dimensions of the physical King's Chamber. Where the forty-degree lines intersect in the larger triangles, or two-thirds up from the base of the Great Pyramid, is the position of the so-called sarcophagus in the rectangle that is the "King's Chamber".

I am more convinced than ever that some sort of structure, or chamber exists at this two-thirds point in the Great Pyramid.

Toward the end of the season in the House of Mystery Vortex, I began to notice an odd, very slow, six-degree of arc movement of a compass on certain lines. I believe this movement, or oscillation is depicted in illustration #22 where an apparent corona seems to contract and expand. At the axis of the Vortex is another anomaly that will be explored later in detail, and it is also found in this diagram as the *floor center*, which is at the forty-degree convergence of the small middle pyramid.

In the illustration the numeral nine, shown as ninety-degrees, cycles back to one (or ten) and the whole thing starts over again. In this universe, unless this numerical rebirth sneaks in to our perceptions as the precession of the equinoxes, we can't see it because it occurs in hyperspace. It's not really possible to see the precession of the equinoxes, because it is a slow swing of the wobbling axis of the Earth that alters our local view of the cosmos by one-degree every 72 years, and an event that takes 26,000 years to occur.

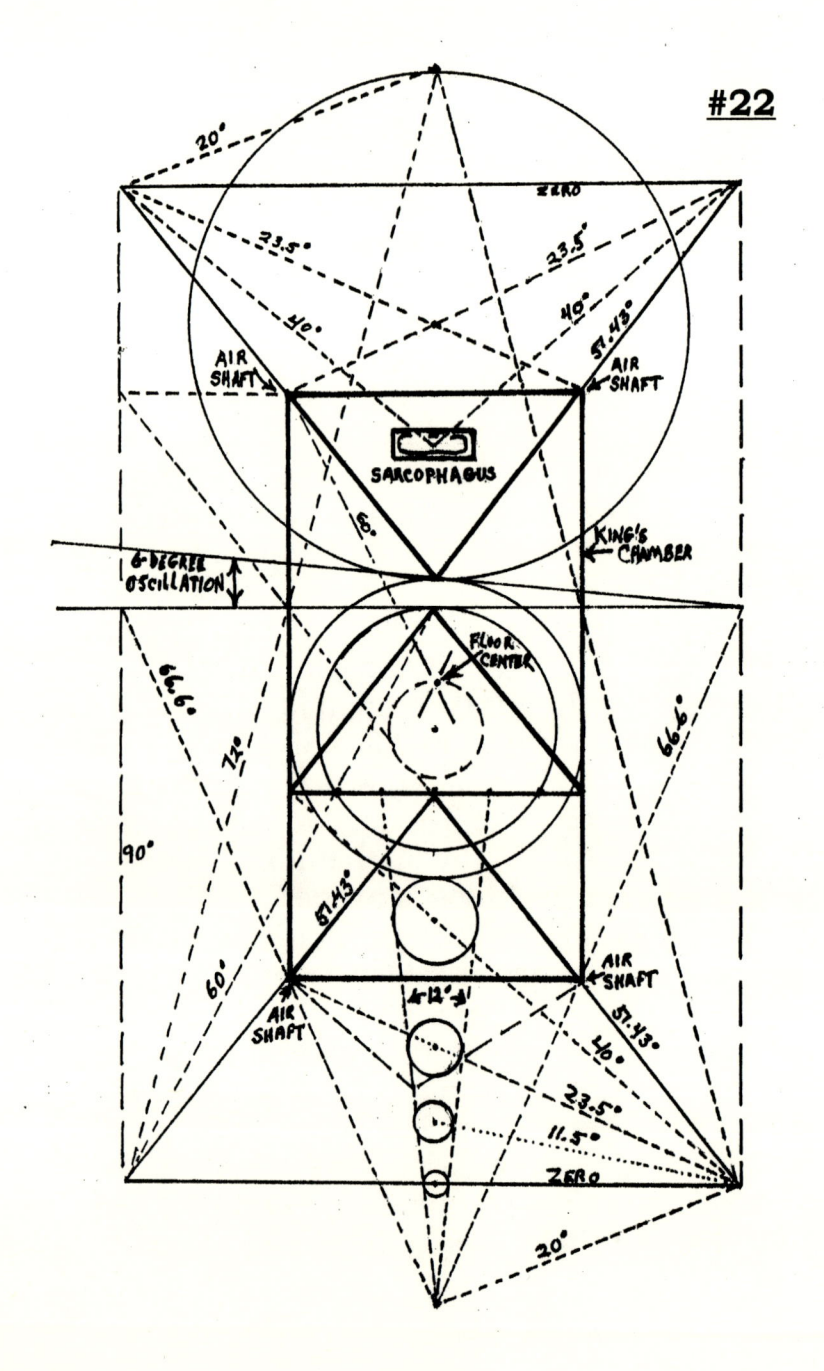

#22

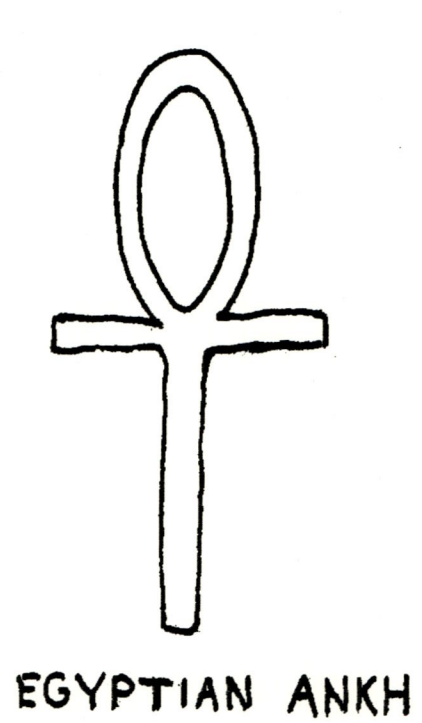

EGYPTIAN ANKH

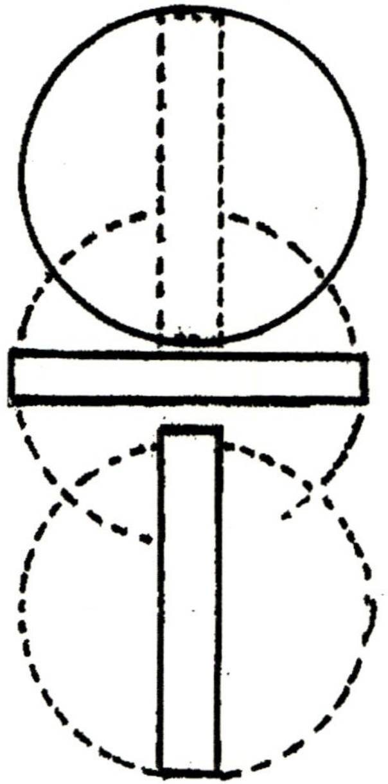

THREE OROTHOGONAL VORTEXES

#23

197

The question is: Does Planet Taylor's year equal 72 of our years, or 26,000 of our years?

The Great Pyramid was no more a tomb than Grandma Moses was a basketball player.

There are three vortexes implied in diagram #22. Think of these three vortexes as disks at right angles to each other, and diagram #23 is a simple comparison between them and of a familiar Egyptian symbol for life called the, *Ankh.*

It is also instructive to make pyramid models, the pointy tops of which correspond to one-third and two-thirds of the way up from the center of the base to the apex of our Great Pyramid model. To do this, go back to the original circle on which the four 60-degree triangles are already laid out. In this exercise the baselines of all three pyramids will remain the same, but the angles of the new triangles are different. Since the length of the base is known it's easy to fit the new layouts inside the corona lines. The original baselines touch the outer corona line. The short King's Chamber pyramid touches the inner corona, and the forty-degree pyramid is formed from having its baseline touch a line one-third the width of the corona.

The two double-circle rings are one-sixth the diameter of the inner circle. The solid line triangles are 60 degrees of a circle. The dashed lines are 72-degree triangles. The dotted line triangles are 48 degrees from the baselines, and have a 23 and a half-degree gap to cut out. This two-dimensional

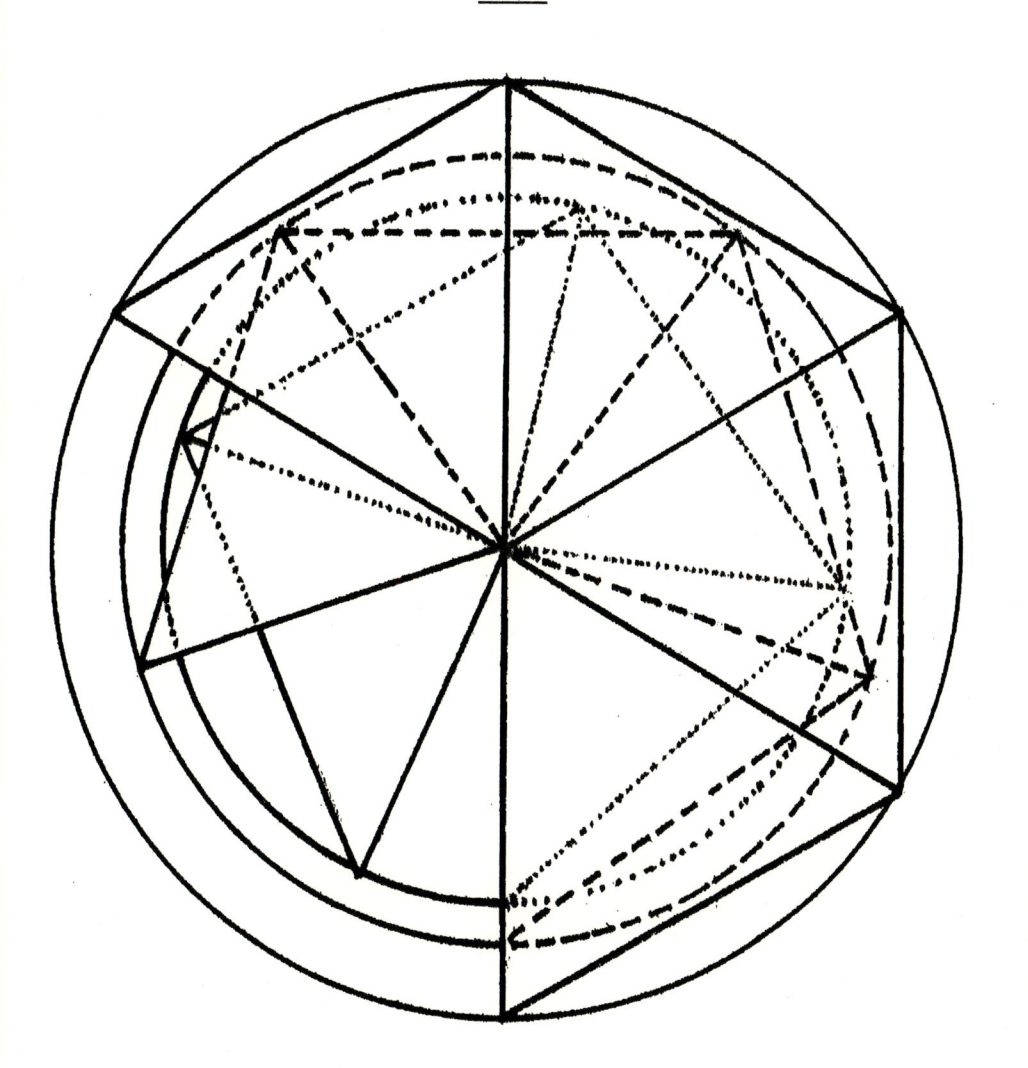

#24

gap is the same as the three-dimensional inclination to the top of King's Chamber, and is also *the same as the Earth's tilt to the plane of its orbit.*

When cut out and taped together these three pyramids, nestled inside each other like egg cartons, make dowsing rods dance in a way Paul Bunyan might have discovered his doing over the Great Pyramid. The rods also react out to 12 times 12 the distance of one-third the diameter of the square base. This three-inch pyramid forms a vortex 24 times larger than itself.

72-degrees minus 60-degrees is 12-degrees. 60-degrees minus 48-degrees is 12-degrees. 12 times 12 builds a zone of influence.

Let's try some more symbolism. Moses lived 40 years as a prince of Egypt, 40 years as a commoner, and 40 years as a savior to his people. Drop the zeros and there are three sections of four. Three *times* four equals 12, and three *plus* four equals seven. Seven divided into 91 is 13. So what? Well, other than those 12 disciples plus one Master, I'm thinking about the square *footage* of the base of the Great Pyramid.

It is an even 13 acres.

Is that a plug for junking the Metric System, or what?

One may be inclined to look at all this and say, "Well, isn't this interesting. Just look how smart those Egyptians were to figure out this stuff. And look at how they were able to fit it in so neatly with things like the Earth's tilt. The obliquity of the ecliptic, isn't that what Litster called it? And all those 20-degree and 12-degree lines? Weren't they clever to work that in to the their big ole pyramid? And that equinox thing…yes sir, that took some figurin'."

I think it's safe to say that the Egyptians, or Atlantians, or Martians did not make a pyramid, and then adjusted it so all these numbers, lines and angles would fit into it. Whoever built the Great Pyramid reverse engineered it to depict exactly what a certain part of the Universe is up to, and they found the blueprint lying all over the Planet.

John Litster located that same blueprint on the ground four and a half miles outside of the town of Gold Hill, Oregon. Revisit diagram #14 for a moment to see how Litster positioned demonstration platforms on intersections of some of these lines and angles. It's not likely he copied the diagram in Egypt, because he missed a few spots. The tours only use about a third of the entire area, and there are unmarked strange points inside the Vortex and its corona that are covered by brush and trees. Litster probably knew of these spots, but didn't develop them because the existing places are enough to enlighten without confusing.

The big debate should be about the placement of the House of Mystery inside the circle. Once the Great Pyramid's interior structure is compared to the Vortex, it becomes fair to ask how the old assay shack ended up occupying the space reserved for the King's Chamber?

Only one of two possibilities is acceptable.

One) The story is true as told. The mining company put the building in a convenient spot to serve the business, and in bad weather it slid off the foundation.

Two) The story is made up. Litster copied the Great Pyramid blueprint, and built the shack where it is, or moved it there.

Common sense and linear logic demand the second explanation be true, because the first explanation requires natural acts that stretch normal coincidence beyond the breaking point.

I, however, opt for explanation number one, and I do so because I know what's coming.

5

THE MOTOR IN THE MAGNET

Mort and I were camped out around my kitchen table, beverages and snacks at hand while we solved the world's problems. Mort had become one of our Reno group by virtue of divorce, and he was at my kitchen table because of the same dubious virtue. While awaiting a judge to award him ten per cent of his assets, and a hundred per-cent of his liabilities, he was keeping his head dry under my roof

Kitchen tables, and a good Mexican *Cerveza* have always provided great platforms from which to launch ideas, and this night was a splendid example why world leaders need to sit down with me from time to time. We had wiped out huge social and economic problems with no difficulty, and the conversation was revisiting the recent phony oil crisis rip-off. This debate occurred a year or two after Nixon opted for private citizenship.

"You know," Mort began, "I'll bet there's ways of makin' a car go without gas."

This was a subject on which I considered myself an expert, and during the next 30 or 40 minutes we discussed a legendary device that allows a ten-gallon per mile Cadillac to squeeze sixty miles out of a gallon of gas. Most consider these stories apocryphal, but I had reason to know better. As a kid, I'd been to the horse's mouth, and seen such an apparatus.

"Those rotten oil companies won't let these things on the market," Mort complained. He hung his head and slowly shook it in disgust.

I was about to disagree and blame those rotten banks, when he suddenly glanced up with a dreamy look.

"I always wondered," he said. "I mean, it seems to me that we should be able to make a motor with nothin' but magnets. Whaddaya think?"

"I think it won't work," I answered, and proceeded to render the standard arguments against such nonsensical ideas; like entropy, and actions creating *equal* reactions.

"I know all that stuff," he said, "but I can't help wondering what if?"

I went to the refrigerator. Discourse, when concerning the fascinating mental chewing gum of, "what if" , is known to be thirsty work.

Mort stayed with me for almost two months, during which time we turned the concept of a free-running permanent magnet motor inside out and upside down. It was a quasi-serious pursuit, which provided wonderful mental exercise, but during his final exit on his way to his own address, we shook hands and lamented that it was too bad that magnet motors just won't work.

He left with a photocopy of a United States Patent I gave him, which I hoped would make up for our magnet failure. It was Pat. #2,026,798, issued in 1936 to a Canadian citizen by the name of Charles Nelson Pogue. It was for a device called a vapor carburetor. There is an undocumented claim that in 1937, Pogue's carburetor made a Ford V-8 deliver over 200 miles per gallon on a test track. How this is possible is not a secret; vaporize gasoline *before* it goes to the intake manifold, and *meter the vapor instead of atomized raw gas.*

Mort said he would build the carburetor some day. I lost track of him and don't know if he even tried, but I spent the next two and a half decades trying to make the magnet motor go.

I collected books, magazine articles, and when I could find them, copies of relevant Patents. I also acquired hundreds of different kinds and shapes of permanent magnets, which ended up being scotch-taped into a few hundred experiments. It wasn't an obsession, even though it sounds like one. Months would go by and I wouldn't even think of magnets, then I'd read something, or wake up with an idea and plunge back in until the next failed experiment

There probably isn't a kid over six, or an adult who was once a kid, who hasn't played with magnets, and been fascinated watching and feeling the effect magnets have on one another. Most of us have wondered how a magnet can pick up gobs of paper clips, or affect another magnet with no visible connection. One magnet will leap toward another, or jump away. It's the first, and the best demonstration that an observable physical link isn't always necessary to influence a tangible object.

The end result of this kind of fascination and sense of wonder has provided a society dependent on electricity. Terms used to measure electricity like; Volt, Ohm, and Watt come from the names of people who used to play with magnets. Early experimenters were able to demonstrate that an electric current would flow in a wire by moving a magnet across it. From this, it was only a short step to show that work could be accomplished at a distance by feeding that current back across another magnet. A direct current generator, and a direct current motor are two identical pieces of equipment. Put physical labor into one, and get physical labor out of the other at a different location, but at a net cost of energy, which most feel is acceptable considering the convenience.

There have been, and still are dissenters who feel the manner in which electricity is generated is incorrect, and wasteful. By using devices like slip rings, or commutators, the polarity of electromagnets in generators or alternators is switched instantly from a pull, then a push, then a pull, then push, pull, push, and so on. This is a functioning system on which the whole world is running, therefore conventional wisdom sees it as not broken, and in no need of fixing. There are variations in electrical manipulation, such as Tesla's alternating current, but the basic generation of electricity has only become sophisticated and innovative, rather than intuitive.

It's almost as if there is an edict that comes from the same legal tome as Murphy's Law. *If something is being done in a certain way, then it should continue being done in that certain way.* Hopefully, this is just a human failing rather than a conspiracy, but either way it has surely had costly consequences.

A few brave heretics have dared look beyond the push-pull, on-off, negative-positive generation of electricity, but have found themselves fighting an entrenched dogma, if not a stubborn economical system. Over the years, I have run across the faint trails of some of these people, and have managed to collect a half-dozen U.S., and Canadian Patents granted for machines that claim to produce a current flow without an outside force turning a generator. It should be kept in mind that patents are not issued for devices of any nature, which are judged not to work.

During our kitchen-table brainstorming sessions, Mort and I would not have been surprised to learn others had beaten us to the prize, but we would have been astounded to learn that the first claim goes back to Canadian Patent #7,572, issued in 1877. The inventor's name was, Wesley Gary, and his machine was featured in a long article in *Harper's New Monthly* magazine in 1879.

The Gary invention is but one of a type that use movable pieces of iron shielding between magnets to achieve constant circular or reciprocating motion. I have built variations of this type, so I know they work. The problem with the design, I discovered, is the moving parts involved cut way down on efficiency.

The best of this type of magnet motor was U. S. Patent #1,724,446 issued in 1926 to H.L. Worthington. His machine used horseshoe magnets and employed rollers as shielding, rather than awkward flat pieces of metal.

As with the Vapor Carburetor, there is no secret as to how these things function. The means by which they work has nothing to do with switching polarity. It involves collapsing the magnetic field into a highly ferrous metal like iron, which has been inserted between two magnets. Even though the magnets are arranged with the same polarity facing one another, they can be brought very close together because they are attracted to the metal rather than being repulsed. When the iron, or soft steel shield is suddenly yanked out from between them, they repel violently from one another. The repulsion is captured by gears or levers, and at a certain short distanced the shield is reinserted for the next attraction to the metal.

The first trick is to get the metal as close as possible between the north-north, or south-south poles without touching either magnet. Even though a magnet might be but a hair's breath from a piece of steel, the two will slide horizontally as if greased. If the magnet touches the metal, it's like instant super glue, and sliding them apart requires quite a bit of energy.

The second trick is to time the shield removal according to the needs of the machine's design, and make sure it is done as quickly as possible. In most cases, this is done by the use of an electromagnet, or solenoid, which means electricity has to be diverted back into the system. A battery is also needed to start the thing. Most descriptions I've seen on these devices claim only one-sixth of the energy made is needed to operate the solenoids.

Even though we're talking about a mechanical device, we are again looking at a six to one ratio.

These are legitimate magnet motors, but still not what Mort and I envisioned. It seemed to me that the idea of shielding, though not the changing of polarity, was just too close to the idea of the mechanical commutator. So I continued my search of the true, one-size-fits-all permanent magnet motor. By speaking of a "true" permanent magnet motor, I omit the similar description sometimes given to direct current motors.

One day in 1980, an article in *Science and Mechanics* magazine made me sit up straight in the chair. A magnetic, and electronics engineer by the name of Howard Johnson, after a grueling fight with the Patent Office, had been granted Patent #4,151,431 for a magnet motor. It had only one moving part! I was at once unhappy to have been beaten to the finish line, and elated to see that my quest for the impossible had been vindicated.

I immediately sent for a copy of Johnson's patent, and as soon as it arrived I set about attempting to duplicate the machine. I wasn't trying to improve the device, and wished the inventor well. I just wanted to see this thing go. Years went by, and I never heard about Johnson again. I was also unable to copy his machine.

The possession of a United States Patent grants infringement protection for 17 years, and then the invention becomes public property. It took me at least the full 17 years to figure out that Johnson lied to the Patent Office by keeping most of the pertinent facts out of the document. It was either he lied by omission, lied on purpose, or he didn't know what he was doing, and stumbled into something he himself couldn't duplicate.

In the end, I did discover what made his machine go, but I had to fall off a ladder first.

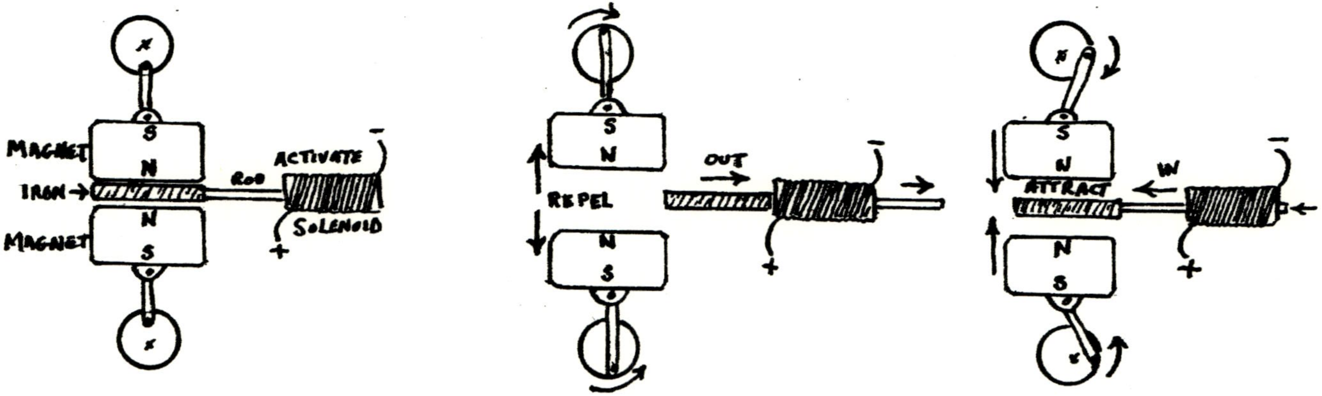

Simple magnet motor using removable ferrous shielding

#25

211

It was a cold February, about a foot of snow covered the ground, and I was about two weeks short of finishing the apple tree pruning. This job consisted of positioning an aluminum tripod orchard ladder in and around the tree, kicking snow from my boots, and then, loppers in hand, ascending to snip off as many suckers as I could reach before going back down to reposition the ladder. I didn't really fall *off* the ladder; the front tripod slid forward in the snow, the ladder opened outward and dropped to the ground. I fell *on* the ladder.

I also fell on my left wrist.

And that's how part of this book came to be written.

With a shattered wrist, it was necessary to employ someone to finish the pruning, and I found myself with time to stare out the window at the snow and think. I was also "blessed" with a very unconventional bone break, which caused unbelievable pain and aggravation. The doctors called it RSD, *Reflex Sympathetic Dystrophy*. When people asked what RSD is, I just said, "I don't really know, but I'm looking for an enemy sufficiently vile to wish it on."

I went through three fiberglass casts and four plaster splints, because my arm would swell out of them. When I finally said good-bye to the splints and casts, it took six months of physical therapy just to be able to touch my thumb to my middle finger. My wife, Lois, said that it looked like my hand was stuck on the end of my arm crooked. She was, during that time, involved with some people who were selling health magnets, and suggested I try them on my wrist.

I would have tried a witch doctor at that point, but I'm too cheap to buy a product from a multilevel marketing scheme for ten times what it's worth. Besides, I had a shop full of magnets.

I studied Lois's literature and concocted a cardboard bracelet of ceramic magnets. It was on about ten minutes when I noticed the ache in my wrist was moving up my arm. In fifteen minutes the pain was incredible and had reached my shoulder. I ripped off the homemade bracelet, and then stood looking at it as my wrist rather quickly eased back to its normal, bearable ache.

For every hundred experiments I've ever tried, ninety-nine of them didn't work. Usually each failure pushes me to try another. I'm perverted that way. With the magnet bracelet, I was faced with an experiment that had failed in a very dramatic fashion, yet it had actually been a success. If I could have such a negative effect, I reasoned, then surely a positive effect was possible.

Today, I have a hand that is straight on the end of my arm, and a thumb that can even touch my little finger. To be fair, some of the credit for this success has to go to Dianne McFarland, an amazing physical therapist (who once pushed a phantom finger right through my fiberglass cast), but a lot of this improvement came from what I learned about permanent magnets.

For this knowledge, I have to also begrudgingly thank a foot of snow, a malicious ladder, and pain I wouldn't wish on an enemy.

The first thing I needed to know is: What is a magnet? Magnets pick up paper clips, make electricity, and affect positively and negatively a biological entity. But why? My encyclopedia devoted several hundred words to the first question, but contributed little to the answer, and had nothing at all to say about the second question. Scientists are good at *what's*, but *why's* sometimes give them gas.

Science has a problem we all share. In the end, nothing can be *explained*, even though everything can be *described*.

The encyclopedia's several hundred words regarding a definition for a magnet can be boiled down to two words: Electron, and spin.

An electron, one of those little bitty "things" that make pictures on a TV screen, can be called an electric charge in motion, or a tiny magnetic field. In the company of most atoms, electrons are said to be paired, which means that electrons in a pair have spins that are opposite in direction to the other, thus canceling each other's magnetic field. A mechanical analogy is the smooth meshing of gears. Other atoms have more electrons with one kind of spin direction than the other, therefore a macrocosmic magnet results.

Howard Johnson claimed his patented motor worked because he had harnessed unpaired electron spins. Well, big deal. That's the same thing as saying he harnessed a magnet. I should have suspected something right away, but this was an explanation that meant nothing to me when I first read it. Even if I'd caught this evasive language, it wouldn't have told me how he mechanically utilized those magnets, or unpaired electron spins.

The Simplistic answer to what is a magnet, is that a lot of little bitty magnets gang up together and get trapped in certain kinds of materials. This gang of tiny magnets then attracts or repels other gangs of little magnets trapped in other kinds of materials. The reason the sky is blue, Johnny, is because it is blue. Little magnets make a big magnet.

Being sometimes thick of head, it didn't dawn on me that this simplistic explanation when carried out to a simplistic logical conclusion makes perfect sense. If an electron with a counterclockwise spin encounters an electron with another counterclockwise spin they repel. If the encounter is between a counterclockwise spin and a clockwise spin attraction is the result. I blew right by a wonderful shortcut by continuing to think in the same vein most everyone else has been working with for more than a century. Polarity.

Instead of attributing spin to only the electron, and since a magnet is a bunch of trapped electrons, I should have simply carried the spin concept up to the same reality level as the physical magnet.

Forget polarity. Think Spin.

But even this wouldn't have answered the next question. What *is* the "little" magnet?

The physicist's electron is an interesting entity. Electrons don't spin like normal stuff spins. Normal stuff - wheels, planets, balls on the way to becoming strikeouts, etc. spin 360-degrees of arc to get back to their starting positions. But physics tells us that the electron has a spin rate of one-half, and that means it must somehow spin twice the distance, or 720-degrees of arc to get back where it started.

When I first read this I thought the writer had jammed his head into reverse while it was going forward. But after much thought and experimenting, the senseless did begin to make a little sense. If the electron, after what we consider a full circle, flipped 180-degrees and spent the other half of its spin in hyperspace, that would account for 720-degrees, and when it emerged in our space it would be right back where it started. We can even put together a three-dimensional entity to use as a model for this idea. It's called a Mobius strip.

To make this model all that is needed is paper, scissors, and tape. Legal size paper, 8 1/2 by 14 is best, but 8 1/2 by 11 will do. A strip is cut at least one inch wide along the length of the paper, and then each end of the strip is marked with the number 1. On the other side a 2 is labeled on each end. Next, the strip is twisted a half turn and the two ends pulled together so that a number 1 meets a number 2. Lastly, the ends are taped together to make a loop with a twist. If the strip is pulled between a thumb and a finger, all the 1's, and all the 2's will pass under a finger without lifting it off the paper.

This can be thought of as a model of the complete spin of one electron. The electron traverses the number 1 side of the paper for one spin, and then travels along the number 2 side of the strip, at which point it starts over again. Two revolutions are necessary to get the circle all the way around under the finger.

It is necessary to make a wide strip, because the next step is to slit it in half the long way. A hole is made in the middle of the paper strip, scissors inserted, then cut along its length without taking the loop apart. This ends up giving us a strip that is half as wide and twice as long as the first one. The "interdimensional" twist has vanished. The new strip is in the form of a figure eight and displays a quarter twist in real space. This should be thought of as the orbit of an electron through the magnet material. One side of the loop is north, and the other south.

Hopefully the strip is wide enough to slit the long way one more time. When the scissors get all the way around again, the strip falls into two loops rather than remaining in one. The loops will be half as wide as the original, but the same length. Each will be a quarter-twisted figure eight, but they will be linked just like loops in a chain.

If the original Mobius Strip is the three-dimensional metaphor for a single electron *spin*, and the split Mobius is one *orbit* of an electron, then the split strips are the *connected orbits* of two electrons through the magnet material.

If the two strips are wide enough to slit one more time, the result will be four linked, and quarter-twisted loops. I have taken these iterations out to sixteen loops before the paper got too thin to slit. All sixteen were quarter-twisted, and linked.

In a magnet, it would seem that a mess of spin electrons are trapped, or linked in each other's orbits. One-third of them can be said to be in our universe, while another one-third are spinning through hyperspace. The last one-third, somewhere along that quarter-twist, are coming and going between the two spaces, or dimensions. The spin is one-half and covers all sides of the loop, but the orbits are in the form of one-quarter-twists that form the figure eight. The spin electrons are not connected, but travel on either side of the figure eight, so they can be thought of as being connected at a distance. The quarter-twist is

218

assumed a two-quarter-twist because spinning electrons cover each side. This is assumed to be a *two*-quarter-twist, because if we leave everything alone, a half-twist and a quarter twist account for only 270-degrees of arc.

Every time an electron completes a half-turn spin, the orbit may or may not be completing a quarter-turn. No wonder the quantum theory can't pin down the location, direction, or spin of any given electron - the darn thing never knows what universe its front side is facing. It doesn't even have a front side.

After all this, do I yet know what a magnet is? Not really, but whatever it is, it appears to be the product of an irrational universe, that in turn is being created by schizophrenic electrons. About all that can be said, is that a magnet picks up paper clips because it doesn't know it can't pick up paper clips. It also affects people because people, as electrical beings, are made of a bunch of spinning electrons.

Health magnets, like the ones that worked on my wrist, flowed from my quest of a magnet motor, and experiments for one brought me closer to the other. The Johnson patent had irritated me for a long time, but I was starting to get a handle on what he had done.

Johnson's basic design involved gluing square, flat magnets in a row on a piece of high-ferrite material, with all of them having one polarity in the same direction. Between each disk was a gap between a half and a quarter the diameter of each magnet. Above this track was suspended a kind of half-moon horseshoe magnet that was supposed to act as the armature, and move through the combined field from one end of the track to the other. Since I couldn't spend hundreds of dollars on having one half-moon magnet shape especially made, I improvised by fashioning this shape from soft steel, and winding it with magnet wire to make it into an electromagnet.

    I followed the patent drawing exactly, connected the wires to a six-volt battery, and nothing happened. Over time, I learned the shape Johnson used for an armature was unnecessary, and perhaps placed in the patent document to discourage guys like me. I found that any shape of magnet will work so long as it is held above the rack at 90-degrees to the magnets that form the track. For instance, if the track magnets are all facing negative, or north poles up, then an armature magnet at 90-degrees will move toward the direction that its own north pole is facing. There is more to it than that, however.

    The stationary track magnets also have to be spaced exactly to form geometric "switching" positions that are dictated by the length of the armature magnet in relation to the stationary magnets. Johnson neglected to inform the Patent Office of this requirement, and he certainly didn't give any dimensions.

#26

Various aspects of a Mobius Strip

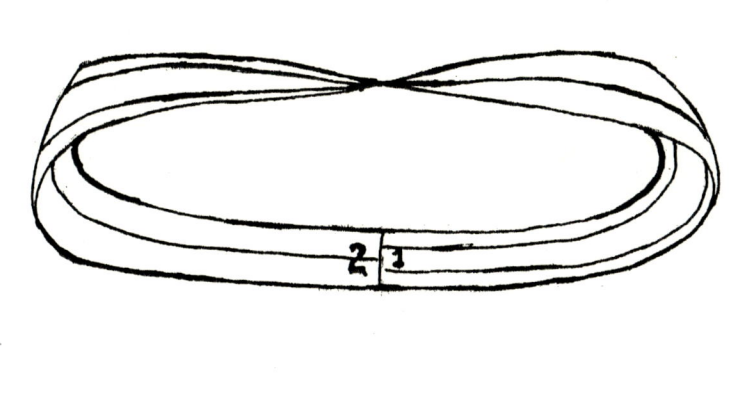

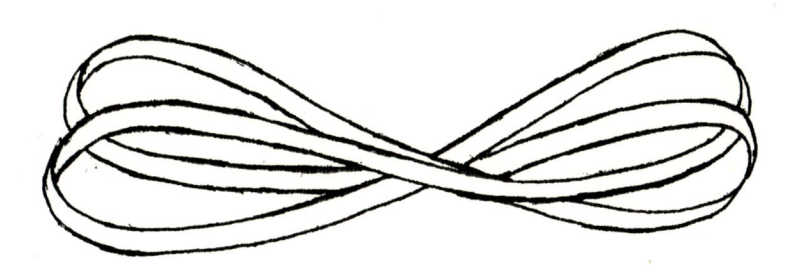

The patent contains descriptions of two types of motors; a linear motor with a beginning and an end, and an endless circular version. Eventually I learned how to make the linear motor function, but when the two ends of the track are pulled together into a circle the motor effect is cancelled. A line of magnets spread over a long distance would run a train to the end of the line, thus making the train the armature of the motor, and the track the stator, but if a powerful train is expected from this pairing, the track would be unbelievably expensive.

I came to understand that successfully completing the circle requires knowledge of the field structure in and around a single magnet. *A minimum of two real-world magnets that exhibit unpaired spins must be made to emulate two quantum electrons.*

This is not knowledge found in anybody's encyclopedia.

It was actually by combining parts of the old iron-shielding motors and Johnson's motor that I stumbled onto the health magnet solution. This solution led me right back to the motor concept, and I was finally able to rip the secrets from Johnson's coded patent document.

It wasn't as easy as one paragraph might imply, however.

If I couldn't solve Johnson's patent, maybe I could improve on the shielding motors? Months of staring at a solution I couldn't see passed, while

I tried all kinds of different things as switching devices. I noticed that steel ball bearings seemed to have promise as shields, but the ones I had were a bit large. Then one day I found a package of BBs in my toolbox and decided to give them a try. The little spheres seemed to do as well as ball bearings, and it didn't matter how big the magnet. Despite their small size, they collapsed the magnetic field on any magnet on which I tried them, and they rolled easily, which meant that very little power would have to be diverted back into the motor.

I considered what sort of design might best take advantage of the BBs, and it was through this exercise that I thought of arranging them on a ring of small disk magnets to utilize a mechanical tripping device. I already knew that a ring of three or more magnets, all with the same poles up, constituted the same pole field as a solid magnet. On my workbench was a large plate of soft steel littered with magnets held in various configurations, and there was a six-disk ring of one-inch magnets all ready to go.

Using guess-and-by-golly as an experimental technique, I placed one BB between every other magnet, and then held another magnet as a armature at ninety-degrees above one part of the ring.

The magnet began pulling my hand around the circle! My excitement grew with each turn of the armature magnet around the ring.

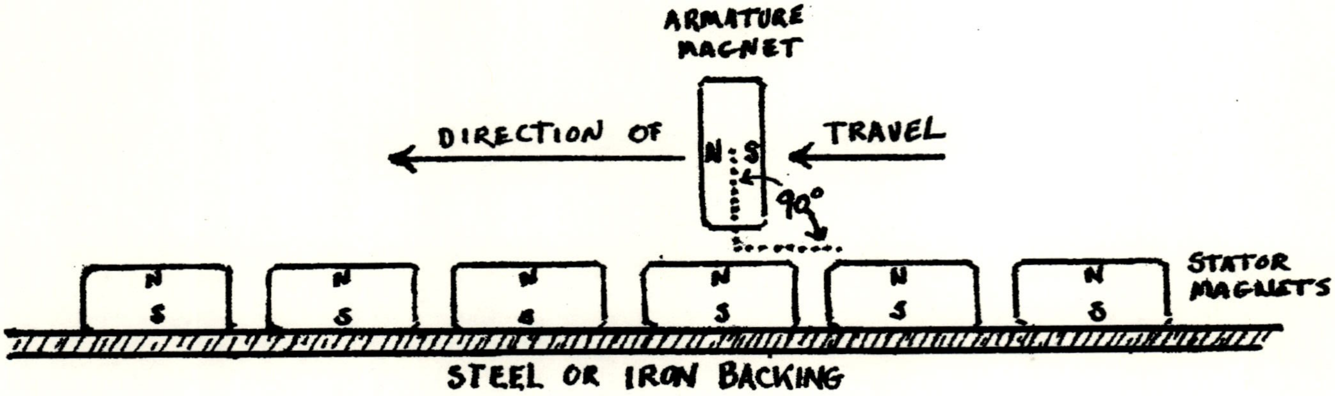

Simple magnet motor as depicted in Howard Johnson's patent

#*27*

During those rare times when things like this happen, I have a terrible habit of dancing in a circle, while chanting, "Yes...yes...yes!"

The problem with my little celebration was that I was holding the armature magnet, and when the dance ended, the ring was clear across the room. When I returned, and placed the armature back in the field of the ring, nothing happened. Each time I lifted it out of the field and replaced it, nothing happened.

I told myself I wasn't completely back to square one, and set out to duplicate the original feat. The feeling of that magnet in my hand circling the others without stopping or veering out of the field was so delicious; I would have stayed up all night.

Happily it didn't take that long. In a few minutes I discovered that the BBs had segmented the ring into three different aspects. When I held the armature magnet over one part of the field between the BBs, the magnet moved in my fingers differently than it did over another part. After a little tinkering, one of those sections caused the armature magnet to drag my hand around the circle.

I was on my way, but not without running into other padlocked obstacles during the course of my experiments. This time, however, I was in possession of the key, so the problems were mostly of mechanics and invention, rather than of perception, insight, or even luck.

I was to learn that the ring of individual magnets, when segmented by steel BBs, is actually the normal state of any solid magnet. Evidently this "normal state" wasn't something others had ever seen. I was able to *see* it because the BBs visually outlined a fundamental geometric truth that is not otherwise evident. Others hadn't seen that magnets have hidden aspects, because no one had ever looked for something that had no reason to occur to them. Even with this accidental discovery, it was not easy to develop the frame of mind that allowed me to accept what was right in front of my eyes.

It takes very little to alter the character of a magnetic field, but it takes a lot to understand that such a thing as character exists inside a magnetic field.

I use the word character in both its natural meanings: As nature or disposition, and as letter or hieroglyphic. The BB-separated segments do not change in terms of their positions within the field, but the aspects, or nature of that which happens inside each segment can easily be rotated from one segment to the next. The size of the segments can also be changed so that any one of them can become dominant throughout the entire field, but to do this the BBs have to change positions. In a solid magnet it is done in other ways. This altering of positions is like changing from letter to letter, as I am doing this instant by typing symbols into coherent forms. There is no language inside magnets complete with syntax, but it seems they are trying to tell us something.

A magnet of any size or shape is a physical substance that has captured a vortex. The shape of this vortex is no different than the Bermuda Triangle Vortex, or the Oregon Vortex. They are segmented in the same way, and all of them manifest a one-sixth-diameter corona. By laying lines across a magnetic field, its world is altered as we perceive it. A vortex in the wild, like the Gold Hill anomaly, is caused by the crossing of lines, but we shouldn't try too hard to discover from what these "lines" are made. The answer will almost certainly be the lines exist because of a relationship to other lines, which also have no manifest substantiality.

A few years ago, I firmly believed there is no demonstrable difference between the negative and positive polarity of a magnet. As far as I was concerned, polarity was just a way to identify, or talk about the opposite ends of the same thing. After all, the north pole and the south pole both pick up gobs of paper clips, and neither pole picks up any more clips than the other. It was a bit of a shock to learn there is a difference, but it was more of a jolt to learn just how different they really are.

I've come a long way. Hand me two magnets nowadays, and in a few seconds I'll find north and south on both of them. They are so obviously different that I've become convinced the two ends of magnetic fields, and also vortexes, are gender specific. The north and south poles may be related to, if not the same as, chromosomes. The north, or negative pole, is male (XY). South, or positive is female (XX).

So that I might coherently talk about them, the three separate segments of a magnetic field needed to be identified with names. Right after my discovery, I called them simply, A section, B section, and C section. I have since renamed them *aspects*, which more accurately describes what each one does, but I have retained the A,B,C labeling. Sections, however, or segments describe the very real physical boundaries, which could also be thought of as *lines of demarcation*.

These demarcation lines radiate straight out from the center of a magnet, cutting the field into "pizza slices" rather than the circular demarcation lines at the Oregon Vortex.

The A aspect allows the 90-degree magnet, or armature to move in whatever direction it is facing without stopping inside the segment, or veering away from it.

The B aspect causes the armature to twist in only one direction around its own upright axis. This is in the nature of a vortex swirl. The armature cannot move forward inside the B segment, and because it is a physical object cannot continue more than one turn into, or out from the vortex.

The C aspect is a combination of A and B. On the outside crust of the "pizza slice", the armature will twist the opposite direction as it will when positioned toward the point of the "pizza slice". This occurs even though the armature faces the same direction in both instances. Exactly between these two outside and inside positions, the armature, in a limited sense, will want to move in the direction of the curve of the field, or curve of the magnet. In this position the armature will not twist from the C segment, but behaves in the same critical manner as it does in the A aspect section.

It is in the unhindered A aspect that the concept of the magnet motor is found.

The B aspect interferes with the idea of a magnet motor and prevents it from occurring.

The C aspect contains both the possibility of a magnet motor, and its prevention.

Howard Johnson's magnet motor had to fit exactly within the geometric confines of A and C, while dealing ingeniously with the down-the-drain vortex aspect of B. B is the infinite in these descriptions, and if it can't at least be set to one side, the magnet motor won't go. My reaction to this was that the electron doesn't let infinity bother it, so why should I?

Not only are the three aspects different from each other, but their placement within the fields are different, and no one is going to build a working magnet motor until the code is cracked.

The north pole of a magnet is segmented in three aspect sections, but those three aspects are only evident when another magnet is thrust into the field at 90-degrees. The aspects begin to show themselves at this point, but they also show their own changeable nature depending on which direction the poles of this 90-degree, or armature magnet, are allowed to face in relation to the field into which it is placed. In the north pole three precise 120-degree segments can be located, but only if the north pole of the armature magnet is faced counterclockwise along the disk rim, or outer edge of the field. Hang on for clockwise.

The south pole of a magnetic is also segmented into *three aspects*. A, B, and C still apply, but along the counterclockwise direction of the armature they share *four sections*. In order to do this, they alternate. The four sections are precise 90-degree angles, and a given labeling might be, A, B, C, B. It could also be, B, C, A, C, or C, A, B, A. In each aspect set-up duplicates are directly opposite one another. For instance, one B will spin clockwise, while the other B will rotate counterclockwise. The positioning of the aspects can be manipulated, but the natural positions are A, B, C, B.

It can be seen in this instance that the symbolism of three added to four to make seven, and three multiplied by four to make twelve is no longer symbolism. This is a tangible fact that has been hanging around inside magnetic fields and vortexes forever.

An odd circumstance occurs when the 90-degree armature is turned to face clockwise in the south pole field. The situation changes from four aspect segments to three, however these segments are not 120-degrees apart as they are in the north pole arrangement The B segment takes half of the circle, or 180-degrees, and A and C share the other half in 90-degree sections. The south pole clockwise aspects cannot be manipulated into different segments in the same manner as the counterclockwise aspects in both the north and south poles.

In so far as the magnet motor is concerned, the north pole allows only one armature direction to be used, which normally is counterclockwise. The south pole can be used as a magnet motor in either a clockwise or counterclockwise direction, but the armature magnets have to be set up differently.

For a long time, I didn't know why the north pole, or negative was unidirectional, and then one day while trying to learn this very thing, it was revealed.

I knew that even though the aspects could be changed from segment to segment, the segment lines, once found and marked on the face of a magnet, do not change. I also knew that the north-south dimension of the armature, when crossing or straddling these lines causes the entire A, B, C aspect arrangement to move from one segment to another. Whenever I inserted the armature into the north pole field facing clockwise, I would only get a variation of the aspects, which then resulted in the armature stopping or twisting out of the field.

While idly playing with my toys one day, the magnet in my hand surprisingly made one complete circle of the bigger magnet's stationary field, and then abruptly stopped.

While holding the armature steady, I breathed deeply, and fought the urge to dance.

Does it want to do anything other than just stop, I asked myself?

The most important thing I had to learn when I first started to play with magnets was to hold them loosely enough so the direction of their movement was conveyed to my hand, but tightly enough not to lose control of them. Most of the magnets I use are ceramic, and therefore are quite brittle. I have a large stack of broken ceramic magnets, because they got away from me and hit the floor, or violently slammed into another magnet.

Slowly, I eased my grip on the armature magnet and felt it twist outward away from the center of the stator magnet. It turned completely around, 180-degrees, and stopped twisting.

Now what? I asked myself, *Anything else?*

The armature again wanted to go on around the stator, but in a counterclockwise direction rather than clockwise. As it finished the first circuit I thought it might stop, but it continued on. It went the second time around, then three times, and after the fourth, it stopped. Something deep inside was beginning to protest.

No way! The skeptic in me pleaded.

In this new position, it twisted 180-degrees again and headed off clockwise around the stator. It made two complete revolutions, stopped, twisted, and took off counterclockwise.

You've got to be kidding! I knew where it was going, and I was going with it right to the end. No victory dance.

There were three more revolution iterations. Counterclockwise for eight turns. Clockwise for five revolutions. Then seven revolutions in a counterclockwise direction. At the conclusion of seven turns, the armature stopped, twisted 90-degrees instead of 180, and seemed to display no more intent to move.

One.
Four.
Two.
Eight.
Five.
Seven.

I was too stunned to dance, or even think.

I made a couple of false starts trying to duplicate what had just happened. I knew the general area where the show had originally started, so it didn't take long to discover that the south pole of the armature must align precisely beyond one of the demarcation lines before it would do the clockwise

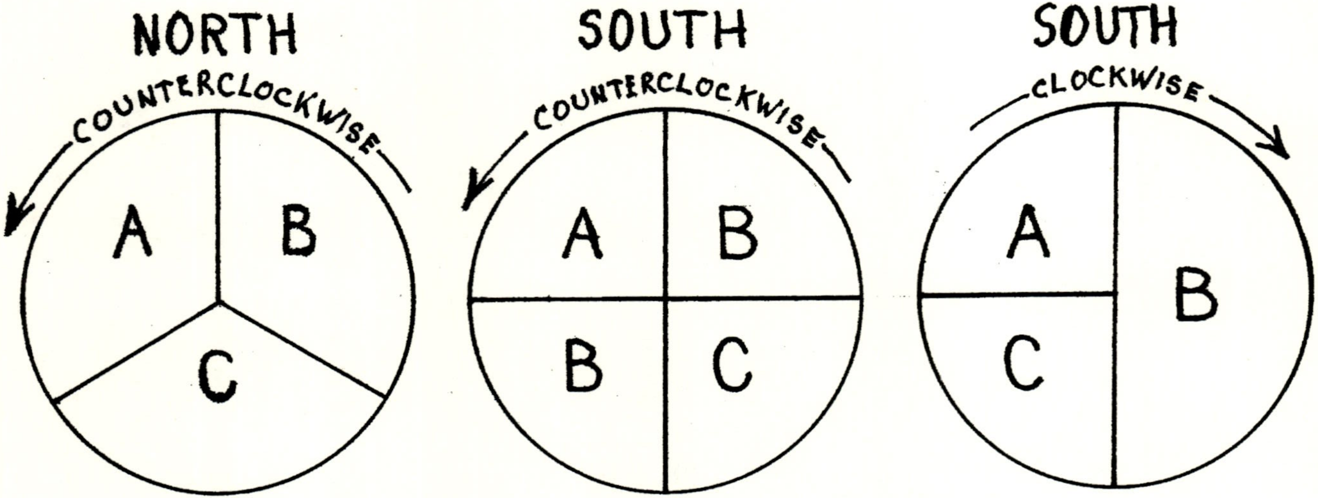

MAGNETIC FIELD ASPECTS

#28

trick. After a few run-throughs there was no denying the obvious.

A magnetic field physically contains the mathematical result of dividing seven into one, or seven into the circumference of a circle:
142857!

During the euphoria of the discovery I didn't notice that this weird way of running the equation didn't seem to contain ∞, or infinity.

If I'd ever had even a small doubt that the Great Pyramid was not a tomb, I threw it out. It is evident that whoever designed the Pyramid knew reality is not only describable by numbers, but that reality may actually be a *construct of numbers.*

Much later, I learned that when the armature magnet reaches number 7 and turns 90-degrees, it really wants to go to the boundary between positive and negative. Once there, it twists 180-degrees, continues into the south pole field, where it pivots 90-degrees. The first time this happened, I was surprised, but not overwhelmed to feel the magnet travel around the south pole field six times, stop, twist, and go around three times, stop, twist, and travel nine times around, at which point it turned outward by 90-degrees, and headed back toward the north pole field, turning 180-degrees at the boundary between north and south.

So ∞ is contained in this physical equation. It's just that infinity must use both poles of a magnet to find all nine whole numbers, before it can start over again.

I am never sure which direction the armature magnet will turn once it reaches the south pole field. If it turns counterclockwise, nine revolutions are counted off first, but if it twists clockwise, then six revolutions count off. Three is always in between six and nine.

The secret of the magnet motor lies in the fact that the motor is in the magnet.

I can only assume Howard Johnson knew this secret, or enough of it to construct a working model, which he and his lawyer physically took to Washington, D.C., and used it to force patent examiners to grant a patent. The Patent Office originally declared Johnson's invention a perpetual motion device, and denied his first application. It is expressly written in law that perpetual motion machines cannot be granted patents because they are impossible, and therefore do not exist.

The one big clue he did put into his patent was a reference to a permanent magnet being akin to a room temperature superconductor. He didn't, however, provide detail as to how get the superconductor, or the motor out of the magnet.

Since Johnson patented his machine in 1979, a logical assumption would be that by 2000, four years after his patent ran out, the world would be less dependent on oil. The reader is invited to conjecture why this is obviously an illogical assumption.

The reader may also take the information thus far encountered, and attempt the rest of the research it will take to lift the motor out of the magnet. Have I already done this? Sure, I know the rest of the secret, but I'm not going to waste it on a Patent. I have Patents for other things, and no good has come of them. But just in case I change my mind, a description of how to make a functioning permanent magnet motor is not included in this work, because there is another Patent Law, which says if a device is copyrighted, it cannot be patented.

Sorry.

A kind of slight of hand has been going on in the area of power generation for a long time, and for those who may be worried the world is running out of energy, be advised that by the time oil becomes scarce, Johnson's device, and many others like it will miraculously appear.

One of the offshoots of my research over the last few years is the knowledge that some of my discoveries are rediscoveries, and if the knowledge of the pyramid builders is factored in, all of it may be old news. Even though it might be old news, a huge majority is learning new things. One of those new things involves a craze that is sweeping the land.

As I write, health magnets are being hawked everywhere. Some of these products, despite what I consider the ignorance of the designers, help many people. A lot of these "devices" don't do a thing, some actually harm, and most of them are garbage. Sometimes the most expensive of these concoctions are the most useless.

My wife, the person who suggested I try magnets on my wrist, acquired a large magnet pad that could be used to sit on, or spread out and reclined upon. She kept it on her side of the bed, and bragged how good she felt in the mornings. For a year or more, proclaiming great success, Lois slept on it. Then one morning, and for the next two mornings, she complained of feeling odd, and of being tired. Her sleep was sluggish, and without dreams. She was getting up with a headache, and her body ached in every joint. There didn't seem to be any sickness, she displayed no fever, and by midafternoon the symptoms had abated. Each morning, though, her condition worsened, and it showed.

As my grandmother used to say, she "looked like something the cat drug in".

At about this time my injury was just beginning to respond to a magnetic application of my own. I was learning new things almost daily, but I still remembered vividly the negative experience with my cardboard magnet bracelet.

"You still sleeping on that magnet pad?" I asked.
She nodded. "Yeah?"
"Try a night or two without it," I urged.
She never used it again.

The pad had somehow gotten into a very negative field configuration, and went from a benign or even helpful phase, and had turned on her. Her whole body was reacting just the way my arm had done, and her sympathetic nervous system was getting more and more out of whack with each passing night.

A few weeks after this, my next door neighbor, a young man by the name of Mauricio, knowing of my work with magnets, came to me and asked if I knew where he could borrow a magnet pad. He was having back pains, and someone told him to try such a thing. Thinking the pad might react to him in a different fashion, I retrieved it from the corner into which it had been tossed, and bade Mauricio to give it a try.

I laid it on the floor, and he stretched out on it. Ten seconds later, he leaped to his feet. From the agility of his ascent, I thought for a moment it might be an instant back cure. Then he began to complain.

"Oh no," he said, glaring down at the pad. "That thing made my whole body ring, and my head is spinning."

I convinced him to try other ways to lie on it. He turned it over, and even tried to lay on it sideways, but the effect was the same. The pad had managed to make itself into an eighty-dollar piece of garbage that was capable of doing harm.

Dianne, my physical therapist showed me a smaller neck pad she had used for quite a while, until it started giving her headaches. She wanted me to fix it. I told her to bang it up against a car fender, but other than that, I had no idea how to fix such a thing.

At about that same time, my father-in-law who lives with us, and who is closer to one hundred than he is ninety, had gotten sick. We seriously thought this was the end. Among other things, he had developed an unbelievable case of hiccups that had gone on night and day for more than a week. With the double lesson of the magnet pad recent in my memory, I recalled he was wearing a pair of magnetic footpads in his shoes. When he wasn't looking, I took the pads out to my shop where I tested them with my usual arcane methods.

I got no results at all from either foot pad, but when they were placed side by side, my dowsing rods went nuts, swinging violently in my hands. We took the pads away from him, and the next morning the hiccups were gone. Two days later the old boy was out in the garden pulling weeds.

Most of the companies that make and sell these body pads, or wraps, use a combination of several magnets spaced near each other with the poles alternating north, south, north, south. Usually the advertising for these things is pure hogwash, like, "Sixteen powerful magnets placed in strategic scientific patterns." For one thing, they all use either rubberized magnets, or in some cases ceramic magnets, neither of which can logically be considered "powerful". For another thing, science hasn't a thing to do with "strategic" placement. For the most part, science doesn't believe in these things, and they are just slapped together in patterns that look interesting, like star shapes and other forms.

By accident, some of these products actually help, but mostly they don't do a thing except convince the mind they are helping. Somehow, during the course of using them, the combination of magnets can get locked into a bad configuration, which is akin to altering the aspect placement in a single magnet. A magnet's character can be changed with almost no effort, and being placed close to a human body can and does change the character of a magnet.

I recommend that someone wanting to try magnet therapy, use only one magnet, and to start off with, use only the north, or negative pole. Unlike the combination of multiple poles that can get locked into a bad, or even a good symmetry, a single magnet's configuration can be easily reversed.

Sometime after the experience of my negative bracelet, I learned how to deliberately duplicate it, and to do so in one small magnet. I called it my evil magnet, and kidded people not to get on my wrong side or I'd slip one under their pillow. Just touching the thing gave me the willies, but I needed a neutral party to test it to make sure I wasn't dealing in wishful thinking, and fooling myself.

There was an old family member hanging around the house at that time that I thought might help. Her name was Misha. She had four legs, a stub tail, and long whiskers. Anyone who has ever lived around cats knows they have odd habits. They will pick certain spots in which to nap, and in a week or two abandon it for another spot. It seems to me that cats know where the lines of the world cross, and prefer to lie there. After a time, the lines of the world move, cross someplace else, and the cat follows.

For three evenings in a row, Misha had come into the living room from her food dish, lay near the fireplace by a stuffed toy giraffe, take a bath, then nod off for an hour or two curled up next to the toy. On the fourth evening, before she got there, I sneaked an evil magnet under the stuffed giraffe, and settled down with the evening news to wait.

Right on schedule, Misha, tongue licking her chops, walked across the floor toward the fireplace. Three feet from the giraffe, she stopped dead, her mouth gaping open in that odd way cats have when they're puzzled by something. She stood like that for about 30 seconds, and then walked a wide circle around the stuffed animal to the opposite side of the fireplace. She settled down a good four feet from her old spot, but couldn't sleep, and kept getting up and turning around. Finally, she abandoned her spot and hid in the hall closet.

Feeling like an awful cad, I got up and removed the magnet. It made no difference. Misha never went back to the spot, though she looked at it several times after that.

Seeing Misha stop three feet away from my evil magnet, and watching dowsing rods react two or three feet above magnets led me to test for the field's limit. Since it was obvious the field could be detected even though the testing device wasn't connected to the magnet, I wondered if an altered magnet, like a pyramid, was projecting a field well beyond its physical size? I really wasn't surprised to discover that it was, and the extent of the limit, though jarring to the intellect, fit right into everything else I was learning.

The horizontal, circular lines of demarcation out from the magnet worked out as six feet from the center, with a two-foot corona. I was using the usual one-inch ceramic disk magnets, so the math was fairly simple. Arbitrarily segmenting the magnet into twelve spaces across its diameter, and then multiplying that times 12 gave me the first demarcation line as a 12-inch diameter circle, which I had found. Then twelve times that yielded a 144-inch diameter, plus a 24-inch corona. I have no good idea of what this large field consists. It's not gravitational, magnetic, or electrical, but it is there. I suspect it may be biological, and as we'll come to see, its character changes at least one more time as it expands outward beyond the ability to determine or detect a physical limit.

I also suspect this 12-foot field is the primary reason *some* magnets work with a living body, human or animal, to treat and even cure certain ailments. I emphasize *some*, because to work properly a magnet has to be manipulated to project the field. On its own, all a magnet does is make electricity and pick up paper clips.

Magnets do work to alleviate pain, and even to combat certain diseases like colds and flu. They work best when they can be used in only one of their A, B, C configurations, and B is not one of them.

All that is needed is a simple permanent magnet available from a hardware store, or a place like Radio Shack. It can be a round disk or square, but not a horseshoe magnet. It doesn't matter if it has a hole in the middle, because just like a vortex, its center is an eye-of-the-hurricane dead zone. It must be magnetized north on one·side, and south on the other. If the magnet is not stamped as to its polarity, the needle on a cheap compass will point to its north, or negative pole. (That's negative in the electrical sense.) The typical refrigerator magnet should not be used, because they are normally magnetized north and south on the same face like a tightly packed horseshoe magnet.

There is an easy way to reconfigure a single magnet that doesn't require tools other than the human hand. Since no magnet comes with it's aspect segments labeled, it's wise to assume when it's first picked up that it is not in its normal, "off-the-shelf" state. A single magnet can be locked into a configuration just like a pad of several magnets, but only if both of its poles are changed at the same time. It took me quite a while to learn that when only one pole is altered the magnet will, during a period of time, revert to its normal state.

I once spent most of an entire day timing the reversion of a magnet with an aspect configuration that was out of balance. When a human hand, or any part of the body, touches a single pole of a permanent magnet that pole is changed, but not the other pole. Left alone, the magnet will revert in an average of three minutes and seventeen seconds to its normal condition.

The first thing that needs to be done is every time the magnet is to be used one pole face should be touched, and then nothing more done for about four minutes. This assures that any locked-in bad effects are dissipated. Chances are this procedure will be unnecessary, but since a neon light doesn't flash BAD, it's a prudent precaution.

At all times during these preparations the magnet should be handled only by its sides. The pole faces are touched deliberately.

After the short wait, and holding the magnet on its sides between the thumb and a finger, it should be placed in the palm of one hand. Most of us will put the north pole face down in the left hand, but others may, after experimenting, have better results with the south face down. I mention this to alert southpaws. Once the magnet is laying in the left hand, the right hand is placed on the magnet. There's no need to squeeze, all that is required is a single light touch. The hands, reflexologists rightly tell us, are like magnets. The palm of a left hand is usually negative, and the right palm is normally positive.

When the magnet is lifted up, and only after it is lifted, it becomes locked in a generally beneficial configuration. Holding the altered magnet on the sides between thumb and finger, isolate the pain spot, and tape the magnet north pole against exposed skin. It must be remembered to do this without touching either pole.

A rule of thumb is that pain should always be treated with the north pole. A virus should be given a dose of the north pole, but bacteria hate the south polarity. With a cold or flu, especially when accompanied with a sore throat, the magnet should be taped to the base of the neck right where the clavicles form that big U. The magnet goes where the problem is. If a leg hurts, find the sorest spot on the leg and tape it down. It the problem is a headache then the magnet goes over the place that seems to be the source of the greatest pain. If something like a sinus infection accompanied by colored residue in the handkerchief is the complaint, then the south pole goes over the point displaying the strongest sense of soreness.

These are not instructions, only "rules of thumb", and nothing I say can be guaranteed. The biggest problem with the one-size-fits-all magnetic health products is that one size does not always fit all. Even with these suggestions a person may have to experiment. The idea of locking in an aspect is not something that needs experimentation, however, and most random successes probably result from the accidental manner in which magnets are ignorantly handled.

The need to experiment usually involves determining whether to use the north or south polarity, or if perhaps the aspect should be set twice instead of once. It also becomes a matter for experimenting when considering how long to leave the magnet on a spot. Some feel a minor ache or pain leave in minutes, while others keep it on for days. Generally, there is more danger from getting a rash from the tape if it's left on too long than trouble from the magnet.

If a complaint fails to get better, or seems to get worse, the magnet should simply be taken off. One of the wonderful advantages of magnet therapy is there does not seem to be any lasting side effects, but there's also no reason to endure discomfort.

Sometimes a person will actually sense the field working. When this happens the sensation is either in the form of coolness or warmth, and it is not odd to find the feeling isn't even at the magnet site. Remember, the overall field is affecting the sympathetic nervous system. Magnetically, men and women are different. Men, when they feel something, generally experience coolness. Women tend toward warmth. No one should lament if they don't feel anything overt. Some of us are just more sensitive than others.

The ability of magnets to convey a sense of temperature goes back a long way. Aristotle claimed magnets are cold. Hippocrates took an opposite view and said they are hot.

I've been asked if there are concrete uses other than motors, and medical possibilities to which this odd knowledge of mine might be put. If the people in white coats ever recognize I'm on to something, there is no telling where experimentation might take us in this field. But beyond this remote possibility, those of us in shirtsleeves are forging on.

For instance, one of my more speculative experiments has revealed an astounding, perhaps unbelievable aspect to magnets and the body magnetic. By accident (a familiar form of discovery) I performed an experiment that seems to confirm something of which I had never heard until after I did it. I was ignorantly fooling around the edges of what's known in quantum science as Bell's Theorem.

John Stewart Bell, a physicist of mostly high repute, is responsible for causing some of his colleagues sleepless nights and bad dreams. More than twenty years ago, in theory, Bell solved a problem that had many a quantum physicist tied in knots. Without getting deep into mathematics I don't pretend to understand, Bell's Theorem proves that reality takes place somewhere far away, and then after that's done we get to experience it wherever we are. It's called non-locality, and it's a concept right up there with singularities as something many scientists wish would go away.

Basically, non-locality says that an event can be affected, or caused by something that is nowhere near the event. It is action at a distance without strings, wires, or even a nebulous radio wave to connect action with cause. Not only does Bell's Theorem say this sort of thing is possible, it demands that this is exactly the way the universe, and all reality is put together.

Quantum theory is a fun place to muck around in, but watch out for quantum mud in the brain gears.

Even though no laboratory experiment has laid bare phenomena to substantiate Bell's contention, no one has been able to argue their way out of his box either. No other theory has disproved his theory, nor has the theory been directly proven by developing, for instance, faster than light communication.

This kind of thing, most argue, is still the venue of science fiction. On Star Trek, the Captain dials up Federation Headquarters, and talks real time with the Admiral, even though they are separated by a hundred light years. If we could travel across Planet Byrd several light years in a few hours, why not instant communication via a similar route?

So there I was, barricaded in my mad scientist shop with a large torus shaped speaker magnet, innocently mapping all its aspect segments with a white-leaded pencil. When the map was complete, I leaned back to admire it, and wonder if any sort of concrete use might come of it?

During one experiment, I noticed that when I placed the fingers of both hands on these lines, on either side of the magnet at the same time, I got a cool feeling up my spine. When I separated from the magnet, this rather pleasant feeling persisted. By testing the magnet, and then myself, I found it and I reacted exactly the same way to the test gear, even though several feet existed between us.

While I was thus involved, Lois came into my tinkerer's den to tell me something. The magnet with the white markings was on a bench close to where she was standing, and she picked it up for a closer look.

My pleasant feeling instantly disappeared. I quickly retested both the magnet and myself, but found no more similarities. By touching the magnet, Lois had evidently cancelled whatever affinity the magnet and I had for one another.

I understood how she might have changed the magnet by touching it, but she had changed me from across the room!

I again placed my fingers on the same marks in the same way, and the same feeling returned. The magnet and I once more were connected, which I quickly proved to myself with the dowsing rods, and with a third magnet freely dangling from a string.

I asked Lois to touch the magnet again. She did, and again the connection instantly vanished.

After she left the shop, I set up the experiment again, and tried to cancel the connection myself. I learned all I needed to do to put everything back to normal was gently lay a fingertip on any of the dozens of magnets lying around the shop. I was able to destroy the orientation of the magnet across a distance in the same fashion that Lois had altered the configuration of my nervous system from several feet away.

I performed the next experiment from across the street. A couple of hundred extra feet didn't matter. I then moved three blocks away and still the magnet had returned to normal after I got back to the shop. I then settled down to think, and to run the math.

The first assumption was that I had discovered a way to find the line of demarcation in what I was sure to be the next ring in an infinity of concentric circles. Since the magnet I was working with was more than three times the size of my one-inch disks, I determined via the 12 X 12 X 12 equation that if I touched another magnet well out beyond 500 feet, the magnet in the shop would retain its connection with me.

The next day, I took the experiment on the road. I connected to the large magnet, and then left it in the shop while I drove off in the car. At one mile I pulled over to the side, got out away from the metal of the car, and tested myself. I seemed to still be connected. I touched a magnet, checked myself, expecting to see nothing changed, but found myself back to normal. I drove to the shop, reconnected with the speaker magnet, which had also returned to normal and climbed back in the car.

I began checking myself every five miles. Finally, at thirty-five miles I determined that I was still reacting the same as if I was in the shop. I touched the magnet I'd brought along, then tested myself again. Nothing.

On the drive back, I came to accept what I expected to find. Forty-five minutes later the test on the magnet confirmed it had reverted to being perfectly normal. Thirty-five miles isn't a hundred light years, but it isn't just across the room either.

I have come to call this phenomenon twinning, or pairing. The magnet and myself were behaving in the manner of paired electrons in a chain-linked, twisted orbit through a magnet. There can be only one acceptable explanation from a possibility of two.

One) I subconsciously fooled myself completely with subjective tests.

Two) I proved Bell's Theorem by demonstrating action at a distance without physical connection.

This experiment obviously operated at a distance, and therefore should be considered a true quantum effect. When I disconnected myself from the magnet that was left in the shop, it must have happened instantaneously. If there are aliens buzzing around out there in the Galaxy they are probably not communicating via standard speed-of-light radio waves. That means these projects of ours that listen for alien cultures with the big dishes are searching on all the wrong frequencies. The aliens probably don't use "frequencies". Their communication devices were paired before the ship left home, and to listen in on them we would need a third device that had been paired to a common link.

The human body is an electrical instrument, and in a sense it is also a magnet. Part of the idea of the health magnets is to become in tune with a given field, and get a boost from it. Much of magnet therapy is accomplished because the field meshes with the sympathetic nervous system, cleans it up, unblocks it, and keeps it humming. I learned when my arm went nuts, that when those web-like tendrils of the autonomic nervous system get out of sorts it can ruin a perfectly good day.

It is also a system, which when it's up and running at full efficiency, can be spotted twelve feet across the Oregon Vortex's yard by a pair of copper rods in the hands of a so-so dowser. The magnetic lines crossing where that young girl was standing amplified her aura many times over, and yanked the rods around in my hands as if she had physically reached out and grabbed them. That was not a subjective experience, and I've been using the rods long enough to know when I am tempted to influence them.

It doesn't really change anything, and maybe no one cares, but reality isn't what we think it is.

Bell's Theorem is correct.

Reality is non-local, and it is assembled where we are not.

Its head is usually hidden, but every now and then Reality peeks out over the event horizon and haves a good guffaw at our expense.

The House of Mystery Vortex is one of its little chuckles.

We can expect a deep, rolling belly laugh any time now.

6

A TERRALINE MAP

So I left the old life, which wasn't that bad, and moved 240 miles east to spend my dotage engaged in the gentlemanly art of growing apples and other hard fruit for which the world would be happy to pay a fair price.

Hah!

This is a difficult story to get on paper, because I have to dwell a little bit on a sojourn of six plus years of pain and aggravation in apple country. It's a little like falling on the ladder, though. If I had not moved into turmoil, this would be a much duller tale.

Okanogan County in North Central Washington is indeed apple country. Over the years the climate there has helped produce the absolute best Red and Golden Delicious apples ever harvested. Lois wanted to grow apples. I looked at the demographics of six people per acre in Washington's largest county, and being inclined toward a less cluttered landscape, decided growing apples wouldn't be too bad.

All it took was a decision.

As soon as the offer on the farm was on legal documents, my life made an immediate about turn, and I began an incredible slide into the most frustrating set of inauspicious circumstances imaginable. Just trying to sell out where we were so that we might take this "easy semi-retirement" turned out to be a scenario written by the Marques De Sade. I've longingly looked back more than once at the time when I could have bailed out for the loss of a mere ten thousand dollars, and stayed right where I was.

We fought fickle buyers, idiot bug inspectors, a contractor who cost us six thousand dollars because he forgot to use ten cents worth of glue on a sewer line, utterly stupid appraisers, unsympathetic bankers, uncaring real-estate brokers, bureaucrats who couldn't keep track of paperwork, and all manner of other busybodies who did their best, by accident, if not deliberately, to keep us from our goal.

The Universe was telling us to stay where we were, but we fought on, and we persevered, and we made it to the farm.

And then things went to hell.

No piece of equipment was spared major breakdown during our tenure. In the house, not one appliance survived. At six in the evening on Christmas Eve, with the temperature at 5 degrees, the furnace died. There are four separate mechanical devices thirty feet down in the well, and they all died at separate times. The tractor died. The hydraulic pumps on the tractor died three times. The sprayer pump died twice. Most of my time was spent with a shovel unearthing irrigation lines that blew up for no other reason than I turned a valve handle. It got so that I didn't want to get out of bed for fear of finding a mechanic at the door with his hand out for another thousand-dollar bill.

I have had things go wrong in my life, but usually an incident happens, then a decent amount of time occurs before the next one. It appeared we had bought a hyperactive gremlin to go with the apples.

We got through the first harvest by dint of sheer bullheadedness, and looked forward to those packinghouse checks to get us well.

The worldwide price of apples died.

Once I had spent a few months as a resident of Okanogan County, and was able to see it from the inside out, I was beginning to wonder if I had moved to another country?

Another country, Canada, is just a few miles to the north, and going into British Columbia from this part of Washington can be an odd experience. The border crossing seems more than an a passage beyond an imaginary boundary. It's like stepping from the inside to the outside, and not just in terms of culture. It's more like a literal passage from one set of circumstances to another. In Canada, the land seems more friendly, green and productive. The cities and towns more clean and prosperous. For many miles to the north from the border the Okanogan valley retains the same name, but the pronunciation and even the spelling changes. The Canadians call it the Okanagan Valley. Instead of Oak-ah-nog-on from the American side, it is Oak-eh-nag-en on the Canadian.

When crossing the border from the north along Lake Osoyoos the landscape, though basically the same, fades into duller browns with humdrum gray rock outcroppings which are somehow less interesting. Towns to the south seem drab in comparison to those in the north, and the intensity of the people loses something undefined. Most of the only natural green is in the form of sagebrush, but pines and fir pepper the hills high above the valley. It's unlikely any of these observations can be objectively proven or photographed, it's just an impression that seeps into the bones the longer one is there.

The Okanogan Valley has its moments. In the spring it comes alive with fruit blossoms, the summer is radiant with green, and the early fall colors are the red and yellow of ripening fruit. Unless one is simply passing through with an appreciative passing glance, these things are known to be true only because of huge irrigation projects. In the early spring, when hundreds of farmers clad in rubber suits are riding tractors and spraying a witch's brew of poisons, the traveler upon entering down into the valley from the east or west is met by a stench of chemicals rising up the valley walls.

Most places accept human habitation graciously, but the invasion of people into the Okanogan Valley appears pasted on. This is farm country, but it appears to persist in spite of the land, rather than because of it. To me a kind of quiet desperation seemed to ooze up all around, and I was becoming part of it.

One of the odd things I noticed almost immediately was the number of people who were having joint replacements. Knees and hips don't seem to last there. The reason, I heard from many, was because it is in the nature of orchard work to wear out hips and knees, yet I ran into others with artificial joints who had nothing to do with orchard work. Prior to coming to the Okanogan I only personally knew one person with an artificial joint, yet within six months I'd met six or eight and heard of many others.

I had been living on the farm just about six months when my ears started to ring. Tinnitus it's called, and it's annoying to be in a quiet spot and have to listen to the constant buzzing, ringing, and roaring of the interior of one's own head. As I met more people, I found literally dozens of others with the same complaint. With the exception of one woman, all the sufferers were men, and all of these were people who were, like me, transplants to the Valley. The only people who appeared to get along well in this area were those who were bred, born, and raised there. A native, I learned, has these kinds of troubles only after he or she leaves and takes up residence somewhere else.

I would joke with people and tell them that all these tribulations were the revenge of the local Indian Tribe. They had put a hex on the white man for taking the land and spreading insecticide from one end to the other. Some laughed. Some nodded thoughtfully, as if I had made a logical statement. Then I saw something outlined on the land itself, which made me wonder about the veracity of my own jest.

Our house was on a slope above the valley floor and it looked down on other houses, orchards, and Highway 97. Just beyond the highway, the Okanogan River was hidden by a line of Cottonwoods. Across the river is a towering upthrust of gray rock and brown dirt, speckled with sagebrush and stubborn scrub pine. Much more than a hill, it is a small mountain that dominates the western sky and rises quickly to about 1,500 feet above the valley floor. Lois enjoyed this view, and it did provide welcome early shade on hot summer afternoons. I saw it, however, as an oppressive monolith disapprovingly looking down on me. I ignored it, because to look on it was to hate it, and I had enough going on in my life without wasting emotion on a huge pile of rocks.

One morning, about three years after we moved in, I stood at the kitchen window, a cup of coffee in hand idly looking out at the pile of rocks. The morning sun was beating on its side, and suddenly I became aware that the rocks, brush and shadows had formed a silhouette of what looked like a bear. It was huge, hundreds of feet long, and the full body of a bear. It seemed to be in the pose of walking up the side of the mountain and looking back over its shoulder...at me. It was an interesting phenomenon. I'm as good at picking Mickey Mouse out of a bank of cumulus clouds as the next guy. Look at them just right, and coffee stains on the drain board look just like Alfred E. Newman. I knew as soon as the sun rose a little higher that my bear would disappear.

At noon it was still there, and not only that but it was accompanied by a large lion's head farther up the cliff. Over the next few days, the lion's face became surrounded by other lion's heads, as if the whole pride had been summoned to gaze down on me. Even though the bear remained on the mountain all day regardless the angle of the sun, the lion faces did change, but in the afternoon they morphed into a single human face frowning in my direction.

It was an almost morbid fascination to study these totems. I wondered why I'd never seen them before? And they were not just my apparitions. I was able to easily point them out to everyone who happened to visit. Once I found them up there, they never left, and no matter how hard I tried, no other recognizable shapes could be formed from any of the other shadows and bumps on that hill.

Although it was fun to joke about an Indian curse, or even a malignant gremlin, I really didn't take these things seriously. But something had to be causing the unrelenting string of mechanical breakdowns, accidents, and other unhappy events that had invaded my life.

About this time, I became convinced that I lived smack in the middle of some kind of negative force, and with my growing study of magnets, I was sure it must be some sort of vortex phenomenon. With this in mind I set out to map the farm with my dowsing rods. Soon I had staked out the edge of a very large circle as it cut through the orchard. When the line was long enough to determine the center, I thought I might have the culprit.

The house sat at the end of a long, straight driveway of about 150 yards. The driveway came off Highway 97 at precisely 90-degrees, and the highway itself ran absolute due magnetic north for a few miles in either direction. The neighbors and me were watching with fascination another phenomenon that was happening along this stretch of pavement. If a person was going to nod off at the wheel and run off the road, have a mechanical breakdown, get a citation for anything, or just run out of gas, the area about 300 yards on either side of my driveway was where it would happen.

We employed the standard arguments, such as, we were just looking for these things, therefore we saw them when otherwise we wouldn't have. It didn't seem to help, because we could drive miles in any direction, never see another vehicle pulled over to the side, and then in the space of a week see four incidents right in front of our property. Whenever there was an unexpected knock on the door it was not surprising to see a stranger needing a telephone. We finally started keeping a full gas can close by.

On one of my physical therapy visits, Dianne was working on my wrist in one of her little rooms, when Mauricio stopped by the open door and gave a halfhearted wave. He was all bent over because of his back, and was there for an appointment. A few minutes later, my neighbor from the other side of the orchard, an old fellow who had just had his third joint replacement hobbled by the door on crutches on his way to wait in another room.

Dianne glanced over at me with one eyebrow arched quizzically. She asked if I knew the lady she had just worked over before I got there.

I shook my head, and asked why she wanted to know.

For a few seconds, she continued to rub and yank on my wrist, and then answered, "She lives just across the highway from you."

She paused, and I noticed she was biting her lower lip. "I'm sure glad I don't live in your neighborhood."

The center of my orchard vortex map turned out to be the middle of the property line alongside the highway. This was where the three-inch main irrigation line to the orchard came up out of the ground so that the big gate valve and sand filter were accessible. This main line then went back underground and ran dead magnetic east through the property for about 1,200 feet.

It looked as though I may have located a source for my troubles, and perhaps for the odd hapless traveler, but it was a local problem and had nothing to do with the countywide desolation that was slowly creeping throughout the land. I questioned old timers, asking them if they had experienced more troubles in the last few years than before. Every one agreed, and they also were able in a general way to date the beginning of their woes.

In the "good old days" the irrigation system consisted of high ditches and wooden troughs along the valley's sides. It was a gravity fed system, and worked just fine, but it was also wearing out and needed some five-million dollars worth of repair. Rather than repair the old, the irrigation district decided to build a brand new pressure system along the valley floor. With cost overruns, the new system ended up costing about 72-million dollars. An orchardist with a hundred acres of trees who used to pay about three thousand dollars per year for water, suddenly was looking at nine or ten thousand, and the cost was rising because the lines were plagued with nothing but gremlin-like troubles.

I was ready to accept that the new irrigation project had somehow messed up the overall vortex field, but I also thought I had a local version making things worse right in my front yard. Hoping to be able to do something about it, I made a scale model of the farm's irrigation lines, and then with a magnet under the model, I brought out the test gear. The reaction I got was so violent that I was sure I had my gremlin.

I knew that simple lines can change the character of a magnetic field, and I had some mighty long man-made lines out in the orchard cutting across the force lines, or Terralines as Litster called them, of the Earth's magnetic field.

The next problem was what to do about it?

I went back to work on my model. The water lines were PVC, or plastic, and the other connections, like valves, were all either brass or aluminum, so the lines were constructed from nonferrous materials. I made the model from nonmagnetic copper wire, cut the main line of the model, and inserted a piece of steel between the severed ends of the copper wire. The model ceased giving my dowsing rods fits.

The irrigation water was off for the season. In desperation I climbed in the truck, drove down to the valve stanchion, and with a hacksaw sliced clear through that three-inch plastic line. I then shoved a piece of sheet metal in between the cut, drove back up the hill, and went looking for my vortex line in the orchard.

It was nowhere to be found!

By the time I took this draconian action the farm was just coming up on two years of having been for sale. Within two months the place was sold. I went to the hardware store, bought a three-inch galvanized steel nipple, and spliced it into the line. I didn't want to leave the new owner with my old gremlin.

We moved seventeen miles north to the town of Oroville, which is about five miles from the Canadian border, and settled into a house with no fruit trees, but with a mad scientist shop in which to continue my research.

My ears had been ringing for more than five years. Cutting the water line hadn't done a thing for them, nor I was to learn, did moving north help.

During these five years I lost the ringing sensation in my ears twice. Once when we drove through Nevada to visit relatives in Las Vegas, and then on to the Grand Canyon. For most of two blissful weeks I experienced silence. I stood on the Grand Canyon's South Rim, and without competition from my ears, was able to heard the rush of the Colorado River a mile below.

Within a day of returning home, my ears were no longer on vacation.

The second time was when I spent an entire day on the wind machine at the farm. I was up there because it needed fixing, of course. The wind machine was an old Ford V-8 engine perched atop a steel thirty-foot gas tank. When it ran, it spun a twelve-foot propeller, which blew air across the spring blossoms to keep frost off them. When I finally climbed down, I noticed my head was almost completely silent. The only thing I can attribute this to was the fact that I spent all those hours on a huge, steel magnetic sink. It was an interesting observation, but didn't do me any good. I couldn't spend my whole life on a steel four-foot diamond-plate platform thirty feet in the air.

It was from the Oroville house that me and my trusty vintage 280-Z set out on that 700-mile solitary September drive to the Oregon Vortex. I traveled Highway 97 through Washington, and then through most of Oregon, and stopped for the night at the town of Chemult in South Central Oregon.

The next morning, I crossed the Cascades near Crater Lake, and then spent the rest of the day bugging Maria at the House of Mystery. By the next morning I was in Northwestern Washington visiting my sister, and then some old friends up near the Canadian Border.

I could still hear my ears, but I had to listen carefully.

On the fifth day, I crossed into British Columbia and headed east across the Cascades on Canadian Route 3, the Hope-Princeton Highway. It was a gorgeous fall day, and I pulled into a roadside stop to use the facilities. This happened to be the place where, several years ago, a gigantic slide had occurred, so I took a few minutes to walk around and study the aftermath of that violence. I heard the skree of a hawk or an eagle in the far distance, and then realized my ears were dead silent. I stayed at this place for almost an hour joyously listening to nothing, but knowing that as soon as I climbed back in the car it would be less than four hours before I would be back in Oroville, and the Okanogan County Vortex.

I think this was when I made the decision to move to the Gold Hill Vortex.

I reentered the United States at a little border crossing called Night Hawk, and drove ten miles on a curvy back road into Oroville. As I rounded a corner and started down a short grade alongside Oroville's golf course something popped in my head. It wasn't dramatic, just a little soap bubble, bloop, and my ears began a faraway hissing. Three hours later it was a full-blown ring and roar.

The next day, I got out my Okanogan County map, and found the spot where I felt that "soap bubble" break. By lunchtime, I had found something incredible, and to this day that discovery keeps expanding outward.

As I said, Okanogan is the largest county in Washington, State, and I'm not picking on it when I say it is also the weirdest. It consists of mostly wilderness, and about a third of it is taken up by about half of the Colville Indian reservation. Though spread out a little, most of the human population lives in towns and farms along Highway 97, which runs right up through the middle of the county, and alongside the Okanogan River. The valley, and therefore the road and river, runs in a generally magnetic north direction. The most southern town is called Pateros, and the most northern, Oroville.

Smack in the middle of the county is the little town of Riverside.

Riverside, I discovered, is dead center in the middle of a vortex that covers almost all of Okanogan County.

On the map, I thought I saw something that reminded me of the layout of the Gold Hill Vortex. Beyond that I cannot say why I put the big speaker magnet on the map so that Riverside was visible through its center hole.

I dangled a small magnet from a string near the magnet on the map, and it suddenly began bouncing back and forth in the same fashion as it would if I had altered its aspect configuration. I held the pendulum magnet over the center of the donut shaped magnet, and it began to orbit around it. This does not happen with two regular magnets. Hang one magnet close to another and it will normally find a spot it likes and stay there.

 I moved the speaker magnet to another spot on the map, and the pendulum magnet did nothing. Back over Riverside, the two magnets again reacted to one another.

 I had given up dancing, besides, I had no idea what any of this nonsense meant. I had heard of people who claimed to be able to dowse maps, but I had always maintained a skeptical distance from that kind of thing. But here I was, in essence, map dowsing with magnets.

 Deciding to withhold judgment, I did on the map the opposite of that which I had done in the orchard. I already had the center, Riverside, so I went in search of the circumference. It wasn't long before I settled on a 54-mile-wide diameter vortex, which I assumed had a 9-mile corona making the phenomenon 72-miles across its entire diameter.

 I found this by studying the terrain, and by the application of a little pyramid math.

 A little over thirty miles east of Riverside is the town of Winthrop where two rivers join, the Chewuch and the Methow. The Chewuch begins in the northern wilderness and flows in a gentle curve to Winthrop where it melds with the Methow, and continues on that same curve to the southeast. These two river beds can be followed perfectly with a drawing compass the point of which is anchored in the map at Riverside. Several miles south of the town of Twisp, the Methow leaves this arc to drop south and empty into the Columbia River at the town of Pateros. The sweep of the arc it had been following becomes a deep valley until it opens just above the town of Brewster, cuts across Highway 97, and then continues eastward on the same arc, but along the river course of the northern Columbia.

For about half of this huge circle, which extends in a circumference of more than 220 miles, the compass can be swung along the natural curve of rivers, roads, and valleys using the town of Riverside as the pivot point

Except for local minor zigs and zags, Highway 97 follows a magnetic north route. This occurs not just through Okanogan County, but for more than a 150 miles from the Canadian border to the city of Wenatchee, where the Columbia River and Highway 97 diverge from the magnetic northerly route. The road and the Okanogan and Columbia Rivers run magnetic north from Wenatchee because a long valley runs north from Wenatchee.

Highway 97, four and a half miles south of Riverside, turns to the northwest by 40-degrees, passes right by the town, and four and a half miles further on turns back to magnetic north. It appears as though something has twisted the land from the river's natural inclination to flow from magnetic north. This section of road is newer and follows an easier route than the old road did alongside the river.

This line formed by the highway stood out like a flashing sign. Its length, nine miles, was the exact measurement I would expect the corona of a 54-mile vortex to be. It allowed me to put together a usable picture, but it was later, after I had a chance get more detailed measurements of the Gold Hill anomaly, that I realized just what was going on in both places.

The ends of the Riverside road jog reveal the diameter of a circle that is the equivalent of the *nine-foot* eye-of-the-hurricane dead zone at the axis of the Oregon Vortex. This dead zone, however, is *nine miles* across its diameter. There is a difference other than size. Rather than swinging the 54-mile vortex circumference from the actual center, which is the town of Riverside, the pivot point is located on the nine-mile circumference line itself, and moves along the arc even as it is drawing the line.

This causes two things that are different from the Gold Hill Vortex. The first is that the Okanogan Vortex oscillates across its entire diameter by nine miles, and apparently forms its own corona. Secondly, the imaginary compass pivot point is dragged around a perfect 27-mile circle causing it to draw the vortex's imperfect 170-mile circumference line of demarcation. In terms of the land on which it sits, the Okanogan Vortex is unstable. One pass of the compass point around Riverside equals only one-half a pass around the larger vortex, so just like our schizophrenic electron, the Okanogan vortex line of demarcation must *go around twice to get around once.*

In terms of the land on which it sits, the House of Mystery anomaly is a stable phenomenon. The large "electron" orbiting at a radius of four and a half feet out from the axis does not make a perfect 27-foot circle, and when it phases into hyperspace after one orbit, its double becomes the "electron" in our space that we interpret as that 19-inch wobble. When the original "electron" phases back into our space it will have gone 720-degrees to make what we perceive to be 360-degrees. Except for Litster's expansion and contraction along the radius, the larger line of demarcation remains fixed.

As might be expected, I went hunting on maps for more of these 54-mile vortexes, and the obvious starting point was Gold Hill, Oregon. I wasn't surprised to find the magnets reacting to each other, and I was also not surprised to learn that the Gold Hill phenomenon was oriented to the negative, or north polarity, which is the opposite of the south, or positive polarity of the Okanogan vortex.

After making sure of the Southern Oregon map reaction, the search was blind. I would put the big magnet down anywhere on maps, hold the pendulum magnet near it, and then if there was no reaction move the big magnet again. The next hit I received was in Southeastern Washington, just northeast of the Tri-Cities area of Kennewick, Richland, and Pasco. Directly to the west, the corona passes through the Hanford Nuclear Reservation. It was another south polarity, 54-mile diameter vortex, but its line of demarcation was rotating in the opposite direction of the Okanogan vortex. As the crow flies, the two centers are about 150 miles apart.

I now had a benchmark to use in the search for others that might exist. On the Washington State map I looked out 150 miles from each vortex site. There was one place that fell into this range, which I had been avoiding simply because it was too obvious, and it was exactly 150 miles from Riverside:

Seattle.

The magnets reacted when the large one was placed right over Seattle. It is a negative, or north polarity vortex zone. Now I had three of these zones of influence, as I had begun calling them, on the Washington map. I drew straight lines between their centers, which formed an isosceles triangle with its long base from Seattle to near the Tri-Cities, and the two shorter lines from each base point back to Riverside. The triangle is tilted on the face of Washington State. Halfway along the base, a 90-degree line runs magnetic north right to Riverside.

I had reached a point in my research where I was no longer incredulous at some of the things that happened. When I laid a protractor on the base lines, I didn't even blink when I saw an angle of inclination toward Riverside of 51.43-degrees of arc.

Highway 97 begins its long northward run at the city of Wenatchee at about the same place as the Columbia River turns to the southeast. A 20-degree line drawn from either base point intersects Wenatchee. At 23.5-degrees of arc lines from these points stop at a small community called Orondo about 15 miles north of Wenatchee.

At Orondo, Highway 2 leaves Highway 97 toward the east. The road winds a little as it comes up out of the valley, but then runs dead straight east toward Spokane, only making a few wiggles before it intersects the triangle line from Riverside to the Tri-Cities area.

Northeast of the bowl which Wenatchee occupies is mostly wilderness, and a good topographical map shows a solid ridgeline of mountains proceeding in an amazingly straight line to the northwest. This ridgeline is at 45-degrees of arc from the magnetic north line of both the Colombia and Okanogan River valleys. The line

#29

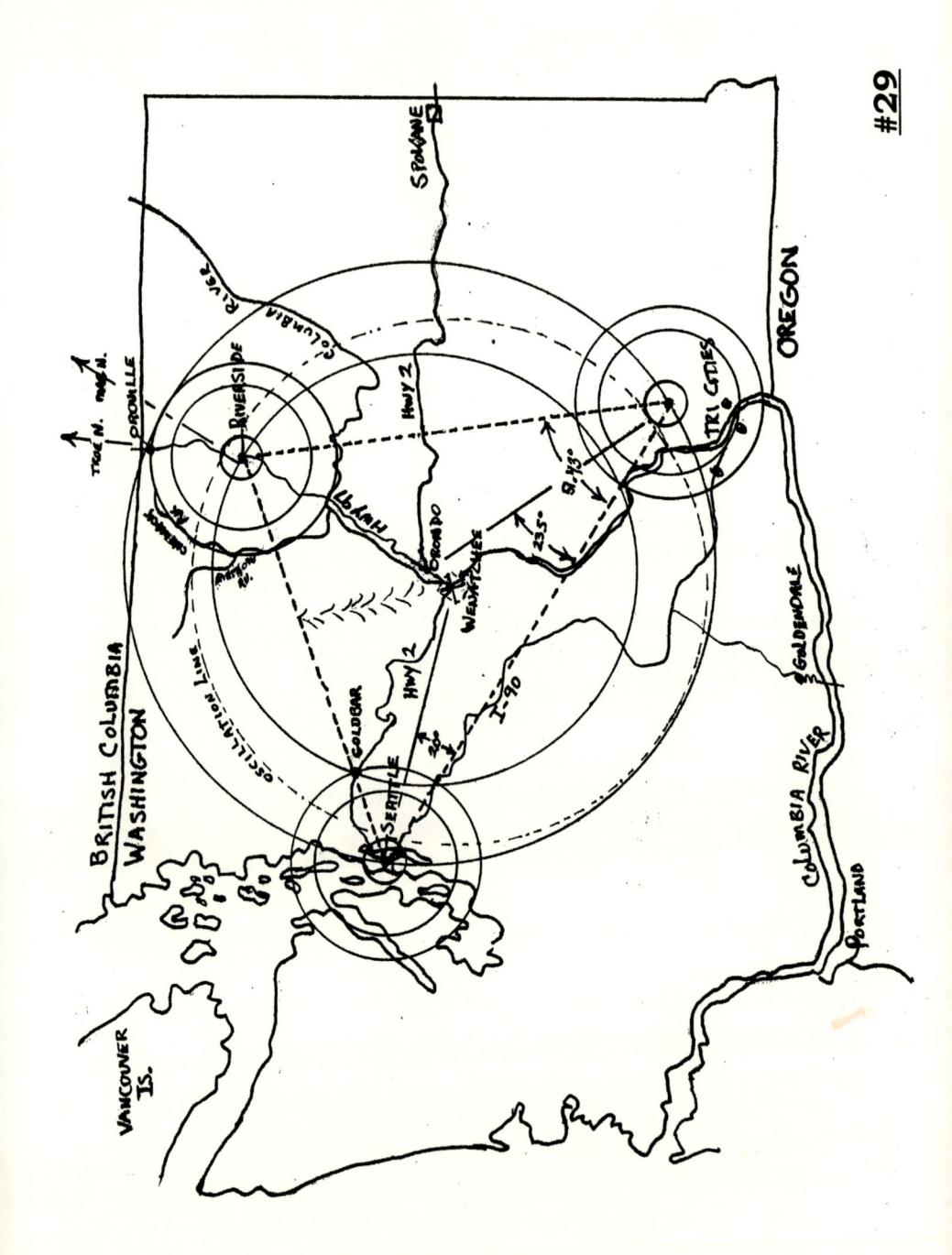

made by the cut through which Highway 2 runs from Orondo is at 60-degrees from the magnetic north line. Though these lines begin at different points along the north-south line, they intersect the opposite triangle sides at exactly the same distances from Riverside.

Long before these cities and towns were built, and long before paved roads connected these cities and towns, these exact lines, angles and points were built as rooms, passageways, and "airshafts" in the Great Pyramid of Egypt.

If we ask which came first we end up with chickens and eggs, so let's extend the concept a bit: Which has more meaning, the map or the territory? Which affects our consciousness more, the vortex or the world?

7

A VORTEX MAP

Without immediate success, I searched the Oregon map trying to fit Gold Hill's Vortex into an isosceles triangle configuration similar to the one in Washington. I was about to concede Oregon's vortex as a stand-alone phenomenon, when I got a hit from the speaker magnet as it lay a little east of Gold Hill. After some tinkering, I located another 54-mile vortex that nudged Gold Hill's corona line. It is a positive field with the perceived center in the northern end of Upper Klamath Lake near the town of Modoc Point. Both vortexes lay on a true east-west line, but not magnetic east and west.

Oddly, things like this were making sense to me. Since these two vortexes are the same size as those in Washington, I felt they must be part of some larger matrix. If I were dealing with only magnets, and not the oddity of finding these things on paper maps, then I would have to say that what I found in Southern Oregon would be at right angles to that which I found in Washington.

This "omnipotent" map view from above would be of the pyramid's apex, so I positioned the big speaker magnet on edge halfway between the two positions on the map, effectively putting it at right angles to both. When the little pendulum magnet was dangled in the field that was now orthogonal, or at 90-degrees to the map, it began bouncing on its string in a wildly abnormal way

I had also spent a good deal of time hunting on other maps without success. The map of the State of California had yielded not so much as a wiggle from my vortex finder magnets, but with this new discovery in Oregon, I had an idea.

Suppose the 450-miles from the Seattle negative vortex to Gold Hill was extended into California? I drew a line true south from Seattle between the middle of the vortexes in Southern Oregon until it left the map in the Pacific Ocean beyond San Francisco. At a little more than 450 miles from Gold Hill the line ended in the Pacific at the mouth of Monterey Bay.

Monterey Bay is about as perfect a half-circle as one might expect nature to provide. I was suspicious. It was almost too perfect, but I plopped the speaker magnet offshore on the California map, and dangled the pendulum. It resolutely bounced back and forth. It looked as though the entire half-moon of Monterey Bay is part of another 54-mile, negative polarity vortex.

In *Notes and Data,* John Litster wrote that his Terralines are found elsewhere, like on the summit of the Siskiyou Mountains 35 miles from Gold Hill. He mentions an area of approximately 30,000 square miles as having been "checked". He didn't say how this wide an area had been checked, but it's likely I was using a variation of his method. Almost in passing, he tossed in the name, Monterey Bay, and said he knew of seven other Gold Hill type vortexes (1953 edition).

It was a few months after the Monterey Bay discovery that I reread *Notes and Data* and came upon this mention. Maria said Litster spoke about a vortex off Santa Barbara near the California Channel Islands. Actually, I told her, this vortex encompasses San Miguel Island.

I had already found it.

Litster was evidently unaware of the anomalies in Washington, because had he known of the big "Great Pyramid" triangle up there, he would have realized that the Monterey Bay and San Miguel Vortexes form the baseline of another 51.43-degree triangle, the apex of which is to the west in the Pacific. The San Miguel and Pacific Vortexes are both positive polarity, but with opposite direction spins.

In 1941, Litster traveled to Santa Cruz, California on the edge of Monterey Bay to help develop another vortex for public viewing, which came to be known as the Mystery Spot. He may have regretted providing this assistance, since the Mystery Spot has been in active competition with the House of Mystery ever since.

The Mystery Spot is smaller than the 165-foot House of Mystery Vortex, but it does have a twin in Oregon.

I once thought the Oregon anomaly was the absolute center of the bigger vortex, but that assumption caused problems with some of my measurements. I am constantly being reminded to pay attention to the obvious. The town of Gold Hill itself turned out to be the center of the larger anomaly, and the House of Mystery site is only a satellite at four and a half miles from the town. The radius of the larger vortex out from the town of Gold Hill is 27-miles, and at 40-degrees from true north of Gold Hill is a spot on this 27-mile radius line that was once called Uncanny Canyon. This is or was a real vortex, smaller than the House of Mystery Vortex, but was said to be just as intense. In the 1970's the Lost Creek Dam was built right on top of this vortex, and some say the concrete at the site cured with a swirl in it. Others say its effects can still be felt on top of the dam.

Thirty-one and a half miles from the center of the Monterey Bay Vortex, back along that 51.43-degrees of arc from the Pacific Vortex is the California equivalent of Uncanny Canyon. It's called the Mystery spot.

#30

Map of nine-mile diameter encircling town of Gold Hill and the line of demarcation where the Oregon Vortex sits

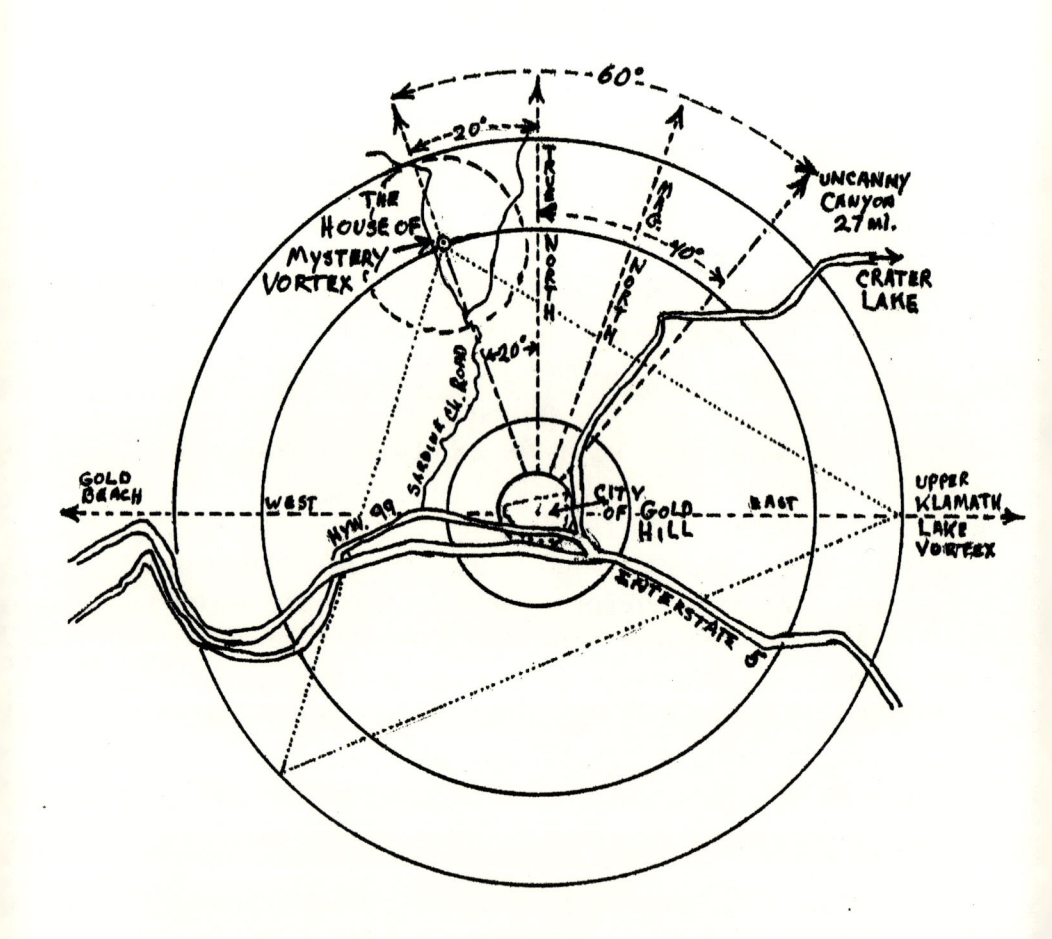

If these measurements hold true, then somewhere along the nearly 170-mile circumference line around Seattle, at 31.5 miles from the center, and at 20-degree increments from magnetic north, there might be another Uncanny Canyon, or Mystery Spot type of vortex in Washington State.

The difference in mileage from the centers of the larger vortexes between Uncanny Canyon and the Mystery Spot is four and a half miles, or half the diameter across the nine-mile corona. I can only assume this is the result of dealing with three negative polarity vortexes, one of which is at right angles to the others.

Ultimately all these configurations must be seen as spheres. The big triangle in Washington and the figure eight in Oregon, both make the same size vortex spheres on an even larger scale. They measure 216-miles across the diameters, have 36-mile coronas, which when doubled to 72-miles make complete vortexes with diameters of 288-miles, and circumferences of 905 miles.

The Gold Hill and Upper Klamath Lake pairs, which form the larger figure eight, share a portion of the other's corona, and half way between the vortex's demarcation lines is the center of the 216-mile diameter vortex. This pivot point is in the woods four or five miles north of highway 140 about halfway between the cities of Medford and Klamath Falls. On a radius of 108-miles, the 679-mile vortex circumference line passes close to the town of Cottage Grove to the northwest, and provides a stark example of how these things can sometimes be located on maps without magnets.

Roads on maps of mountainous country tend to show topography by default, because road makers follow the easiest routes through the countryside. On an Oregon road map Interstate-Five betrays some of these vortex lines. For instance, Gold Hill sits alongside a freeway that runs due east and west, even though it is a north-south highway. The pavement was laid down to take advantage of the Rogue River Valley, so I-5 takes a sharp left just north of Medford, and doesn't turn right until the city of Grant's Pass. Highway 140, though it doesn't connect with I-5, eventually follows this same east-west line across the mountains to Klamath Falls. Both highways, with occasional wiggles, line up with Modoc Point on Upper Klamath Lake.

North of Grant's Pass, I-5 turns northeast at Stage Road Pass, and runs straight for about seven miles until it turns north again at Azalea. Nine miles north at Canyonville, the road jogs slightly northwest until it finds its northbound track on the way toward Eugene. Azalea is 27-miles as the crow flies from Gold Hill, and the highway from there to Stage Road Pass follows the curve of the vortex, until it cuts back toward Canyonville nine miles away. Nine miles, of course, is the width of the corona.

Fifty-five miles north near a little town called Curtin, the freeway makes a northeasterly jog to Cottage Grove, where it cuts due north to make another little dip into Eugene 18 miles later. A small part of the circumference line of 679-miles passes from Curtin to Cottage Grove, and the 18-mile jog toward Eugene is exactly twice as long as the 9-mile identical jog from Azalea to Canyonville.

Vortexes affect terrain. It's not the other way around.

I've heard of dozens of other vortexes from visitors to The House of Mystery. I was told that North of the Bay of Fundy in New Brunswick, Canada is an old barn where one can get the same feelings. Michigan and Wisconsin supposedly each have one, and South Dakota and Colorado. Many fakes like the ones at Knotts Berry Farm, or at the Bonanza replica ranch at Incline Village at Lake Tahoe exist, but the most repeated story has to be one of the most amazing simply because it is so repeated.

A huge number of people from widely divergent places have shared with me the story of "Gravity Hill", or "Magnetic Hill". It goes like this:

"There's this stop sign in (X) at the bottom of a hill. While stopped, if you put your car into neutral it will roll backwards *up* the hill."

Oregon supposedly has three of these places. California has four or five. New Jersey has two, Montana, North Dakota, Minnesota, Arizona,

#31

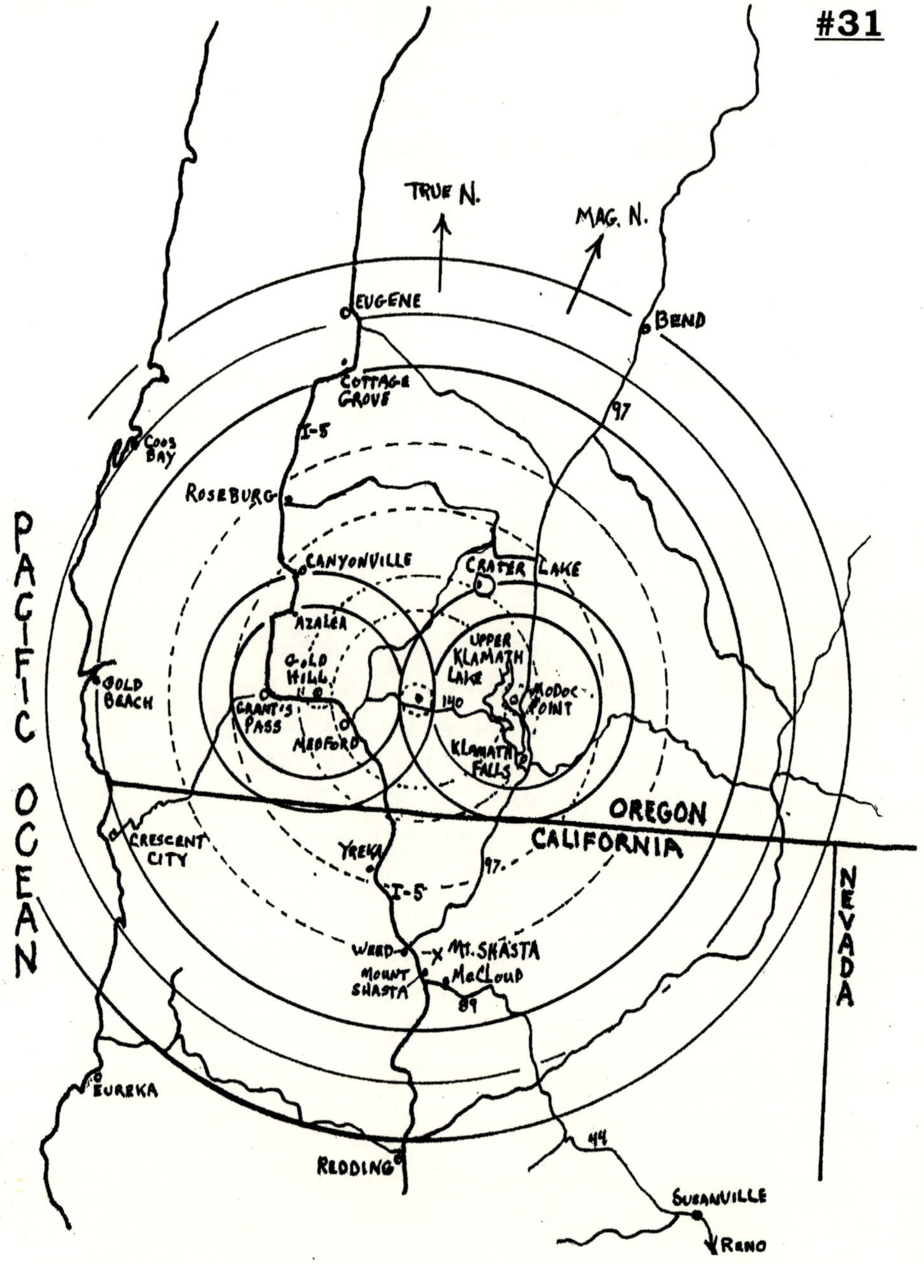

TRUE N.
MAG. N.
EUGENE
BEND
COTTAGE GROVE
97
I-5
COOS BAY
ROSEBURG
PACIFIC OCEAN
CANYONVILLE
CRATER LAKE
AZALEA
UPPER KLAMATH LAKE
GOLD HILL
GOLD BEACH
GRANT'S PASS
140
MODOC POINT
MEDFORD
KLAMATH FALLS
OREGON
CALIFORNIA
CRESCENT CITY
YREKA
97
NEVADA
I-5
WEED
Mt. SHASTA
MOUNT SHASTA
McCLOUD
89
EUREKA
44
REDDING
SUSANVILLE
RENO

Alberta, Ontario, Georgia and many other places each have at least one.

One day a man told me about Gravity Hill in Ogden, Utah, and even gave me instructions on how to find it.

One hour later another man said, "You know, we have this place in Utah called Gravity Hill where cars roll uphill."

"Yeah, I know," I answered laconically, "its in Ogden."

"Oh no," he quickly corrected. "It's in Salt Lake." He then told me how to get there.

Another day a man with an odd accent began telling me of a place near where he lived called, Magnetic Hill.

"Where do you live?" I interrupted.

"Jerusalem," He answered.

He must be on to something. I've since had two more people from Jerusalem who told me the same thing. I didn't ask for directions.

These are almost certainly apocryphal stories. For one thing cars, like golf balls, do not roll uphill, yet there seems to be uncounted numbers who swear they've seen it happen. The phone rings at the House of Mystery, and a voice asks, "Is this the place where water flows uphill?" Or, "Is this the place where boulders roll uphill?"

Human kind is utterly fascinating. How much smarter than ants, I sometimes wonder, are we? A couple at night on a New England road is abducted by a UFO, given a traumatic physical examination, and a few years later hundreds of thousands claim a similar horrible experience.

There are no real Magnetic Hills, but I hope there are at least a few hundred optical illusions that make it look like cars are rolling uphill, because if there are not then we have a really big mystery to think about.

There are plenty of real vortexes, inside of which reality is felt and perceived differently than outside, without having to make them up. The positioning, and even the names of some of these places, though, strains credulity. For instance, if we follow that line from Gold Hill to Uncanny Canyon, an angle of 40-degrees from true north, across the southeast corner of Washington, diagonally through Idaho, and Western Montana, it passes through or terminates near a whistle-stop town called Hungry Horse, which is about ten miles from the west entrance to Glacier National Park.

In Hungry Horse, Montana there is a little roadside attraction called, The House of Mystery. Though less known, it is a real vortex. I don't know if the name choice is deliberate plagiarism, or an accident, but the Montana House of Mystery is about the same distance from Seattle, as Seattle is from the Oregon House of Mystery.

Without making the list any longer, suffice it to say that these groups of triangles, and figure eights exist across the map in precise coordinates from each other. The distance ratios vary because of the Planet's curve. The farther north these areas are the closer together they become. Vortexes are everywhere, and indeed, vortexes may be all there is.

These places are linked by straight lines and curved lines. The straight lines were popularized in the 1920's by one Alfred Watkins, an English beer salesman, who took his divining rods to the English countryside. He determined that places like Stonehenge, Avebury, and others across the Channel through France and perhaps to Egypt, were connected by what he termed *ley lines*.

Watkins decided that ancient man must have possessed greater geographical knowledge than they've been given credit for. My own guess is that ancient man put his monuments where the "lines of the World" cross, rather like our cat, Misha, who sensed them as good places on which to rest and take baths. The vortexes naturally make *ley lines*, and they may even influence geography itself. Ancient man did not need a flying machine in order to line up his monuments. He may not have even known the monuments lined up.

The curved vortex lines were described about 800 years ago by a man who apparently didn't know anything about vortexes. Leonardo Fibonacci was an Italian Mathematician who is known today for a particular set of numbers called the Fibonacci Sequence. He took the number 1, added to it another number 1, and the 2 thus provided was then added to the last 1. The resulting 3, he added to the 2, which makes 5, and the sequence continues in this fashion: 1, 1, 2, 3, 5, 8, 13, 21, 34, 55, 89, 144, and so on. Some of these numbers seem familiar, and in fact they describe a spiral when each number is plotted on straight lines radiating out from a common center on precise angles.

Long before Fibonacci, the Greeks plotted these spirals, not as numbers, but as geometry. They called it the Golden Spiral, or the Golden rectangle, or the Golden Section. They seemed stuck on the word Gold, and as we will come to see, its a word that in several languages seeps out of the subconscious to get stamped on to the very rocks and dirt of this planet in an amazing, unbelievable fashion.

The Golden Rectangle can be divided by a line into two parts, one part a square and the other part a smaller rectangle. A curving line is drawn from one corner of the square to an opposite corner, and then the next smaller rectangle is divided into another rectangle and square, which supports the next curving line from corner to corner. Continuing in this way from rectangle to square to curving line, so long as there is enough paper to draw it, yields a shape that is found in all kinds of architecture, but more importantly, found in nature. Sea creatures such as the Conch or

#32
Golden Spiral

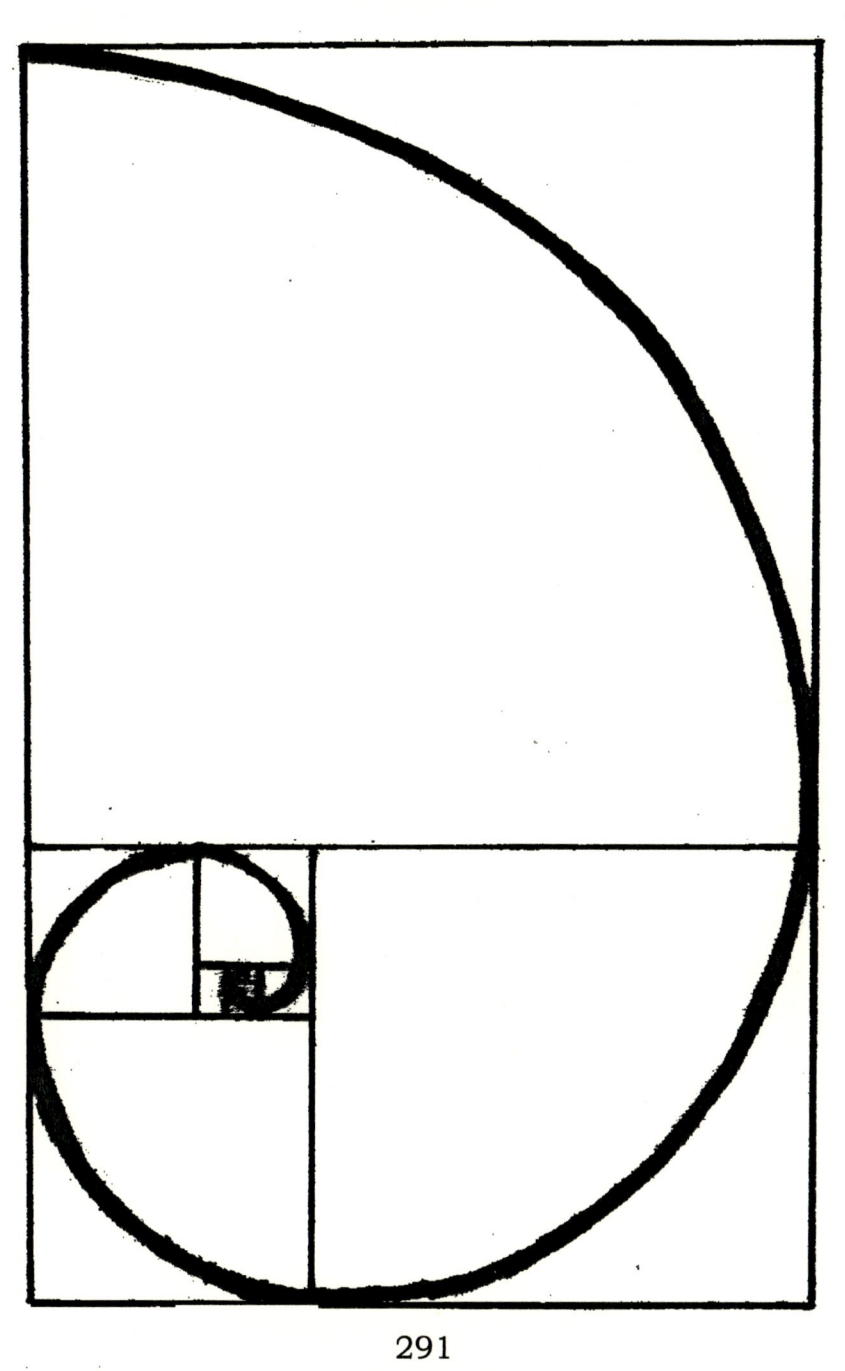

Nautilus shellfish, and other animals like snails produce the most prominent natural objects.

With a pyramid, or a vortex, the Fibonacci Sequence produces a Golden Spiral by dividing its base, or diameter by seven finite Fibonacci sections. The Great Pyramid's base is thirteen square acres, therefore the *radius* of the base is segmented into thirteen equal spaces whatever its size. Across the diameter, counting the two center spaces as one, there are 26 points but 25 spaces. There are 13 concentric circles, and 13 is the seventh number in the sequence. The twelfth number in the sequence is 144.

In the same manner that no radius line touches the true axis of the Gold Hill Vortex, the first number 1 is plotted on the number one line, allowing for a center "dead zone". (At the Vortex, that would be four and a half feet from the axis.) The second number 1 is located on the same line, but at either 120-degrees, or 90-degrees from the first radius line. The determining factor of whether to use 120-degrees or 90-degrees is polarity and direction of spin.

Once the Fibonacci numbers, 1, 1, 2, 3, 5, 8, and 13 are plotted on straight lines of either 90, or 120 degrees of arc, the missing numbers, 4, 6, 7, 9, 10, 11, and 12 fall on the intersections of the Fibonacci spiral lines and the concentric ring lines. Radius lines crossing these points furnish all the angle ratios found in the Great Pyramid and the

#33

Fibonacci Sequence plotted as a Golden Spiral within a north-polarity magnetic field

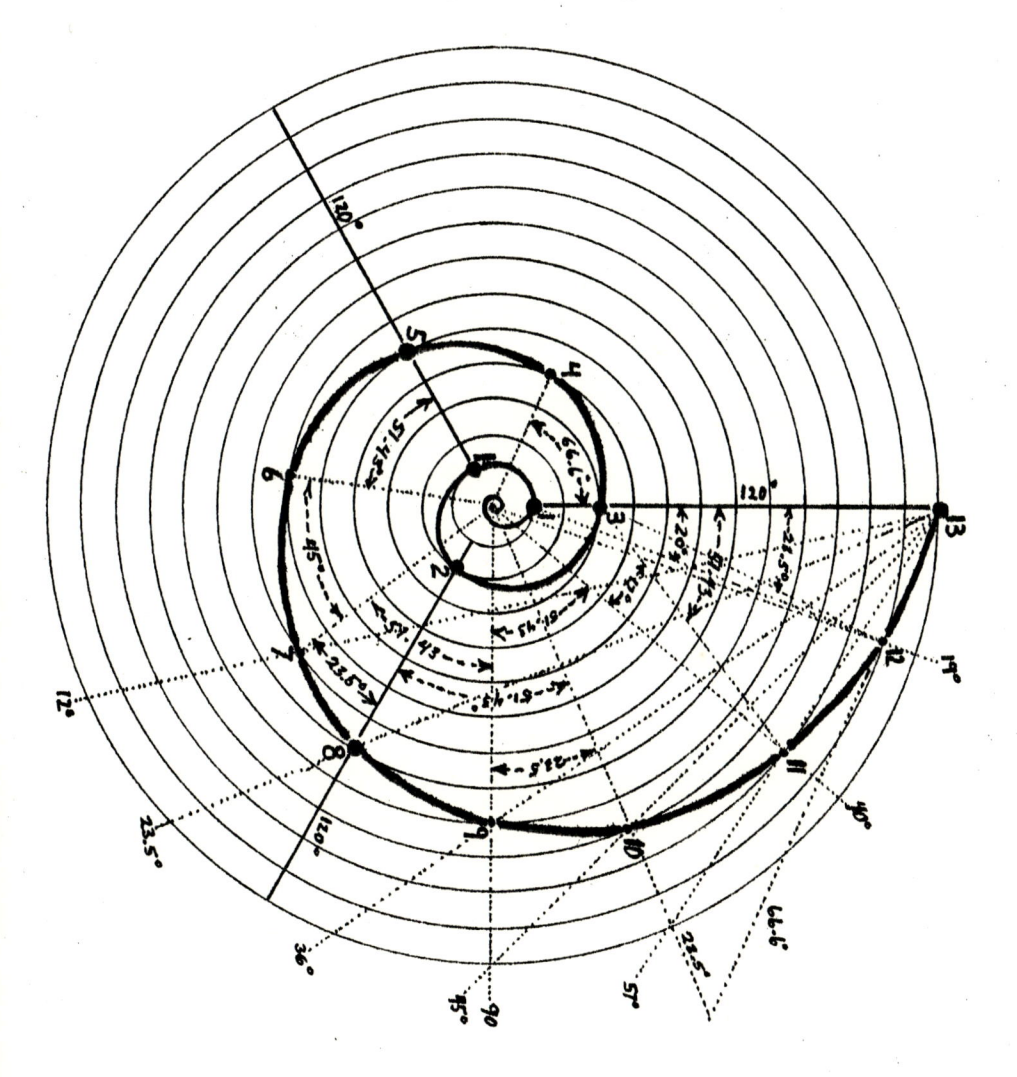

#34

South polarity - counterclockwise

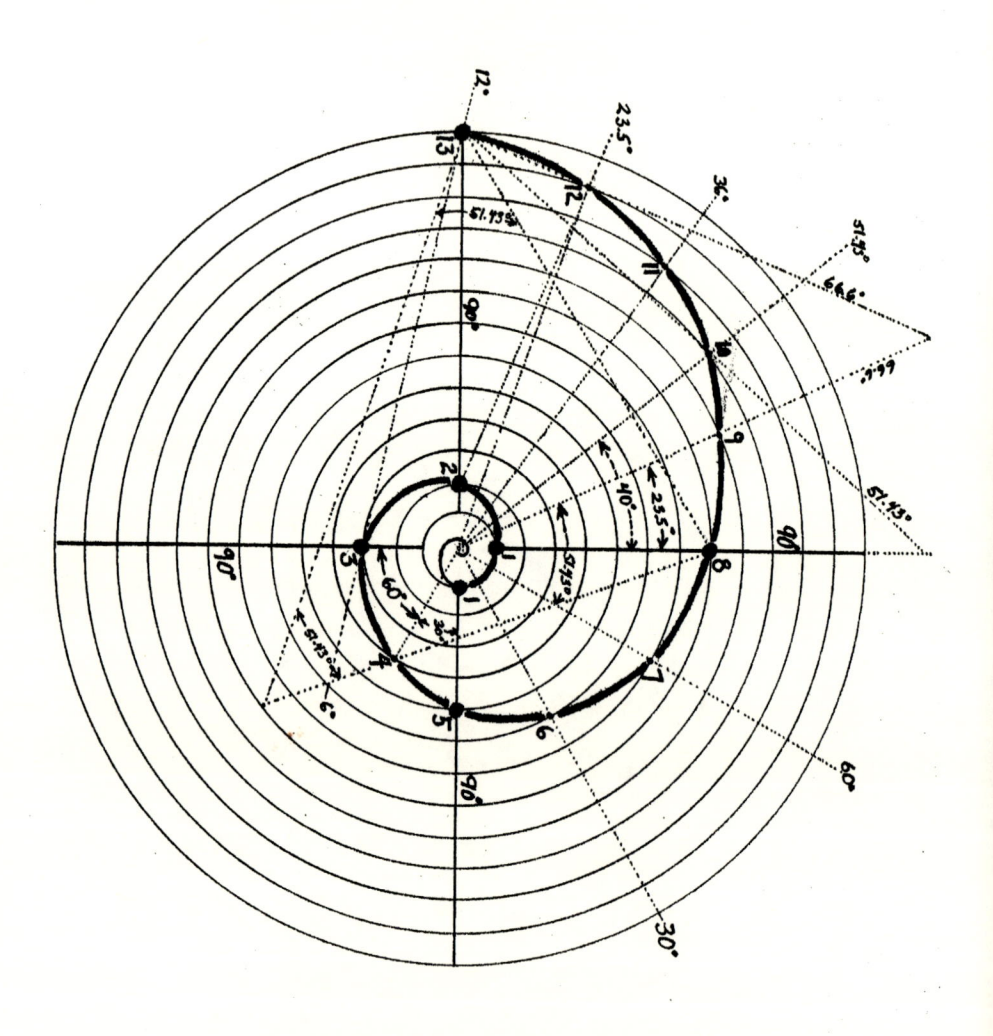

294

#35

South polarity - clockwise

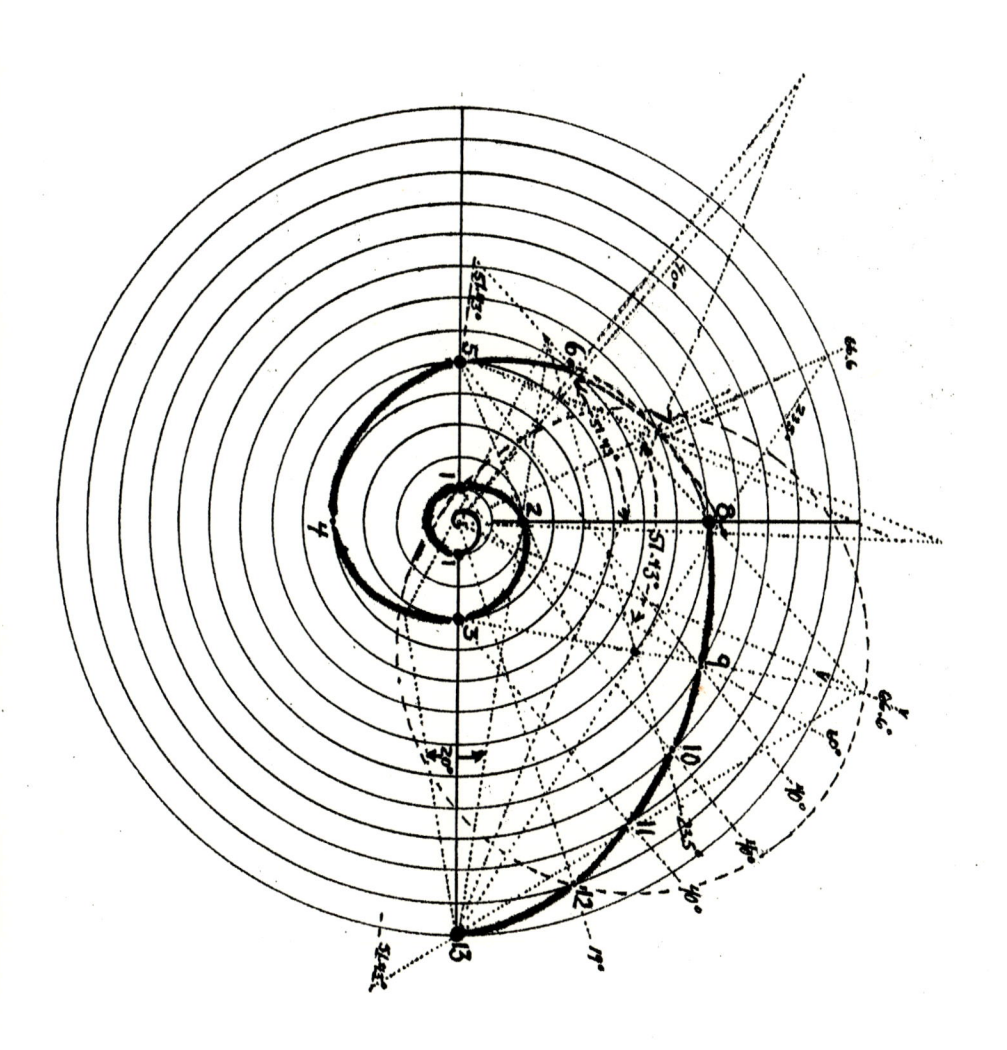

295

#36

South polarity encircling north polarity center

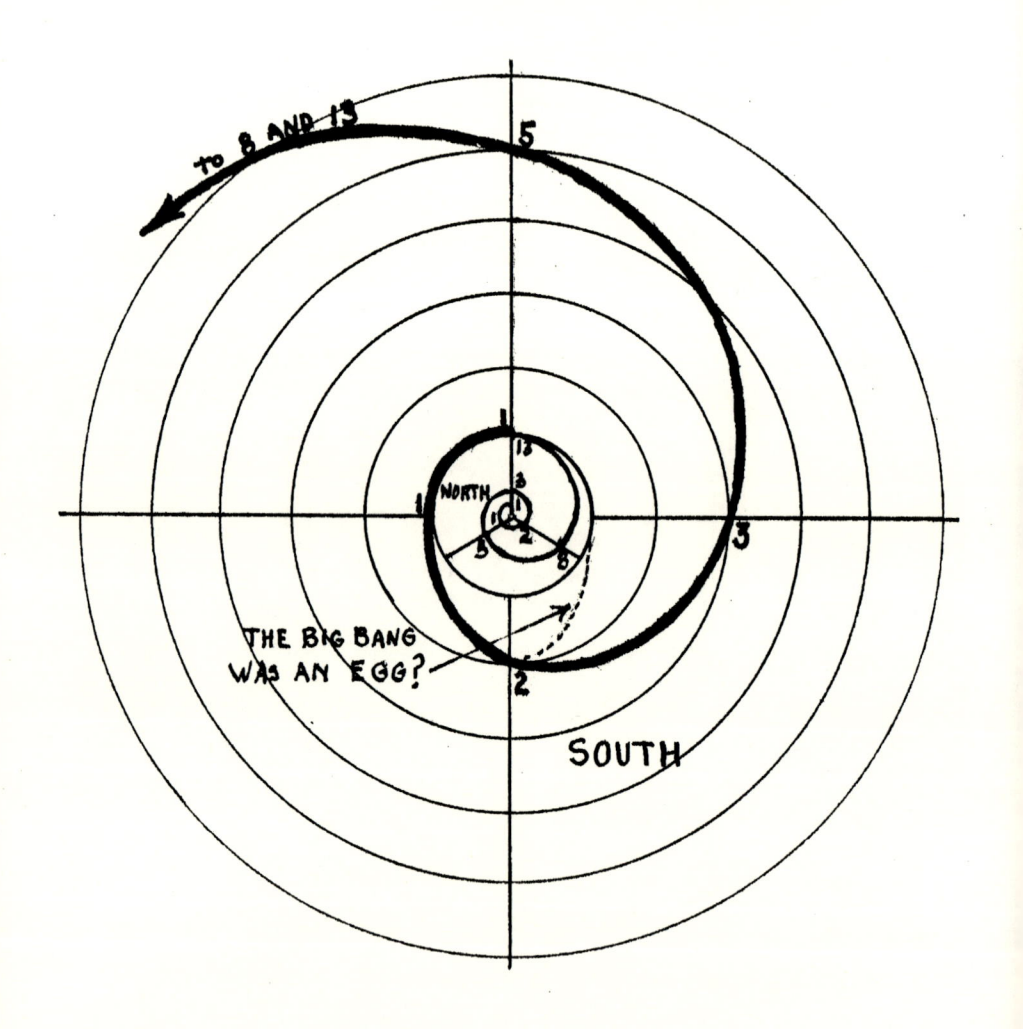

296

Gold Hill Vortex, and they do so regardless of whether the spiral was plotted on 120-degree lines, or 90-degree lines. In the case of the south pole positive polarity, 180-degrees and 90-degrees clockwise, this description continues to hold true.

One diagram is missing. I have no idea how to even begin a two-dimensional drawing of the 142857∞ clockwise negative polarity spin. I don't believe such an illustration is even possible. However, I have constructed a mathematical grid that shows the repeating nature of such an irrational number, and it fits in perfectly with the Fibonacci Sequence as it applies to the Golden Spiral. The Greeks and Romans came at the same thing from two different directions, and now a Norwegian is going to try and cement them together.

For this feat I need to revisit my allegorical treatment of the story of Moses. Three *times* four equals twelve, and three *plus* four equals seven. I call this the Nelson Coordinates:

Set up two rows of numbers like this:
1, 2, 3, 4, 1, 2, 3, 4, 1, 2, 3, 4.
1, 2, 3, 1, 2, 3, 1, 2, 3, 1, 2, 3.

Each row has twelve separate numbers. Counting both rows prepare thirteen vertical spaces so that there are 144, plus 12 spaces in the grid. Just as in the Fibonacci Sequence, the object is to add only the last two numbers. For instance, in the last two vertical spaces the two numbers are 4 and 3, so 7 is the next number in the third column. Then 7 and 3 are added, and the zero from the resulting 10 is dropped, making the next iteration 7 and 1. All zeros are dropped. We still live in that nine-based universe. After ten more columns are filled in with what look like random numbers, the twelfth, and thirteenth rows read:

8, 7, 6, 5, 8, 7, 6, 5, 8, 7, 6, 5
8, 7, 6, 8, 7, 6, 8, 7, 6, 8, 7, 6

In the 8, 7, 6 row where's 4 and 5? In hyperspace. They add up to nine which is also missing.

When the grid addition is continued, the twenty-fourth, and twenty-fifth rows are the same as the first two rows, 1, 2, 3, 4, three times, and 1, 2, 3, four times.

Every row adds up to either 3, 6, or 9, which is the sequence in the magnetic positive polarity pole, after 142857 has worked its way through the negative pole.

Vortexes are composed of three elements: Concentric rings. Spiral lines. Straight lines. Wherever these three lines cross more vortexes are created, and wherever one vortex infringes on another's "space" reality shimmers into existence. Each vortex is a finite structure, but part of an infinite number of structures. Each line of demarcation is reached after seven Fibonacci iterations, but between 12 and 13 numbers, a new,

3 TIMES 4 = 12 (1 2 3 4)   #37
3 PLUS 4 = 7   (1 2 3)
Add last two numbers in each column.
Drop all zeros.

1-	1	2	3	4	1	2	3	4	1	2	3	4	30 = **3+**
1-	1	2	3	1	2	3	1	2	3	1	2	3	24 = **6=9**
2-	2	4	6	5	3	5	4	6	4	3	5	7	54 = 9
3-	3	6	9	6	5	8	5	8	7	4	7	1	69 = 6
4-	5	1	6	2	8	4	9	5	2	7	3	8	60 = 6
5-	8	7	6	8	4	3	5	4	9	2	1	9	66 = 3
6-	4	8	3	1	3	7	5	9	2	9	4	8	63 = 9
7-	3	6	9	9	7	1	1	4	2	2	5	8	57 = 3
8-	7	5	3	1	1	8	6	4	4	2	9	7	57 = 3
9-	1	2	3	1	8	9	7	8	6	4	5	6	60 = 6
10-	8	7	6	2	9	8	4	3	1	6	5	4	63 = 9
11-	9	9	9	3	8	8	2	2	7	1	1	1	60 = 6
12- **1**	8	7	6	5	8	7	6	5	8	7	6	5	78 = **6+**
13- **1**	8	7	6	8	7	6	8	7	6	8	7	6	84 = **3=9**
14-	7	5	3	4	6	4	5	3	5	6	4	2	54 = 9
15-	6	3	9	3	4	1	4	1	2	5	2	8	48 = 3
16-	4	8	3	7	1	5	9	4	7	2	6	1	57 = 3
17-	1	2	3	1	5	6	4	5	9	7	8	9	60 = 6
18-	5	1	6	8	6	2	4	9	7	9	5	1	63 = 9
19-	6	3	9	9	2	8	8	5	7	7	4	1	69 = 6
20-	2	4	6	8	8	1	3	5	5	7	9	2	60 = 6
21-	8	7	6	8	1	9	2	1	3	5	4	3	57 = 3
22-	1	2	3	7	9	1	5	6	8	3	4	5	54 = 9
23-	9	9	9	6	1	1	7	7	2	8	8	8	75 = 3
24- **1**	1	2	3	4	1	2	3	4	1	2	3	4	30 = **3+**
25- **1**	1	2	3	1	2	3	1	2	3	1	2	3	24 = **6=9**

299

larger sequence is started on the same line as 1 and 1. The old sequence can be considered the "dead zone" of the bigger vortex swirl, because the infinite number of structures are connected only at the lines of demarcations, and *not from their centers*.

Call it a field: Gravitational, biological, magnetic, planetary, solar, galactic, or universal. A vortex is pretty much the same boring thing no matter where it's found, but the way they all interact combine to make structures that are infinitely interesting. Tiny vortexes are electrons that make atoms, which are larger vortexes that make molecules, which are even larger vortexes that become stuff like us, so that perhaps through us they can behold themselves.

Vortexes hold each other in place. For instance, the Seattle negative Vortex anchors both the Okanogan and Tri City positive vortexes to an oscillation of no more than the width of their own coronas. The entire triangle acts like a pendulum with Seattle as the fulcrum point.

Gold Hill is a different kind of fulcrum point in regards to the Klamath Lake Vortex, which rotates toward and away from Gold Hill much in the same way as the driver pushes and pulls the wheels of an old steam locomotive.

Once we start looking beyond our world of solid objects, vortexes and the influence of vortexes seem to be everywhere.

There are three *linked* vortexes on the Giza Plateau, and they have names: Khufu (Cheops), Khafre (Chephren), and Menkaure (Mycerinus). It's been noticed by others that the configuration on the ground of these three pyramids match exactly the three bright stars that form the Constellation Orion's belt. If these pyramids, or at least the positions they occupy relative to a true north alignment on the Earth is gauged to the time when Orion's Belt was in a matching celestial position, then either these pyramids, or the marks for their foundations were put on the ground around 10,500 BC.

Starting with Plato's account of the sinking of Atlantis, legends abound about lost civilizations. Catastrophes like the story of Noah's Flood, or the loss of a continent called Lemura, some claim to have been caused by the Earth tipping erratically, and violently on its axis every now and then. Suppose one of those lost civilizations figured out how to stop this erratic behavior of the planet, and was able to stabilize the axis tilt to a dependable, pendulum-like 23.5-degrees of arc? Maybe someone learned how to ballast the Earth's geometry by linking a natural anomaly to a contrived anomaly. Perhaps together, the three Giza pyramids may cast an influence that reaches around the Planet, and anchors a huge vortex we call the Earth? I say this, not just because of that 20-degree magnetic north line that crosses the

#38

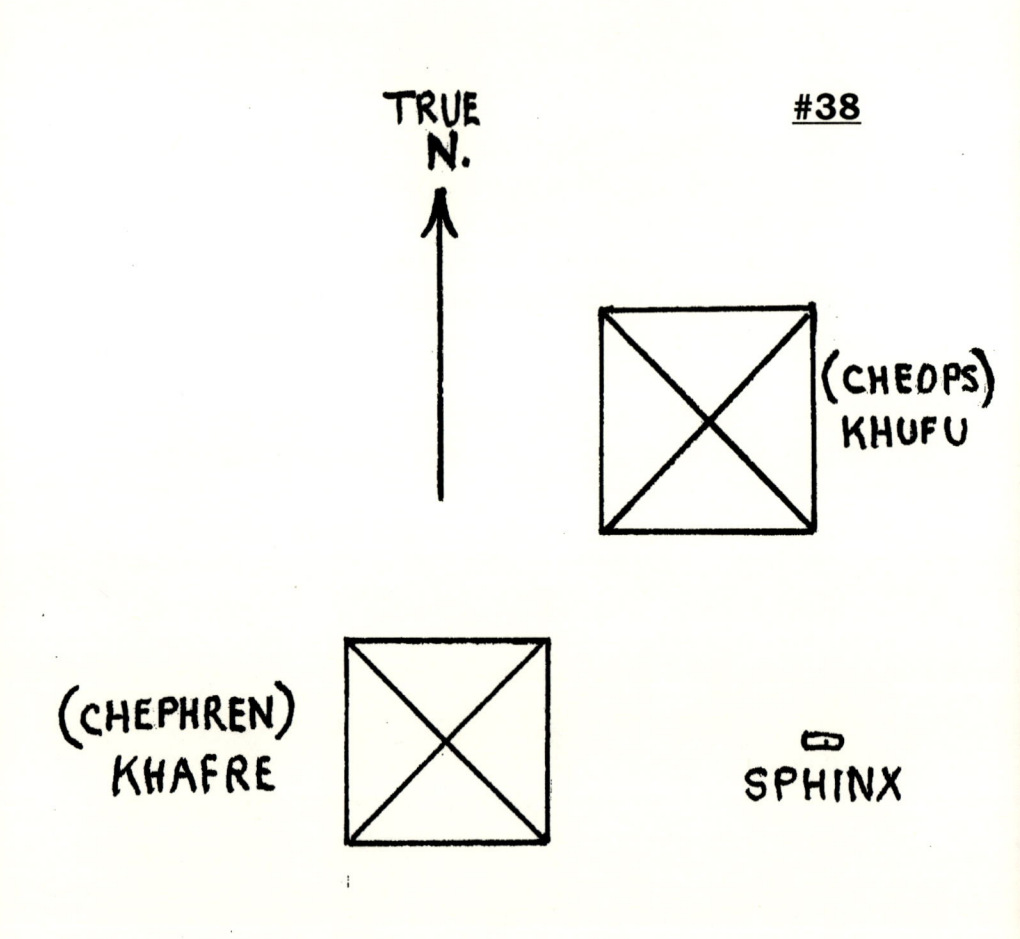

TRUE N. ↑

(CHEOPS) KHUFU

(CHEPHREN) KHAFRE

SPHINX

(MYCERINUS) MENKAURE

globe from Gold Hill to the Nile Valley, but also because of that which the Oregon Vortex is a part.

On a map, let's center a square representing the base of a big pyramid on Seattle, and align a flat side about 22-degrees off true north. We'll center another such square on Upper Klamath Lake, and align it 20-degrees from true north. Lastly we'll lay a slightly smaller square at the mouth of Monterey Bay, and position it about 18-degrees from true north. These alignments are to correct for compass declinations to magnetic north, and when this is done, the placement of the squares on a fair-sized chunk of the Western side of the North American Continent presents a mirror image of the placement on the ground of those three Egyptian pyramids at Giza.

Seattle is Khufu (Cheops).
Upper Klamath Lake is Khafre (Chephren).
Monterey Bay is Menkaure (Mycerinus).
Seattle is negative.
Upper Klamath Lake is positive.
Monterey Bay is negative.

The West Coast group is aligned magnetic north. The East, or Giza group is aligned true north. The two groups are aligned 20-degrees off from one another. Both groups are connected by 20-degree lines to the Bermuda Triangle, and to the Yucatan Peninsula, and are connected across the North Magnetic Pole by a 20-degree line from true north. When we locate the North Magnetic

Pole above Hudson's Bay on a globe, then tip the globe so as to look at it from the axis, the North Magnetic Pole from the axis measures *one-sixth* the distance to the equator if the view is considered to be two-dimensional.

The North Magnetic Pole of the Planet Earth is the equivalent of that big "electron" orbiting the axis of the House of Mystery Vortex!

There are two differences: One's a lot bigger than the other (I'm getting to that), and one's in our space, while the other is in hyperspace. The measurement *ratios* are the same right down to the precession of the equinoxes wobble.

I know that much of this information is not the kind of fodder found in textbooks, and I would have given up this seeming weirdness long ago if this stuff hadn't just kept falling into place. One number, angle, or real-world observation after another continued to support the next number, angle, or observation. I would have been happy with just the knowledge gained from magnetic fields, but the data flowed over into the idea of greater vortexes. Every thing dovetails into the other.

Consider John Lister's measurement of the Vortex's diameter? He called it 165 feet 4 1/2 inches, or in decimal terms, 165.375 feet. My own tinkering and math doesn't quite agree. Once I had wrung everything out, my figure was 165.34375 feet, or about 165 feet 3 11/12 inches. The difference is only seven-twelfths of an inch.

Seven-twelfths?

There is still enough of a skeptic in me to wonder if I subconsciously engineered this result. I don't think so, but it looks a little pat.

165.34375 feet, off by a few twelfths or not, was a real-world number, and so far as I could tell, those bigger vortexes of 54 miles, with 9-mile coronas were also numbers from the "real world". But I was still in a quandary, because the two didn't seem to connect to anything. One day, while half daydreaming, I was playing a little 7 and 12 bingo with my calculator, when I entered this simple equation:

12 X 165.34375 = 1,984.125

That meant nothing to me, so I let it ride:

12 X 1,984.125 = 23,809.5

This was also a number of no interest, so:

12 X 23,809.5 = 285,714

I remember staring at this result for a long time, repeating the numbers to myself slowly.

2...8...5...7...1...4...?

The result of dividing 7 into 2? Could it be *that* 285714?

I suddenly came awake. My finger hit the divide sign, and then tapped in the number five thousand two hundred and eighty.

165.34375 is an expression in feet, and so too is 285,714. 5,280 are the number of feet in a mile.

Breathing hard, I mashed the equal button.

The LCD window of my calculator screamed, 54.1125 miles!

So, defenders of the Metric System, try to match this one.

A direction, and an unlikely destination was beginning to come into the open.

I backed up the 12 times 12 equation from the smallest known value I had, 165.34375 feet. When I reached what I thought to be a logical starting point, I moved the entire 12 times 12 equation forward for a series of nine iterations. Why nine? Because, in this Universe, as we've been learning, everything starts over after reaching nine. The results wrung the skeptic out of me for good.

Start at 0.095685033 of a foot. (A tiny bit more than an inch.)

1. 12 X .095685033 = 1.1482204 feet
2. 12 X 1.1482204   = 13.778647 feet
3. 12 X 13.778647   = 165.34375 feet
   (House of Mystery Vortex)
4. 12 X 165.34375   = 1,984.1251 feet
5. 12 X 1,984.1251 = 23,809.501 feet
   (4.51 miles. Gold Hill to Vortex)
6. 12 X 23,809.501 = 285,714.1 feet
   (54.1125 miles. Gold Hill Vortex)
7. 12 X 285,714.1   = 3,428,568.1 feet
   (649.35 miles)
8. 12 X 3,428,568.1 = 41,142,817 feet
   (7,792.2 miles)

Before going to the ninth iteration, I want to discuss numbers 7 and 8. 649.35 miles plus a 109-mile corona on both sides is the total diameter of the Bermuda Triangle. Ivan Sanderson and others determined this as fact long before I started playing with a calculator.

Number 8 was not unexpected. It seems this 6 sextillion, 388 quintillion short ton planet of ours measures 7,926 miles across its diameter, and after subtracting an equatorial bulge due to centrifugal spin, 7,792 miles is at least close enough for government work.

9. 12 X 7,792.2 miles = 93,506.4 miles

It was incredibly tempting to change 93 thousand miles to 93 million miles and proclaim the distance from the Earth to the Sun, but there was a more honest way to decipher the meaning of number nine's product.

93,506 miles is half of 187,012, which is one-sixth of 1,122,072, which should be the diameter of the next higher iteration, which is number 2 on the next series of nine. The Earth is the nut of Planet Byrd's corona, and like the Bermuda Triangle it slides back and forth while drawing an oblong circle on Byrd's surface. Just as the Okanogan Vortex has to make two passes to get around once, the Earth is doing the same in relation to Planet Byrd. We are just like that big "electron" out behind the House of Mystery, slipping in and out of hyperspace, going on and off like a blinking light, and rubbing our bellies while patting our heads.

Flight 19 may have dropped through the last six iterations of reality, and found themselves on a planet we would think of as about thirteen-twelfths of an inch across. Nothing on Planet Taylor got smaller for them, but from our point of view their airplanes would be significantly smaller than viruses, let alone their bodies.

The deeper I get into these kinds of results the more outlandish examples of what Reason would like to consider as coincidences show up. One example is the *nine-foot* dead zone at the Oregon Vortex, and the *nine-mile* dead zone at the Okanogan Vortex. Another good instance of such a coincidence is that ninth iteration, which caused me to mention a desire to change 93 thousand to 93 million, so as to justify the product of the equation to equal the distance from the Earth to the Sun. Quite frequently, an actual number measurement will agree with a ratio comparison. I always wonder if both explanations might be correct?

My habit of celebrating results sometimes prevents me from writing down results. For instance, after returning home from the 1998 trip to Gold Hill, I realized I had failed to measure the actual size of that gap in the line of demarcation. I remembered it *looked* to be less than two-feet, and was *maybe* a foot and a half, and I was mad at myself because I really wanted to know the actual distance.

I tried various mathematical solutions using the measurements I had, such as Litster's 165.375 diameter calculation. After multiplying, dividing, adding, and subtracting that measurement in every way I could think of, it always boiled down to the corona, which left me with either Litster's number, 27.5625 feet, or my number, 27.114582 feet.

The next thing I did with both numbers was to apply my old half-way-to-infinity rule of dividing a number by 2. After four iterations, I ended up with a number that translated to 19.25 inches, or to 19.137 inches. I rounded them off to 19, and decided to keep it. The result looked even better when I finally reread *Notes and Data,* and became reacquainted with Lister's expansion and contraction of 19-inches. Later, after learning the gap I discovered opened and closed, I decided I had simply rediscovered Litster's expansion and contraction point.

While fiddling with other sets of numbers that sometimes made sense and sometimes didn't, I kept running across that same 19, or 19.2 result. If there is a number that doesn't appear to have any direct connection to pyramids, it's 19, but whether it's an actual distance measurement or a comparison ratio, it keeps popping up in vortex measurements.

At the end of March, 2000 a man by the name of Igor Shnaper was on one of my tours through the House of Mystery. I mentioned to the group that the fall of gravity should be about ten per cent less inside the Vortex than outside. Mr. Shnaper said he would be happy to do the calculations to prove or disprove this contention.

To be frank, I had never known the correctness of this assertion regarding the fall of gravity in the area, and had no idea how he might prove or disprove it. After the tour broke up, I took him back into House where a brass plumb bob hangs on a string from a rafter. He measured the length of the string, and then allowed the plumb bob to swing. He counted ten swings, timing them with the second hand of a watch.

He thanked me, said he would take the observations home, do the calculations, and send us the results.

Six days later he E-mailed the following to Maria:

Period = 2*Pi*Sqrt(l/g),
Where Pi = 3.1415
    Period = 1.9 sec
    l = 2'8" = length of the string
    g = gravitational acceleration
       (normal 9.88 m/s^2 or 32 ft/s^2)
Inverting the formula
g = l*(pi/Period)^2
we are coming up with 8.89 m/s^2, or 29.16 f/s^2

Which is about 10% smaller than normal!!!

Mr. Shnaper went on with four more lines of calculation to show how he estimated any error in timing the pendulum swings, and then included his credentials, which included a BS in applied physics from Cornell University, and an MS from Stanford in aerospace.

It was nice to have confirmation of something I've been telling folks on the tours, but I was also interested to learn that the two-foot eight-inch string we used to hang the plumb bob provided a ten-swing period of *19 seconds.*

Coincidences like this are becoming a bit disconcerting, but none more so than some off-the-wall-measuring I did on my little six-inch globe one day.

The Giza Plateau, and the center of the Bermuda Triangle are both on the same latitude line, 30-degrees of arc. The Tropic of Cancer is naturally at Latitude 23 degrees. Suppose, I wondered, if a line parallel to the axis was drawn up from the equator, how far would 30-degrees on the Earth's curvature be measured from that perpendicular line? I cut a piece of cardboard so as to square my little globe, and then measured over to the 30-degree latitude line.

The gap was five-sixteenths of an inch. My globe is six inches in diameter, or 96 sixteenths. By dividing 5 into 96 I was left staring at 19.2

segments of five-sixteenths across the diameter of the Earth.

Does, I wondered, any of this have to do with the investigator? Am I making this stuff up? Do I dare put any of this in print, and hope at the same time to be taken seriously? Should I tell the folks the rest?

It's comforting to know the center of the Bermuda Triangle is six plus degrees above the Tropic of Cancer. If it was in the Southern Hemisphere and below the Tropic of Capricorn, and then someone found out I was born in January...?

To make matters worse, where would my credibility be when it was discovered I was born January 19th?

At least I was too young back in December of 1945 to blame for assigning the "Lost Patrol" the flight number of...19.

8

A GOLD MAP

It was twenty-five years later, and this time I was sitting at Fred's living room table, rather than he at mine. There were no pyramids for him to dowse, but I did have my maps spread out, and was showing him where all the best vortexes could be found. He was more interested in where the bad ones might be, though, and asked about a certain town on Vancouver Island that he had recently visited.

From his glowing recommendation, I had a hunch he was considering this as a retirement location. I think his first worry was whether the wife could be coaxed into life along a rustic, out-of-the-way Canadian waterway with no roads in or out. After witnessing my impressive map demonstrations, he might have also been concerned about the possibility of an evil vortex making the plumbing break, and his ears ring.

Fred left the room, and came back with a big road map of British Columbia, which he opened on the table. I positioned my torus-shaped speaker magnet over the mouth of Alberni Inlet, and dangled the little pendulum magnet close to it. He seemed happy with the complete lack of results, signifying no overt vortex nearby.

In the last several weeks before this, I'd been so busy hunting vortexes to the south that I'd ignored the North.

As we sat comparing stories, the Canadian map remained spread out between us, and this was a good opportunity to check it over. I slowly moved the speaker magnet north of Seattle until I got a reaction; up in the "bush" as the Canadians call the wilderness. It was about 120 miles above the border, which made it closer to the Seattle Vortex than I would have expected. At that time, I had yet learned to appreciate that the curvature of the Planet collapsed these distances in the same way that arbitrary longitude lines get closer together.

"Well, there it is," I said. "A long way from Vancouver Island."

Fred leaned forward, studiously checked the position of my newly found vortex, and then commented with a grunt, "Huh?"

I waited, as he remained hovered over the map, evidently puzzled by something. Fred is not a person who can be hurried, but I was about to ask what had captured his attention, when he sat back, and inclined his head toward the donut-shaped magnet in an inscrutable nod.

"Look down through the hole," he said, his voice an oddly flat monotone.

I must have opened my mouth to ask why, when he added, "Just look."

I looked. For the first five seconds, nothing seemed out of the ordinary, and then what he wanted me to see slammed me right between the eyes. It felt almost like a real impact. I was looking at something that had been hanging around just below the radar screen of my perception for some time. It was a strange, minor coincidence I had noticed in passing, but not voiced.

Until that moment it was something I'd not even thought strongly about.

In Southern Oregon, four and a half miles from the House of Mystery, at the center of one of my 54-mile zones of influence, is the town of, **Gold Hill**.

72 miles due west of the Gold Hill Vortex, the same distance as a 54-mile diameter vortex with a 9-mile corona on each side, is the seaside town of **Gold Beach.**

At the same distance as the Santa Cruz Mystery Spot is from the Monterey Bay Vortex center, 31.5 miles, and on a line pointing straight at Riverside, Washington from Seattle is the town of **Gold Bar**.

On a magnetic north incline, and halfway up from the baseline forming Washington's trio of zones, is the community of Orondo, which translated from Spanish is **Deep Gold** (*Deep*, as in profound).

At the time Fred and I were having this conversation I still lived in the town of Oroville, which shares the Okanogan Vortex corona line with the larger Washington Vortex line of demarcation. The made-up name, Oroville, is of course, "Spanglish" for **Gold Town**.

What I saw at the bottom of the magnet's donut hole was a body of water called Carpenter Lake, and at the north end of the lake a dot denoting the Canadian town of **Gold Bridge**.

We looked each other in the eye for a long time before daring to talk about what had just occurred. I searched my memory for some small explanation.

I have read of so-called *L-Fields* that have been proposed to explain how a dumb insect like an ant, a termite, or a bee when banded together become like brain cells with legs and wings. An invisible quantum, action-a-distance connection exists, which turns the colony into a collective genius. Ask a beekeeper how little time it takes for a single bee to die after the swarm leaves it behind.

I mentioned the L-Field theory to Fred by way of trying to comfort both of us. There wasn't much else to say in defense of this colossal coincidence of finding the word **gold** stamped at the exact places to which Pyramid math and the magnets pointed. I ruled out the possibility I may have physically influenced the magnets, because of my true ignorance of the existence of Gold Bridge, and I surely had nothing to do with naming these places.

To think this name-dropping on maps could have happened as a conscious decision was silly, and yet the only conclusion left was absurd.

I wondered if these six references to gold were all there would be? Running across these places on maps was at first accidental, but whatever happened next, because I was no longer honestly ignorant, would be the result of a deliberate search. If no other line, angle, or center of a vortex showed up with a gold name, then maybe the idea of an actual coincidence would stand.

The first thing I did was investigate a place I knew about in South Central Washington, called Goldendale. I don't know if I was relieved or disappointed when this town didn't seem to line up with anything.

This was also about the time I was putting together the "Golden" Section and the Fibonacci sequence connection, so I was also counting spaces out from Riverside, and Orondo to the lines of demarcation to see if anything fell on the spiral lines. At first none of the golden names lined up on these lines, and then I realized I was using the *counterclockwise south* spiral. When I switched to the *south polarity clockwise* application everything changed.

The first numbers of 1 and 1 were easy to find. They constitute 180-degrees of a small circle around Orondo. The numeral 2 shows no language correlation on the map. Number 3 hits halfway between the first 1 and the Okanogan Vortex corona line. 4 falls right on Highway 2 as it points straight toward Spokane. 5 occupies the space that the Queen's Chamber takes up in the Great Pyramid. Numbers 6 and 7 are in the wilderness, but 8 lands right on Gold Bar.

Numeral 13 is Oroville.

The second number 1 in the next higher sequence begins at the Tri Cities Vortex, and the spiraling line, just before it reaches the magnetic north line at the Washington corona, where it begins an even larger spiral, slices right through the town of **Goldendale**.

I am the first to admit the unbelievable, even fanciful nature of the kind of dots I'm connecting, and I have to constantly remind myself that I didn't *invent* any of this. These titles I didn't choose, were presented to me on charts I didn't draw.

Whatever its cause, this is an elegant, spellbinding picture of a part of Nature we haven't yet looked deeply into.

What would happen, I wondered, if I extended the Fibonacci sections into the next larger Golden Spiral sequence?

As in the nature of the nautilus shell, the spiral widens, quickly enters the Pacific Ocean, and sweeps toward Vancouver Island. It cuts the Island almost in half as it passes between the town of **Gold River** and a mountain called **Golden Hinde Peak**.

As it traces across the mainland, it passes north of **Gold Bridge** by the width of a 54-mile vortex, and continues on to a rendezvous with **Golden** British Columbia.

As the line arches south of the border it passes through the vortex that is responsible for Montana's House of Mystery. From there it traverses between **Gold Creek**, Montana, and Orofino (**Fine Gold**) Camp Ground.

The spiral passes from Montana, through Idaho and into Nevada, where it slams into a town on Route 95 between McDermitt and Winnemucca called, Orovada. Since *Nevada* in Spanish means *snowfall*, Orovada probably means a cascade of gold (*cascada de oro*), or **Falling Gold.**

Even the word snow gets mixed up in this crazy quilt of golden places.

A snowflake consists of six radiating arms upon which ice crystals form their well-known, unique patterns. These patterns are believed to be caused by tiny pockets of oxygen, a gas most attracted to magnetism. Magnetic fields, snowflakes and vortexes share a dependence on the primary angle of 60-degrees, and the idea of snow having something to do with magnetic fields, or *power* goes back a long way into the past. Check the enigmatic statements of Job, 38: 22 and 23:

22: Have you entered into the *storehouses of the snow*, or do you see even the storehouses of the hail,

23: Which I have *kept back* for the time of distress, for the day of fight and war?

Our spiral line, which started at Orondo, Washington, has a few more miles to go from Orovada, Nevada. It ends near a lake that is about forty miles northeast of my old stomping grounds of Reno, Nevada. This lake was given an unbelievable unconscious name considering where the Fibonacci spiral line has been.

The Orondo–Orovada spiral line ends at the *north* end of **Pyramid Lake**.

There is only one way into the Great Pyramid: *The north entrance.*

Proceeding south there are more such spirals. From the Gold Hill area the spirals are quite complicated considering its 90-degree alignment with the Washington and Monterey Bay Vortexes. The reader is encouraged to peruse the map provided, and to count the impressive number of times the word gold in at least three languages is used to construct these spiral lines, straight lines, and concentric lines.

Words, in this case, fail while at the same time they astound. Under this assault on common sense, logic is forced to give up the concept of a true coincidence. Reason, however, hangs on to the last, feeling a need to continue using the word coincidence to describe these phenomena, because the phenomena appear illogical given the reality we perceive. This kind of thing should not happen, and yet it clearly has happened.

I'd like to think debunkers are going to have huge difficulties with this stuff.

The problem with finding true coincidence here is this: If two coins are thrown in the air, and after they come to rest on the floor, a straight line between them can be drawn no matter how they land in relation to one another. If three coins are tossed up to fall on the floor, the odds of being able to draw a straight line between all three are immense. If four coins are flipped in the air, a number like ten to the umpteenth power would be needed to describe the possibility of having them arranged in a straight line when they came to rest. If three or four coins line up twice in a row, this is an amazing coincidence. If it happens again?

Now, let's try this one: A line is started from **Gold Bridge**, British Columbia and crosses **Oroville**, Washington. It moves straight over the Planet's curve in a southeasterly fashion to **Orofino**, Idaho. A few miles later, on the same angle it cuts over **Golden**, Idaho.

The straight line then intersects the spiral line that swings down from **Gold Creek**, and **Orofino Camp Ground,** Montana. The lines meet just a little southeast of a town called *Challis*, Idaho.

Challis is not a gold name, but since Gold Hill **represents** *the pyramid of Chephren at Giza, this intersection is the* **equivalent mirror image** *of where the Sphinx would be located if it was built into the Northwest landscape. It is also twenty-degrees of arc from Gold Hill.*

The straight line continues through Utah, and enters Colorado near a burg called *Gateway*, but other than this, without checking local maps, it doesn't make obvious contact with anything golden in either Utah or Colorado.

Just northeast of Albuquerque, New Mexico, the line meets another town with the name of, **Golden.** From here it slashes within a few miles of the famous city of Roswell.

Just inside Texas on Route 285, the line comes to a screeching halt at the town of *Orla*.

We know the line ends at Orla, because in Spanish the word means *border*, or *fringe*. A border is a place to cross, or change direction, and also the line from here all the way to South America encounters no more references to gold.

Looking west from Orla, at a little more than a hundred miles is, **Orogrande**, New Mexico.

When a new line is drawn between Orla and Orogrande, the next place encountered is **Oro Valley**, Arizona.

This straight line continues westward toward San Diego, and into **Casa de Oro**, California.

Let's see, we have, **Gold** Bridge, **Oro**ville,

#39

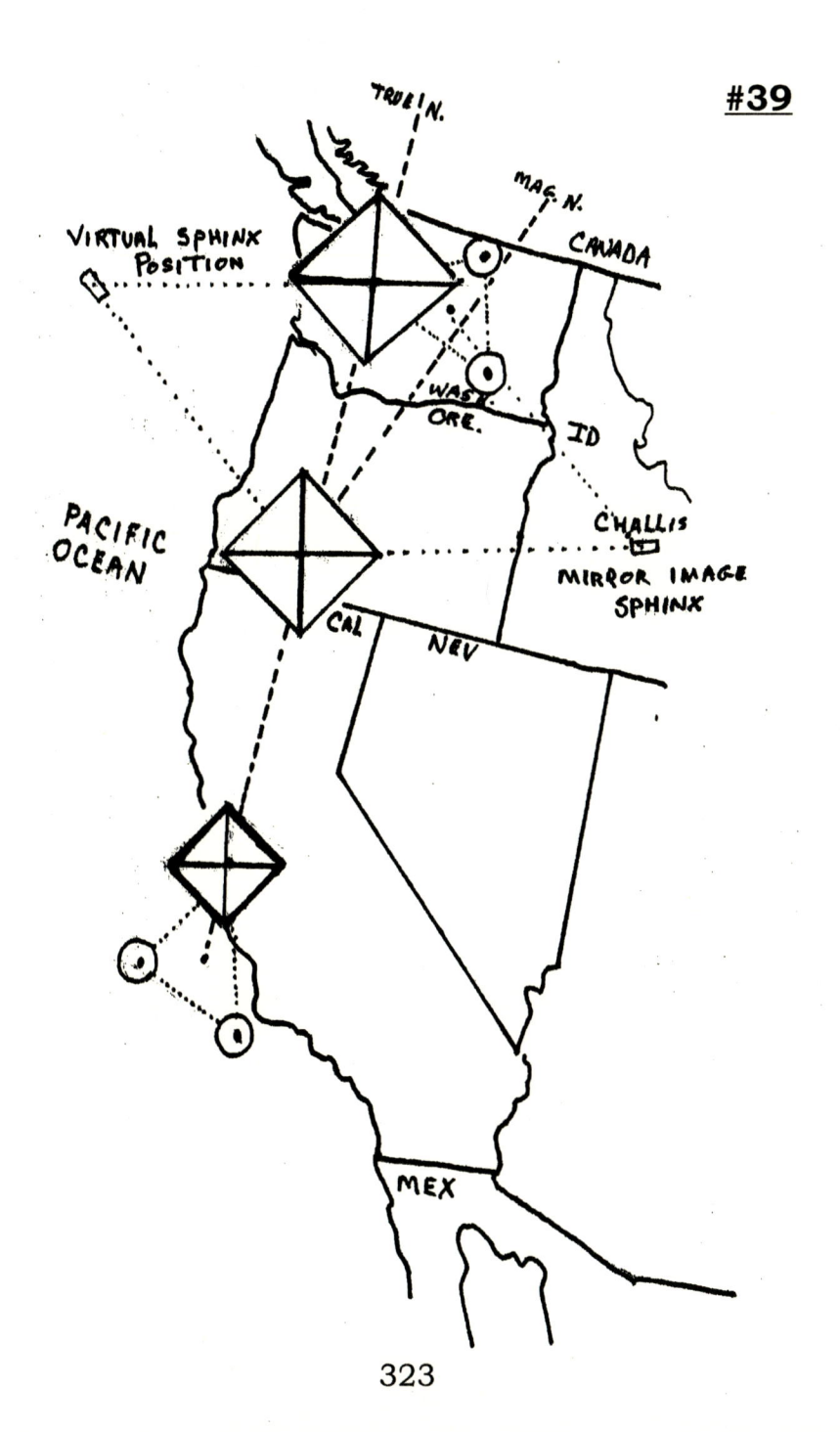

Orofino, **Gold**en, **Gold**en, **Oro**grande, **Oro** Valley, and Casa De **Oro** all on a straight line, which, assuming these places got their names in a random fashion, makes a minimum of eight coins tossed in the air.

If we consider Challis, and Orla as pertinent, then there are ten coins on the floor that have landed in a straight line!

It's true that there are two lines, but when a protractor is laid at Orla, Texas, using the line to Casa de Oro as the base, the line back up to Gold Bridge is at an angle of 51.43-degrees of arc, the angle of inclination from base to apex of the Great Pyramid. If this angle is counted as another coin on the floor, then that makes eleven in a straight line.

To further complicate the issue, I need to mention that Gold Bridge, British Columbia is situated as close to latitude 51-degrees, 26 minutes as it needs to be to represent the Great Pyramid's angle of inclination *from the center of the Earth.*

Coin number 12!

Anything else?

Well, yes.

After the baseline leaves San Diego it intersects in the Pacific Ocean a line coming down from Gold Bridge. This line is skewed from true north by almost 12-degrees, and is 90-degrees from the baseline. It cuts through Seattle, between Medford and Klamath Falls, and then right by the Mystery

Spot at Santa Cruz, into the middle of the Monterey Bay Vortex, and across the center of the larger Pacific Vortex on its way to meet the baseline.

About halfway between this baseline and Gold Bridge is Mount Shasta, and it is from here that a really big vortex circle can be swung from Gold Bridge and the baseline. It should be recalled that there are five Bermuda Triangle type vortexes in the Northern Hemisphere, and the corona of this big circle touches the northern point of the Vortex zone out from Hawaii. The Orla–Casa de Oro baseline also ends at this point. From this same point, a line back to Gold Bridge is 60-degrees from the baseline making this a very large Isosceles triangle. This angle is line number 7 on diagram # 22.

When the Orla–Gold Bridge line is extended farther north on a Great Circle route, it passes through The Klondike **Gold** Rush National Historical Park in the most northeastern section of British Columbia. Still following the curvature of the Earth, the line passes just to the south of Prudhoe Bay, Alaska, and goes on to contact Siberia at 90-degrees from the Magnetic North Pole. From the point where this line crosses that 20-degree line on its way to Egypt beyond the Magnetic Pole, the angle to the northern Siberian Coast near the Island of Vrangelya is 51.43 degrees of arc.

There doesn't seem to be anything golden printed on the map of Alaska, especially near

Prudhoe Bay. However, if we wanted to fudge the line and indulge in slang, the stuff being pumped out of the ground at Prudhoe Bay, and that which the oil companies say is in abundance in the Arctic National Wildlife Refuge is often referred to as, black **gold**.

Going back to the Hawaiian Triangle: If a line from this Triangle's center is drawn through the Klondike Gold Rush National Historical Park, it will be at 72-degrees and constitute the eighth line from diagram # 22. The ninth line from this diagram, drawn from the southern point of the Hawaiian Triangle to the axis of the Earth (150-degrees longitude) is of course 90-degrees to the equator, and it crosses Prudhoe Bay.

For those who wish to check these statements on maps, it must be remembered that the Earth's curved surface has to be taken into account. Cartographers have an inherent problem of drawing maps of a round world on flat surfaces, which they have solved in various ways. If a short distance is involved no one worries about the horizon, but a depiction of a large area such as the expanse of the United States presents an accuracy dilemma. One radical solution is the Mercator Projection, an example of which is the depiction of Greenland on a world map to be the size of South America when it is really only about the size of Argentina. The Mercator Projection shows correct relationships, but incorrect dimensions. It's best to measure these things on globes or Mercator maps, but generally a state road map will work even though such maps are flat.

Meanwhile, the centerpiece of all this measuring, Mount Shasta, has been noted for a long, long time as very strange place. A few people claim the area around Mount Shasta is the last remaining land above water that once belonged to the sunken continent of Lemura. Others go to the Mountain to meditate, and perhaps try to catch a glimpse of those weird people who supposedly used to wander into the town of Weed, clad in flowing robes, and bought things with pure gold.

I had my own strange run-in with this area, which will be recounted later.

These sorts of bizarre, extrinsic things keep entering my life, and then fall neatly into place. Every so often, though, a problem turns up causing me to wonder if I might be fooling myself? The reality-based part of me is almost gleeful at these times, and argues that I should toss out all this nonsense and go get a real job.

I was having a bit of trouble with the Seattle Vortex measurements, and a nagging apprehension about how terribly convenient it is to find one of these things hanging around a city was keeping me from solving the problem. I'd heard of old-timer pilots complaining about instrument fluctuations on a north approach to Boeing Field in Seattle, but I still balked at locating one of these

#40

A larger triangle on the west coast of North America (Note: The 30-degree north latitude line actually travels a little south of Bermuda on its way to Cairo)

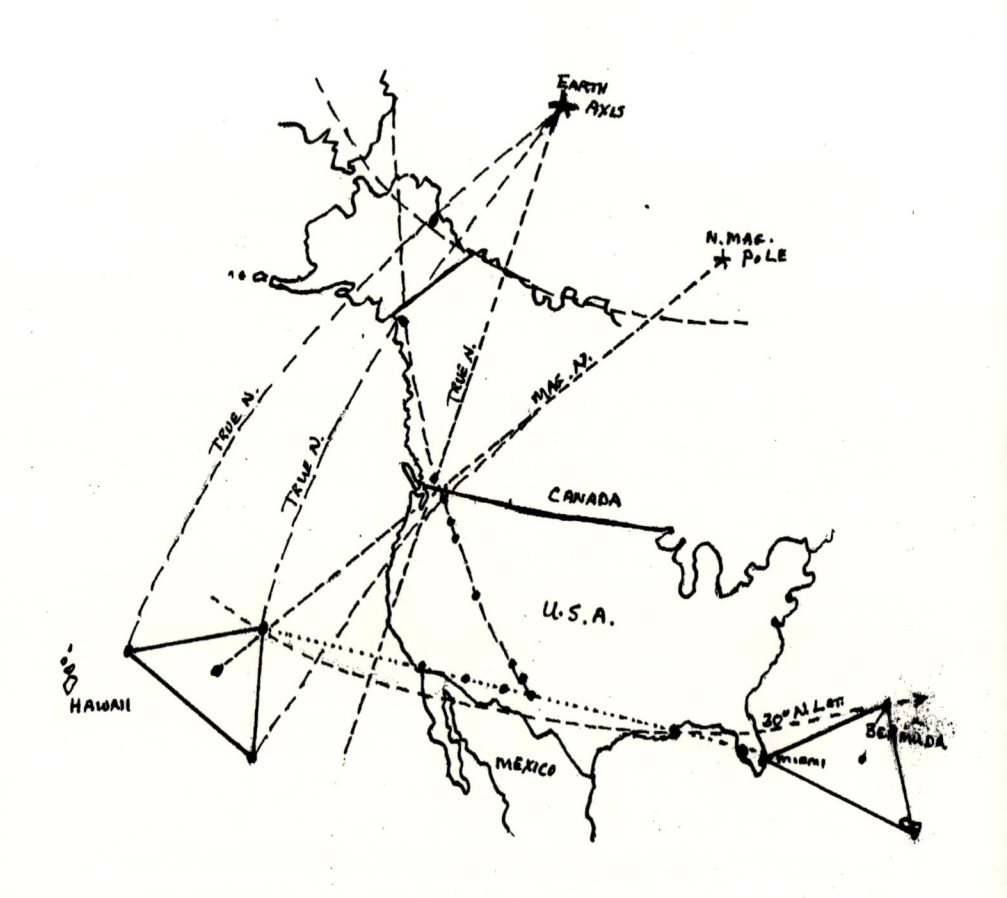

things in a big metropolitan area. The larger Seattle Vortex was found by poking around on state road maps, but the closest I'd come to pin pointing this thing was to place it in Puget Sound just off Discovery Park. The problem was that this point is off by four or five miles in so far as rectifying the position of the town of Gold Bar. It also slightly skews the angle of the line back to the Tri Cities area.

Since I had finally learned the exact center of the Gold Hill Vortex is in the town of Gold Hill, and not the House of Mystery site, I decided it was time to find the axis of the Seattle anomaly.

For this task I dug out an old Seattle city map so as to get close to my work. I'd spent about two years living in this city, and I knew it quite well, but even so I was beset by an odd, intense desire to disregard the obvious.

The first thing I had to do was ignore Reason.

North of downtown, and just west of old Highway 99 is the Woodland Park Zoo. The Zoo looks down across the Highway toward the obvious: A small body of water called Greenlake. The lake is about three-quarters of a mile across, which makes its nearly circular shape an undisguised candidate for the vortex center. The whole lake is a part of Woodlawn Park with lawns and jogging paths encircling it, and beyond the Park boundaries the shoreline is ringed about with streets and dwellings.

When I applied my magnets, Greenlake announced itself as the dead-zone center of the Seattle Vortex. As always though, if what the magnets infer isn't corroborated by the connecting of the lines and angles to other such places, then the results can't be trusted. I immediately found several verifying lines, so the lesson about paying attention to the obvious was learned one more time.

There is a really big "electron" spinning rapidly, but chugging around the lakeshore about every two hours, just like the one orbiting the town of Gold Hill, and similar to the smaller one out behind the House of Mystery.

From Greenlake the distance to Gold Bar is just right at 31.5 miles. The line from Riverside, through Gold Bar, and then Greenlake comes out exactly four and a half miles beyond Greenlake on the west side of Discovery Park. About a half-mile offshore in Puget Sound is a vortex similar in size to the House of Mystery Vortex. Nobody will be walking around having his or her height changed, however. This vortex is over water.

While involved in mapping out the above, another obvious fact gave me a good whack. I thought I wouldn't run up against golden words in Seattle, and then I remembered driving by Greenlake hundreds of times on "old" Highway 99. In 1962 and '63, when I lived there, and Interstate-5 was in the process of being built, Highway 99 was the only good way through the city. 99 was also a city street, known then and now as, Aurora Avenue.

Aurora: the **golden** goddess of dawn. *Aurum*: Latin for **gold**.

In Seattle, Aurora Avenue runs north and south.

I'm sure, as we travel around, most of us speculate how places get their names? Many who drive Interstate 5 in Oregon sometimes question what State they are in:

Portland, Oregon, or Maine?
Albany, Oregon, or New York?
Salem, Oregon or Massachusetts?
Lebanon, Oregon, or Pennsylvania?
Saginaw, Oregon, or Michigan.
Peoria, Oregon, or Illinois?
Florence, Oregon, or Italy?
London, Oregon, or England?

The list of pirated city names in this State is long, and no doubt has much to do with homesickness felt by early setters who toiled the Oregon Trail in covered wagons. People who built these cities and towns came from places with these names.

The titles of towns like Gold Hill, and Oroville have a lot to do with the fact that gold was discovered and mined near them. However, the discovery and mining can't have anything to do with why the names line up so perfectly in relation to these vortexes. Many towns and cities grew up near, or because of gold mines, but don't have names identified with the metal that came from the ground near them.

Though the names usually involve variations of the word gold, other oddities creep in from time to time. Oddities like the Town of Aurora (**Golden**), Oregon, just south of Portland.

A straight line from Aurora to Upper Klamath Lake, where it crosses the corona line that passes above Eugene encounters the town of Nimrod. Nimrod was supposed to be the great grandson of Noah, and Hebrew legend identifies him as a mighty hunter. If we are to consider the Gold Hill–Klamath Vortex as the middle star in Orion's Belt, and Orion is also a mighty hunter, what do we make of this?

Whoever christened the town of Nimrod could have called it anything, or started the town fifty miles away and missed these lines. Aurora itself could have received a different name, or been placed to one side or the other of the north–south line connecting Gold Bridge, Seattle, Santa Cruz, et al.

One of the fun things about working at the House of Mystery is meeting and talking with the many interesting folks who stop by. One of the more intriguing of these is a woman who lives in the area, and complains that a force line from the Vortex runs through her house. She is certain this line comes right out of her fireplace, and evidently interferes with her life. She is something of a fun-loving sensitive, and we all have a great time when she comes by to brighten our day.

   She is Greek. Her name is Aurelia, and, no kidding, it means **The Golden One**.

   I know the general area where she lives, and I have not been able to plot any sort of line from the Vortex in her direction. However, a line from *Aurora*, 250 miles north, which passes down the road *Aurelia* lives on, is 23.5-degrees off the line that goes through Nimrod. As an aside, on its way to her house the line runs through a spot on the map called. Nonpareil (*A paragon, or a* **6-point** *interlinear space in printing*). A line from true north of Nonpareil to Nimrod is about 52-degrees of arc, and a similar line from Aurelia's house is 60-degrees.

   I haven't seen her lately, but I can't wait to point out that the disruption of her fireplace isn't our fault.

   I have searched atlases across most of Canada, Mexico, and the United States, and it appears the gold-naming phenomenon is almost exclusively the property of the western side of the North American Continent. For a time, it looked like Golden and Aurora, Colorado, both of which are suburbs of Denver had nothing to do with any of this. Then I saw that the Denver area is 23.5-degrees off the Orla–Gold Bridge line.

When I revisited Orla, Texas on the map, I saw something else. The distance from Orla to Orogrande when plotted on the Gold Bridge line shows the radius of a line of demarcation of another vortex, which swings from Orla to just beyond Roswell, New Mexico. The radius of this line when chopped into thirds gives the corona width, and when added out from the line of demarcation this *corona* line cuts through a town northwest of Roswell called, **Corona**. It's a town that's also smack on the 51.43-degree Gold Bridge line. When plotted from Orogrande, Roswell and Corona are about 40-degrees apart.

    I am not going to try making a case for this area being a natural portal for alien visitors. I'll let others do this, and my guess is that they'll give it a try. There is a better candidate, however, for this kind of connection, and I fell into it while still back on the apple ranch.

    My neighbor, Mauricio and his family came from El Salvador. His father lives there, but comes north to visit once or twice a year. One day, Mauricio told me that his father, after being in the area for three or four months also becomes stricken with ringing in the ears, but when he goes home his ears quiet right down.

    After hearing this, I got out the magnets and maps, and learned the whole country of El Salvador is apparently a vortex. It is also one of those places on the Earth where magnetic north and true north

#41

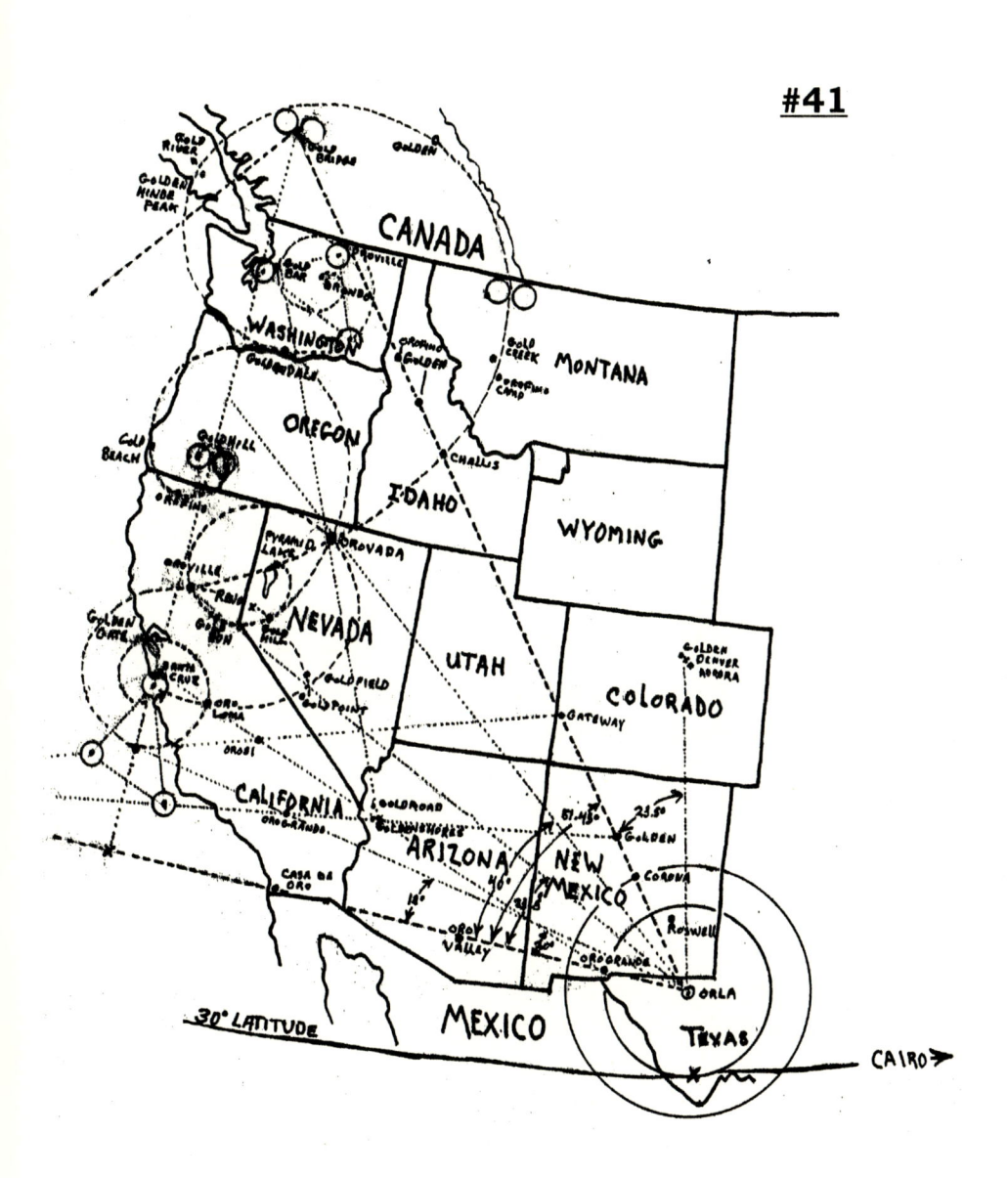

are the same. A longitude line goes due north from El Salvador, through the Yucatan, Pensacola, Florida, up the middle of Lake Michigan, to Hudson's Bay, Baffin Island and the North Magnetic Pole, finally stopping at the axis of the Earth.

I'd been tracking vortexes east, but hadn't gotten to the area around the Gulf of Mexico. All of a sudden the boot of Louisiana, as it hangs out there in the Gulf of Mexico, looked suspicious. It looked obvious. It looked like a circle of just the correct size might tuck right in under Biloxi, Mississippi, and just east of New Orleans. It appeared that a double vortex like the Gold Hill–Klamath Lake configuration ought to sit just off shore in the Gulf, with the eastern twin vortex circle situated due south of Pensacola, Florida. A line down through Mobile Bay, Alabama would cut them right down the middle.

Not only did it look like these phenomena should exist here, my magnets agreed, and some very interesting lines and distance ratios verified my suspicions.

There are quite a few things about this discovery that are significant:

Lines drawn on a *great circle route* to Miami from Gold Bridge, Seattle, and Gold Hill, touch this twin Vortex in different places making a 12-degree angle between them when checked from Miami. A line drawn to the west on a *flat map* from

Pensacola, cuts through Corona near Roswell, into Arizona and between the towns of **Gold Road** and **Golden Shores**, to Orogrande, California, then terminates at the apex of the Pacific Vortex of which Monterey Bay is a part.

The distance from the Pensacola area to downtown Miami is the *exact* distance from Miami to the center of the Bermuda Triangle.

The significance of that stone circle, which was found in Miami, looks huge, but I still don't think it was necessary for ancient man to have flying machines to put these things on *ley* lines.

South of the city of Pensacola, on a long spit of land dividing Pensacola Bay from the Gulf of Mexico, is the town of Gulf Breeze. For a number of years, Gulf Breeze is a place where a person can almost make a reservation to see a UFO up close.

Here, might there be a portal?

At the bottom of Louisiana's boot, a few miles from Grand Isle on Route 1, is the town of **Golden Meadow.** As measured from a true line of latitude, Gulf Breeze is 23.5-degrees of arc from Golden Meadow.

When a line is drawn west from Miami across the Everglades toward Naples it encounters a town called, **Golden Gate.** This line when extended across the Gulf toward Louisiana intersects Golden Meadow, and continues on to Orla, Orogrande, Oro Valley, Casa de Oro and beyond. This line appears

#42

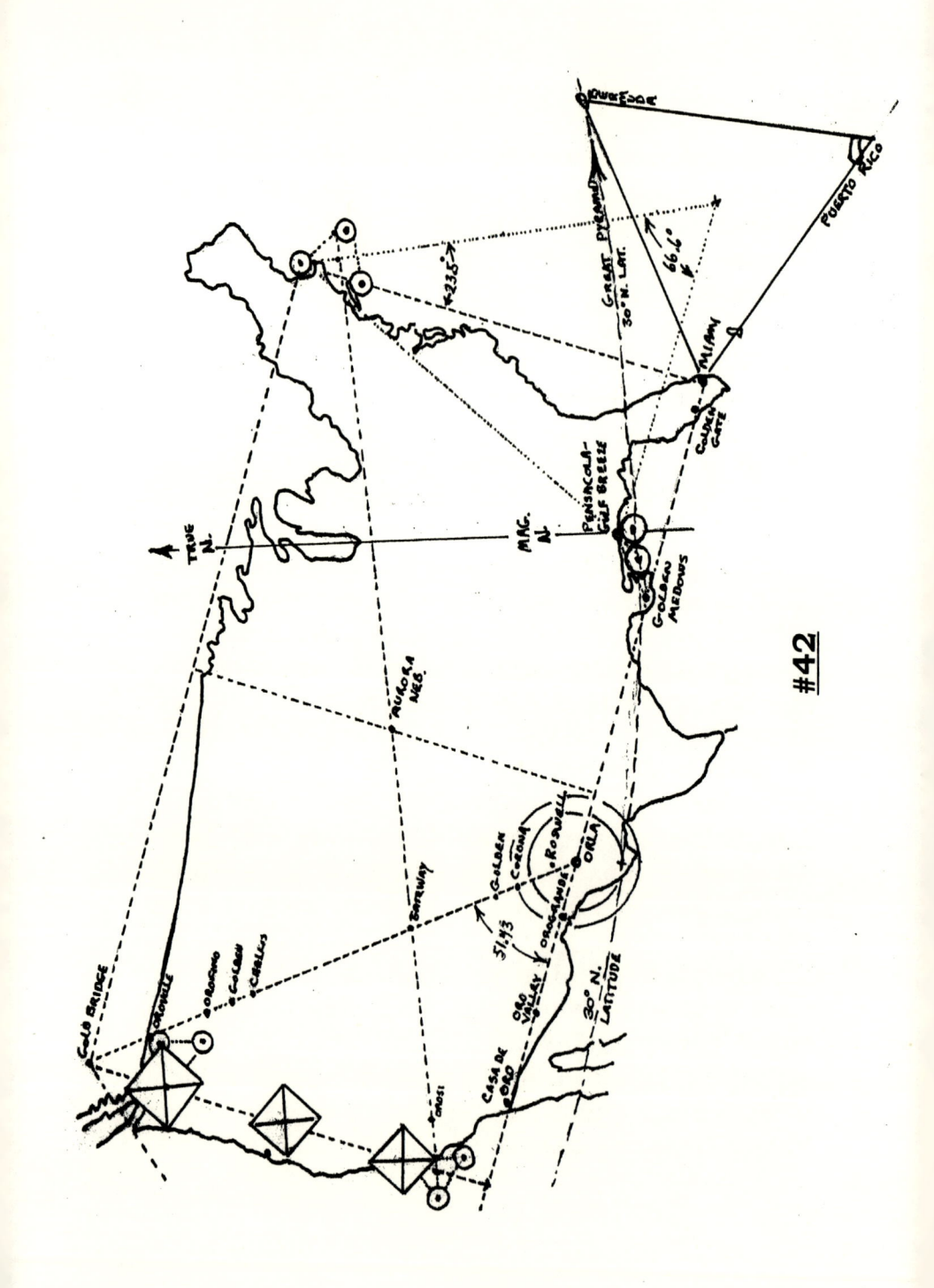

as perfectly straight from Miami to the San Diego area because on flat maps the southern boundaries are in scale.

From Miami to the north, another straight line the same inclination as the line through the Pacific Coast "pyramid areas", skirts the East Coast, and helps form the baseline of another triangle of three 54-mile vortex areas off the coasts of New York and Massachusetts. The northern leg of this trio of vortexes encompasses Cape Cod Bay, and the southern leg is just off Long Island. The apex is to the east in the Atlantic Ocean.

I don't know if this triangle has anything to do with 747's falling out of the sky, but if I were departing Kennedy Airport on my way to Europe via a great circle route, I think I'd like the pilot to go a little farther north before turning east.

A line drawn from Cape Cod Bay to the west terminates at Gold Bridge, British Columbia, and completes a perfect rectangle that can be evenly divided into two squares. This rectangle looks suspiciously like a really, really big King's Chamber, and the exact center of it looks to be comfortably close to a town in Nebraska called...**Aurora**.

I could easily clutter up this map with more lines through more towns called either, Gold(something), Aurora, Aurelia, or Oro(this that or the other thing), but I leave that to the reader if he or she hasn't anything better to do.

I do need, however, to point out that the 30-degree north latitude line scrapes itself on the vortex circle around Orla, and then cuts straight through the centers of the twin vortex circles between Louisiana and Pensacola, continues east to the Island of Bermuda, and finally to the city of Cairo, Egypt.

It could be noted that a town about a hundred miles south of Santa Cruz, which would equal the Great Pyramid's underground chamber of the larger Pacific Vortex, called Harmony, lines up with the California town of Tranquility, Gold Hill, Nevada, Orovada, and we-know-where Montana, but I won't mess up the map with this either, because I think you can see how quickly small coincidences become major implications.

9

THE OPEN END

    I ask myself lately if I've found what John Litster may have thought the world wasn't ready for? Did he know all that I've already recounted, and perhaps more? No one can consciously know everything that another knows, so I don't pretend to understand the details of his work, but is it possible that the totality of my knowledge now surpasses that which he once possessed?
    At times, I think the answer is the second question, and then there are times when the Vortex throws a curve at me.
    I don't claim greater intelligence, insight, or luck. Litster just lived in a different time, and investigated the Vortex lacking data to which I have access. Also he almost certainly saw things from a perspective I don't necessarily share. He probably

made bad assumptions, but it's a sin of which I've been accused, and after attention is drawn to what I've recently been up to, debunker's cream pies will fly in from all quarters.

If there is any validity to the folklore about Litster thinking the world wasn't ready for what he discovered, it may be that it was *he* who wasn't ready for what *he* discovered. All we know is that an educated, intelligent man spent thirty plus years working inside the Vortex, and after thousands of experiments his contribution to our knowledge is a thirty-page booklet of mostly pictures, which contains a text that is almost in code.

Across the field of any knowledge, dogma can sink in, thoughts get trapped in a vortex-like singularity, and room for doubt disappears. Litster may have come to a point where a new thought was a thought encountered before, and the one after that, the same. Whether the disappearance of most of his work was deliberate on his part, the mischief of another, or the accident of a leaky roof, because so little is left, we have to start over.

When looking through *Notes and Data*, I sometimes wonder how he interpreted his own findings. For instance, I take issue with his descriptions of Terralines. "These lines run due East and West and also North and South..." he wrote. A Terraline, according to Litster, measures 57 inches wide where they contact the ground.

They bend when passing through the Vortex site, and where the paths cross the lines oscillate a quarter of their width. I have always assumed by the word Terralines, he meant magnetic lines of force that are part of the Earth's magnetic field. If this is case, I wish I could ask him about the assertion that there are "...East and West..." lines. I don't know of a magnet that produces force lines horizontal to it's pole, which is what an east and west line would have to be.

Once, in an unlikely environment far from the House of Mystery Vortex, I literally saw the tracks of Earth's magnetic force lines.

One of the few places I enjoyed in the Okanogan apple country was a lake about eight miles from Oroville, called Wannacut. It is a high lake, two miles long on a north–south axis, and a half to three-quarters of a mile wide. Evergreen trees, mostly ponderosa pine, cover the east and west sides of the bowl in which it sits. To the north and south is open sagebrush country, and a gravel road passes along the west shore. A few houses, and a small fishing resort pepper the eastern side.

On a warm fall morning, I drove up to Wannacut, parked my truck on a high part of the road for the lake view, got out a notebook, and settled back in the passenger's seat to work on some ideas. It was going to be a hot day, and there was no shade at this vantage point, but I didn't plan to be there long.

Every ten or fifteen minutes a vehicle sped by kicking up a huge cloud of dust, which rolled over me and down the slope toward the water. I was kept busy winding the truck windows up to keep out airborne dirt, and then down to let air circulate. As I watched one dust cloud roiling down to the lake something odd on the surface of the water caught my attention.

Three or four hazy, barely discernible white lines were riding a gentle chop near the shore. They were fairly wide, 100 to 150 yards long, and extending in the same direction toward which I was facing, so that I was looking across their parallel ranks. Wondering what they were, I watched them for a minute, and then had to lean over to roll up the driver's window to ward off a new batch of dirt. When I glanced back down the hill the three lines had grown to five or six, and they had lengthened considerably.

These white, fuzzy "lines" continued to add numbers and lengthen, until after twenty or twenty-five minutes 80 to a 100 of them totally spanned the lake's half-mile width. By this time I was watching through binoculars. The lines appeared to be two or three feet wide with a 20 or 30-foot space between, and the absolutely straight parallel lines slowly became visible as far as I could see along the length of the lake. A slight breeze fanned the trees, and the gentle wind stirred the lake's surface, yet the lines rode the disturbance without breaking up.

Two white gulls flew in and landed on the water. Through the binoculars I saw one of the birds float up to, and then into one of the lines. The hazy line actually parted as the gull's body drifted into it, and slowly closed when the animal went beyond. When the bird was completely inside the line there was a foot or so of clear water around its body.

I was enthralled by these sights, but not so much so that I couldn't figure out what was happening. Within minutes after the lines covered the lake, those nearest me began to fade and disappear. In another twenty minutes the phenomenon was gone entirely, but I was sure it was still there. For reasons that made perfect sense, I was convinced the lines had simply become invisible.

The truck was parked in mining country, and the roadbed sparkled in the sunlight with the reflection of tiny bits of minerals common to the area. Many these minerals were nonferrous copper, or mica pyrites, but some were iron, and therefore attracted to magnetic fields. The surface of the lake had to be carpeted with these minute particles stirred up in the dust raised by car and truck tires, but the ferrous iron was captured on the water in the magnetic force lines while the rest remained evenly disbursed.

The late morning Sun was over my right shoulder, and as it rose higher above the eastern hill the Sun's refraction off the particles made them visible. Also it's possible the magnetic influence oriented the ferrite particles in one direction making them easy to see. Toward its zenith, the Sun's angle between the lake surface and myself changed, so the lines vanished opposite to the order in which I saw them spread. I hadn't really seen "Terralines", but I saw where Terralines were by the trails they made on the surface of Wannacut lake.

By the compass I keep in the glove box, the lines ran magnetic north and south. At no time during the sighting were east and west lines visible. Was the word *Terraline,* then, coined to describe the force lines of the Earth's magnetic field, or did Litster refer to some other substance lying in horizontal filaments to the Earth's North Magnetic Pole?

Though fortuitous, this was a legitimate sighting. If others had been with me at the lake, I could have shown them these hazy lines in the same manner that I was able to point out my pet bear on the side of the mountain. Among other things the Earth is a magnet, and in this case a body of water acted like a giant sheet of paper holding iron filings rigid in a magnetic field.

I don't have to hallucinate these things.

Magnetic force lines exist.

Finding what Litster left out, what his nomenclature refers to, or what he didn't know has been, and continues to be fun, but I do wish he had at least left behind records as to what he thought all this means.

I wonder if he thought that all this means we do hallucinate these things?

Is this what he may have feared?

If electrons everywhere and everywhen are in sync when they phase into what I've been referring to as hyperspace, then shouldn't we all cease to exist until they phase back? Or maybe it's not that we cease to exist, but in a brief instant, we exist *elsewhere* and *elsewhen*. The Universe may be blinking on and off like a strobe light, but we wouldn't know it any more than we are consciously aware of the spaces between the still frames in a reel of motion picture film as it's being projected on a screen in a dark theater.

Perhaps when the electrons that activate a perception of our universe phase into hyperspace the essence of us, our ethereal minds as opposed to physical brains, ride the wave experiencing the universe of hyperspace. When we get back we don't remember what went on there, because memory may only function at ninety degrees to the phase, and doesn't pick up the thread of continuity until our electrons reunite with the atomic nuclei left behind. While we are gone the nuclei of our atoms wouldn't be alone, however, because the paired, or twined electrons have two 360-degree sides to their 720-degree reality.

While gone we might be running another show, and another aspect of ourselves would be operating the machinery here. When we get back, if indeed we even return to the same reality, we pick up the ball and keep dribbling toward the hoop until the next electron phase, which repeatedly occurs faster than the eye-blink of a gnat. Even if this shift, or split wasn't what we might regard as fast in another setting, we wouldn't know the difference. Speed is a function of time and distance, and time has no validity in this process, because distance has no relevance to electrons that communicate with each other across light years instantaneously.

This is where and when Bell's Theorem kicks in.

Nonlocality, or the consciousness of predecessors, assembles reality, and then we surf on into it thinking we were always there. Some one else has surfed out leaving us their past, which until it becomes our present used to be our future. We tinker with it for a period of "time" to prepare someone else's future, which instantly becomes our past. If we land in a different universe that looks almost the same as the one just left, we don't know the difference, because it's just another tick on the clock. If such side-by-side, or one-after-the-other universes exist they would be involved in a smoothly flowing, eternal split, and if space is acting like a super-dividing amoeba then these splits may be what we *interpret* as the linear motion of time. Maybe we do notice a difference, but don't recognize it for what it is.

There may be an infinite number of "places" where we exist as individuals, *and* as the "ant colony". From one end to the other of this infinite collection of linked individuals we might recognize only a few of our duplicates, but we would share the whole spectrum of existence from the ugly and the beautiful, to the cowardly and the brave. The experiences of one individual would subtlety influence the others in an unconscious sense, but the concepts of free will and causality are still valid, because the splits can take any direction desired.

The idea for us as individuals is to recognize that time is an illusion, and that all things can only occur *now*. The present is all there is, all there ever has been, and all there ever will be.

The universe is created now. Not ten billion years ago, and not six thousand four hundred and eighty three years ago on a Monday morning.

Conscious bleed-through awareness of others along this personal lineage will be rare, but should it happen, the memory probably will be misinterpreted as evidence of that which it is not. Reason will allow that such a memory may be a dream, or a hallucination, but when Reason is pushed, and if nothing else will suffice as an explanation, it will accept concepts like reincarnation rather than concede sovereignty over a reality it needs in order to exist.

Another aspect of time that is part philosophic, and part a concept of physics, states that because we cannot be intellectually aware of something until after we have seen it then whatever seen belongs to a past moment. Light has a speed limit of 186,281 miles per second in a vacuum, therefore it travels finite distances, and whatever our eyes see must be something that occurred in our past by virtue of the fact of these distances.

No one argues that an image of distant stars is light that started out years before, and is therefore light from the past. When someone is across my kitchen table helping me solve the world's problems, he or she, though only four-feet away also exists in my past. Even measured in a million parts of a microsecond, my guest is still a finite table's length from me. At the speed of sound, 741 miles per hour at sea level, we hear one another from a lot farther in the past than we're seeing.

In the science literature lately we've been treated to the results of experiments done in scientific laboratories, whereby light shined through a swirling, super cold fluid has actually been slowed down to as little as 40 miles per hour. Any swirling fluid is by definition a vortex. The guys in the white coats are close to making a black hole from almost nothing, and in such a case the past is even farther away.

It's fashionable to say we might feel another's pain, but to really do so we would have to physically cross an impossible time and space barrier. To be able to interact with each other in any context is due to our ability to divide infinity into manageable pieces that have perceivable lines of demarcation.

To say the only moment we have in which to make decisions, or to engage in actions is *now* seems axiomatic, but to take advantage of this statement we must do more than just give it intellectual lip service. If we look at a past object or action, and mistake it for the present we then make our decisions in the past where they can have no effect on the course of our lives. There is a trinity of time we need to understand, and then conquer.

Time seems to have a polarity, and its opposite polarity is space. Time without space is a singularity, and just as north and south together form a magnet, time and space make a whole structure. In a way, then, past and future are the polarities of the present. We cannot act out of free will from a past platform, or from a future position. But if we figure out how to stop the present from mutating into the future long enough to act from a location of the two combined, or *now moment,* free will can be enforced in ways that will leave Reason babbling.

The long defunct Primadonna Club in Reno once had to pay me a huge jackpot on a slot machine, because an errant, unguarded thought stopped my world. In one accidental, vibrant, living moment the present came to a dramatic halt while I stood in front of that machine. Six bars *instantaneously, and in unison* crashed into the pay line...and my gut. For a while I fooled myself into thinking I understood the mechanics of what happened, but though I tried, I was never able to consciously duplicate the feat. I came to learn that there are no "mechanics", only a feeling, and *absolute knowledge* that the machine and I are one and the same thing, and the way to this knowledge and feeling involve unlearning the world.

I have a starkly vivid memory, though, of the time when the steel gates of Reason were tricked open long enough to show there is a way to *now*.

At the end of the discussion, all we have is *now*, and until we understand this we are all alone in the past, waiting for the future.

If this idea is despised, blame Plato.

The philosopher Plato didn't have modern physics and the quantum theory to draw on, but he claimed that the essence of a thing exists before we can sense it.

Blame Albert Einstein for giving us the concept of the photon particle existing forever as one eternal second.

Blame Max Planck for siring the quantum theory.

Blame Werner Heisenberg for his uncertainty principle, which means we can't ever be certain of anything that goes on in the quantum (and maybe nowhere else either).

Blame John Stewart Bell for discovering that all this stuff is put together someplace else before we get to mess with it. And we shouldn't forget to blame all those who can't disprove Bell.

Blame Reason for refusing to deal with infinity.

Or blame me. I'm just the messenger.

In many ways this is scientific stuff. Look at what science says about the porous state of matter, and the exchange of atoms going on in our bodies on a continuous basis. Our atoms are being replaced every day. A year or so goes by, and we're walking around in new bodies; except when viewed by someone who hasn't seen us during that year; then the new us looks old. We get new atoms, yet these atoms have been hanging around since the beginning of time, so they are old atoms. But this means that when we were new babies, we were still made of old atoms. We can't destroy these atoms, only change and exchange them. I may have once extracted an atom from a cake for my sixth birthday, which was then expelled on my seventh birthday, but which I reclaimed yesterday.

Since the body is rebuilt every year, why do we get old?

Could it be that when universes split we just end up in the next perception, which is of a universe where we are older?

Suppose one of us refuses to make the next transition? Can that person just sort of let one aspect of reality exist around him or her, and enjoy a life of what we regard as continuity?

In this case, I don't see the idea of continuity as probable, but I do see the possibility of pausing for a beat inside that moment before transition as highly beneficial. The idea then is to learn how to take our conglomeration of atoms with us without exchanging them, and in that there is a continuity of individuality that seems nothing short of amazing when placed against the reality enforced by Reason.

There is precedence in my *now* moment in front of the slot machine, and in the countless similar moments experienced by others who have accidentally stepped beyond this transition. There is also hope in the depths of a question raised by the fact of atomic exchange:

What is the explanation of why, after the material of our brains has been replaced, we are able to remember events that were witnessed by a physical brain we no longer possess?

If we never before possessed any of these exact same bunches of atomic stuff we have draped around us, is any of this atomic stuff necessary to support consciousness? Where is our consciousness when we follow the electron path through elsewhere, or elsewhere? Is our one mind in the total fractal picture from which each of us has been infinitely copied? Are we The One, and also The Many? Are we at once the frozen single image *and* the moving projection of the movie film?

These are probably not questions for which the world is ready to demand answers, but no panic should be generated by the ideas. If any are concerned about losing themselves, all that needs be done is to check personal history.

We got this far, didn't we?

If all of this is hallucination...so what? It works, doesn't it? Stamp a foot. Does the heel go through the floor, or does it make a thud?

We exist.

Someone has already proven that.

Back in the Seventeenth Century, French philosopher, scientist, and mathematician Rene Descartes, cleared all this up with his famous comeback when asked to prove his existence:

"I think, therefore I am."

After exposure to such a succinct thought, if any are dubious, Descartes brilliantly anticipated the doubt:

"Only one thing cannot be doubted:" he said, "Doubt itself. Therefore, the doubter must exist."

Descartes also thought that a vortex might be the underlying cause for existence. This was stout thinking about tenuous stuff a very long time before Einstein, Planck, Heisenberg, Bell and others stirred up the mud in the otherwise clean waters of physics.

A lot of mainstream physicists seem to be taking carefully planted steps out on the thin ice of a many universe theory, so my conjecture isn't without some agreement among people who also go about trying to figure out why cannon balls fall to Earth. People like, Stephen Hawking, Roger Penrose, John Wheeler, Michio Kaku, and others, through a theory called, Superstrings, dredge up the possibility of several universes being part of why reality exists the way it does. Superstrings, some think, is the Unified Field Theory that forever eluded Einstein.

Still, even with respected names poking around the edges of a many universe idea, some aspects of quantum mechanics cause a loss of scientific equilibrium in the ranks of the faithful. When one attempts to measure something at the ultra tiny level of the quantum, the measurement can not be trusted, because apparently the act of looking at that which is measured causes it to react in an unpredictable manner.

If a scientist, by poking around below the level of the atom, causes movement in the quantum simply by the act of observation, then the next question is:

Does thinking about the observation cause the *formation* of that which is observed?

I was watching a TV program about two physicists who were filling what looked like a 40-foot-long blackboard with chalk squiggles. After months of honing the equations, one finally says, "Well, Dave, I believe that's it."

The other physicist says, "Yes, Herman, I think you're right."

They had just made a fantastic discovery in the realm of mathematics, but knew the cameras were rolling so they didn't dance, and shout, "Yes, yes, yes!"

After the commercial, they packed bags and headed off to the atom smasher, where they spent another week blasting itsy bitsy pieces of matter into other itsy bitsy pieces of matter.

Finally, a photographic plate came out of the bubble chamber that showed a certain two-inch line, which proves that all those chalk squiggles weren't in vain. They had found a previously unknown itsy bitsy piece of matter that the math said had to exist.

As a layman, I have several questions:

There were dozens of similar lines on that same plate, so how do you guys know that particular two-inch line is the particle you were after?

What good will come of this?

Who cares?

Who paid for that two-inch line?

But the big one is:

You guys wanted this outcome so bad, how do you know you didn't collaborate to *create* this new, never-before-seen particle?

This kind of thinking ultimately asks: If stuff in the quantum can be moved, or created by looking at it...or thinking about it...then suppose, since the quantum is our foundation, what would happen if the quantum is raised to the macrocosmic level?

I mentioned something from the Bible once, and I'm about to do it again, because I think there's a lot of good stuff in there, even though it's covered up with awful translations, and bad interpretations. People are playing with snakes and drinking poison because they don't understand that the last person to write down this plagiarized information didn't understand it either. Don't get me wrong; a lot of people who play with snakes and drink poison get away with it. They get away with it because Matthew, chapter 18, verse 19 (that's **19**), is loaded with universal truth:

*If two of you on earth **agree** concerning anything of importance that they should request,* ***it will take place****...*

Agreement is the name of the reality game. Get two or three, or more people together in the name of anything...NASA, for instance, and we go to the Moon. Or two really dedicated guys can manufacture a particle from the quantum soup.

Then there is the case of the eight people formed by the Toronto Society for Psychical Research in Canada who, in the early seventies, got together and invented a fictitious man in the past, gave him a history, the name Philip, and then doggedly tried to conjure up his ghost in contrived séances. They failed miserably for a long time, and then "Philip" suddenly showed up, rapped on a table to answer questions, and ultimately moved the table all over the place. I understand the table was seen on Canadian television going up stairs by itself, and onto a stage. Philip was a great, hard-won success as a séance ghost, but he was the ghost of a fake person.

Eight people got together and agreed on what they were going to accomplish, and then in the face of repeated failure finally bludgeoned Reason to back down and give them a small opening in the steel doors to show them a piece of the reality it was guarding.

"You must have unbending intent," Don Juan constantly told Carlos Castaneda.

Unbending intent means pounding Reason over the head mercilessly until it lets in the universe it is shielding us from. Reason shields us from that universe, because if it lets all of it in, Reason disappears. Those steel doors are simply self-preservation.

This is what probably happened to the seventeen messiahs or so who populate our ancient literature. They all got very good at manipulating this reality by using the underlying structure, or foundation, which was no longer hidden to them.

Then life in three dimensions got boring.

So they left.

"And the things I do, so shall you do..."

This statement leaves out, "Be prepared to lock horns with some really complicated vortexes after you figure out the ones around here."

In computer jargon, the game shifts to the next level of play. Science is not ready for the next level, and may never be ready. No sane, well-adjusted scientist is going to try and prove any of this stuff, because at a deep level there is a fear they will find that which they seek. Should they find validity attached to these ideas of mine the finely structured world they helped put together might shimmer, and then fall apart. No one is going to tear down a house they have spent time, money, and effort to build.

It's not easy to hold this universe together. It needs a lot of clear-thinking, levelheaded individuals to keep everything in place with their clear-thinking level-headedness. These people are needed, especially if reality is an illusion, because a majority of us have to be fooled by the illusion to have a strong enough agreement to keep the universe humming.

I have decided that from now on at the House of Mystery I'm going to treat debunkers, and their utterly silly arguments with the respect they deserve. I'm not being facetious. It just recently occurred to me that good solid, both-feet-on-the-ground debunkers do more to hold this worldview together than anyone. Sure, I think they are indulging in self delusion, but I'm still fond of this world, so I'm glad they are fooling themselves, because by doing so they help maintain an agreement regarding the corporeality of the universe. I kind of like the world the way it is, even though I don't think the world is the way it is.

If it wasn't for debunkers, guys like me would throw this place into chaos, and I don't know if I'm ready for the next game level.

I'm not yet ready to tangle with the idea that time, space, and the things that fill them are creations of the mind being created continuously, even though a segment of myself knows perfectly well that this is a fact.

We seem to live inside a projected world that operates exactly the way each of us individually and collectively expect it to operate. By accepting the reality of the unreal we do not even think about the existence of the real.

Apparently we live in an illusion that's taken seriously, and in the long run nothing that's done to us, or by us is serious, except in that it builds character. If we don't fool ourselves, though, how do we become good people? The dilemma is, do we condemn or congratulate those who warn us about the dangers of a disease like cancer, the menace of eating certain things, or smoking? On the one hand, such admonitions perform a service by publishing warnings complete with graphic descriptions of symptoms. On the other hand they are doing humanity a disservice, because by publishing the information they are creating the problem and showing graphically how to contract the symptoms.

An illusory world would operate on beliefs and expectations. We believe in disease, and fear is certainly a form of expectation.

An illusory world would operate on the basis of intent. If one doesn't intend to get a disease then it's not expected.

I think it's all in the way we pay attention to things around us. Once in a while, like the incident with the slot machine, I step outside and accidentally look back in. However, I haven't yet learned the other thing Don Juan drummed into Carlos Castaneda's head:

You must learn to sustain the effect.

Once, a long time ago, I even accidentally did that, and I think that was because *agreement* was along for the ride.

What I am about to recount is an exact description. It is exact because I wrote it down right after it happened, which, being a sloppy researcher, is something I rarely do.

It was mid-September of 1974 and John and I decided to drive to Reno. This would make the seventh or eighth such trip for both of us together. Usually others would be along, but this time there was just ourselves. We were no strangers to the 850 miles ahead.

The drive was made in my car, a 1972 Datsun 510, and one of those products the manufacturer later tried to *improve* to my dismay.

I arranged to pick up John at his apartment at nine in the evening. Since these jaunts started from Bellingham, Washington, which is 30-miles south of the Canadian Border, we always left at night to avoid Interstate 5 traffic in Seattle, and then Portland, Oregon. We knew the trip would take 14 to 15 hours depending on stops. It was timed to get us into Reno between 11:00 am and noon. Not only did we miss traffic by starting at night, we arrived after most people had left town, and the next throng was yet to arrive. On this schedule we never had trouble getting a room.

I drove the first leg of the trip while John napped in the reclined front bucket seat. Our first stop was usually near the city of Vancouver, Washington just across the Columbia River from Portland. When we were close to the gas station and restaurant we normally used, John was sawing some pretty heavy logs. Since he had a long driving shift coming I wanted him to sleep as long as possible. A check of the gas gauge told me I could squeeze another eighty or ninety miles out of this amazing little Datsun.

I crossed the bridge into Oregon, and drove through Portland at about one o'clock in the morning. Near 1:30, I wheeled off the freeway at Salem, and into a gas station by a Denny's restaurant. We fueled the car, and then ourselves with a quick snack.

Fifteen minutes later, we were back on I-5 south, and I reclined the passenger seat for my nap.

I awoke several times when passing by lighted cities, and was sitting up as we dropped down into Grant's Pass, Oregon. At Medford, we had plenty of fuel to take on the Siskiyou mountain pass, so the plan was to fill the tank in Yreka, California. As it turned out, I was asleep when John approached Yreka, so he kept going. I awoke when I felt the car enter the freeway exit at the town of Mount Shasta.

My watch informed me it was almost 6:30 in the morning. Dawn was tinting the sky pale blue. We were right on schedule, and had time for breakfast at the restaurant just across from the gas station where the 510 got a drink.

We had a quick meal of ham and eggs, got coffee to go, and I took the wheel near seven am. Instead of going back to I-5, I drove south through town on old 99, and then turned east on route 89. This two-lane road rises steeply from Mount Shasta up toward the Mt. Shasta Ski Park, and then drops quickly into the small town of McCloud, which is about ten miles from the Interstate.

At the bottom of the hill the road bends left and through an intersection, which was guarded by a blinking caution light. I drove under the light and east into about a hundred miles of beautiful pine forest.

Beyond McCloud for several miles, the 14,162-foot cone of Mt. Shasta is over the eastbound driver's left shoulder. As I steered through a tunnel of ponderosa pine, I looked at my watch. It was not quite 7:25.

Behind us in the west were high clouds, but ahead the sky had turned vibrant blue, and the morning sun hit us in the face whenever the trees and road lined up with its low angle. I put on sunglasses, and settled back for the two-hour plus drive to Susanville, California.

From Susanville it would be an hour and a half into Reno.

At this moment an ordinary thing happened, which I instinctively interpreted as extraordinary.

Along the road a sign came into view. I was hit with an incongruous, unsettling thought that the sign and the environment around it looked familiar. The thought was out of place because the entire road was familiar to me. I was puzzled by my own reaction. Why should I be concerned about a sign announcing the upcoming road to the town of Westwood?

I can't adequately describe what I felt at that moment. It was something like awe mingled with befuddlement. It was like I knew something I shouldn't know.

My foot reached for the brake, and I steered the car to the road shoulder. I was breathing heavy when we stopped. To the left the sun shined brightly just above the horizon through a thin stand of lodge pole pine.

The road looked perfectly normal, and familiar. And that was the problem.

"What's the matter?" a voice said, and I nearly jumped out of my skin.

I looked over at John. For a long, weird second I wondered what he was doing there? His eyes were open wide, and looked to be what I could only describe as haunted.

The road sign was about a hundred feet behind us. I jerked my thumb to the rear. "You know where Westwood is?" I asked in a voice that was mostly a squawk.

He shook his head. Behind his glasses the eyes were still as big a barn owl's.

"This country look familiar?"

He nodded. "What're you saying?"

"What time is it?" I asked cautiously. I didn't want to look at my own watch.

He looked down at his wrist and frowned. Finally, he looked at me and bit his lip. "Is this right?" he asked, indicating the great out of doors with a nod of his head.

"What time is it?" I repeated.

"About 7:30. What's going on?"

With a huge lump in my throat, I said, "John, we're about ten miles out of Susanville."

I finally checked my own watch, which informed me the time was 7:28 and change.

The last time I had looked at my watch was three minutes in the past, and almost a hundred miles to our rear!

We were no longer on route 89, but on route 44, and I had absolutely no memory of having made the turn.

I was also ravenously and unaccountably hungry. Fifteen minutes later, when we arrived in Susanville, I wheeled into the parking lot of the first cafe along the street. We nearly ran one another over to get inside where we consumed piles of hot cakes, and bacon and eggs. By our watches it had been less than 45 minutes since we finished the last breakfast.

The reason I know these details after 26 years is because we spent almost two hours in that cafe making napkin lists of every thing we had done since leaving Bellingham.

"What time did I say you should be ready to go?" I asked John.

"Nine O'clock," he answered.

"What time did I get to your place?"

"About one minute to nine."

"Where did we first stop for gas?"

"Chevron station near Salem. We had pie and coffee at the Denny's next door. I had apple ala mode, and you had cherry."

"How fast did you drive on the way to Portland?" he asked me.

"Fudging the speed limit by about five," I answered. "You?"

"About the same."

Before we left the cafe, the trip from McCloud to Susanville was relived about three times.

During the 85 miles from Susanville into Reno we started asking one another the definitive questions.

"You remember McCloud?"

"I remember the blinking yellow light, and the...what is that...tractor company on the right."

"How about that big sweeping curve on eighty-nine where we come down the hill, cross the curving bridge, and then up the other hill?"

"No."

"Do you remember the intersection of eighty-nine and two-ninety-nine out in the middle of nowhere where they have those horrible speed bumps warning you to stop?"

"Nope."

"Remember Hat Creek?"

"Uh...no."

"How about the turn off from eighty-nine onto forty-four?"

A long frown, then, "Nothing."

"The long curving pull up out of the Hat Creek area?"

"Don't remember that."

"The rest stop about half-way to Susanville where we usually stop to offload coffee."

"We didn't stop there. As a matter of fact, I think we flew over."

As much as a year later, we still quizzed one another in this fashion, looking for something to rationally explain how we traveled almost a hundred miles in minutes, or perhaps even less than a minute. I now question if it took any time at all?

There are moments when I wonder if John and I are even in the same timeline we started out in that September night in 1974? Are we right now about two hours ahead of ourselves?

What happened to us eight or ten miles east of McCloud, California?

Do we really want to know?

We've both told the story to others more than once, and more than once the suggestion has been offered that aliens probably picked us up. I'm well versed in the alien abduction stories, and point out to those with this theory that we did not *lose* two hours, but *gained* two hours.

We seemed to have hitched a ride on a kind of time machine, but it was at the same time a space machine. If we had chartered a Lear jet in Mount Shasta, the ride to Susanville would have taken longer by air than it did in my trusty little Datsun 510.

There's only one thing I know for sure about this magic transit of ours, and it is that it actually *happened.* I know this isn't saying much, but there isn't much to say, other than if a thing like this can happen, *then the world we're attached to is not something to which we are strongly attached.*

Reason can do nothing but admit this unconventional transport occurred, but after the admission it just turns around and looks the other way. Time and space getting warped in this fashion isn't even reasonable, so why waste time thinking about it?

It was just an illusion the debunker will say. Ok...and what if he is right?

If time and space are illusions, what does that make reality? If we accept that time and space are illusionary doesn't this mean that the senses which tell us about the illusion are also illusions?

If what happened to John and me along California Routes 89 and 44 was an illusion, then the word illusion is itself an illusion.

As my grandmother used to say, "Isn't this a fine kettle of fish?"

Twenty-six years later I can't explain the mechanics of our little detour through reality, but I am now able to plot the course.

That large Oregon vortex circumference line of 679 miles, when swung on a radius of 108 miles from halfway between Gold Hill and Upper Klamath Lake arches east of McCloud, California, and cuts across Route 89 a few miles west of the cutoff to Pondosa, which is our point of disappearance, or more properly, our last position of memory.

A line true north of our **re**appearance point on Route 44 intersects the line that runs 40-degrees from Gold Hill, through Lost Creek Dam or Uncanny Canyon, and to the center of the larger corona which passes near Eugene, Oregon.

A line of 51.43-degrees of arc from our reappearance point through our disappearance point carries northwest just south of Grant's Pass, and for all I know, though Aurelia's fireplace. From here it goes to a union with the demarcation line just south of Coos Bay on the Oregon coast at a spot called...here we go... *Seven Devil's Wayside*.

I don't make the maps. Okay?

These vortexes, from the smallest to the largest, are in motion within themselves. It's a confusing, sometimes contradictory appearing motion along lines straight, spiraling, and at right angles to each other. At times, whatever it is in the continuum that is in motion meet at intersection points, and there for a brief moment, a harmonic resonance is set up through the entire structure.

Reality shakes.

At the House of Mystery site, it's the little canopy that Litster built out in the yard that shakes, and sometimes when many things line up at once, it shakes violently. During this moment of resonance, maybe mosquitoes get transported elsewhere and elsewhen, but people *should be* too big to be affected dramatically. (A recent experience causes me to qualify this statement.)

#43

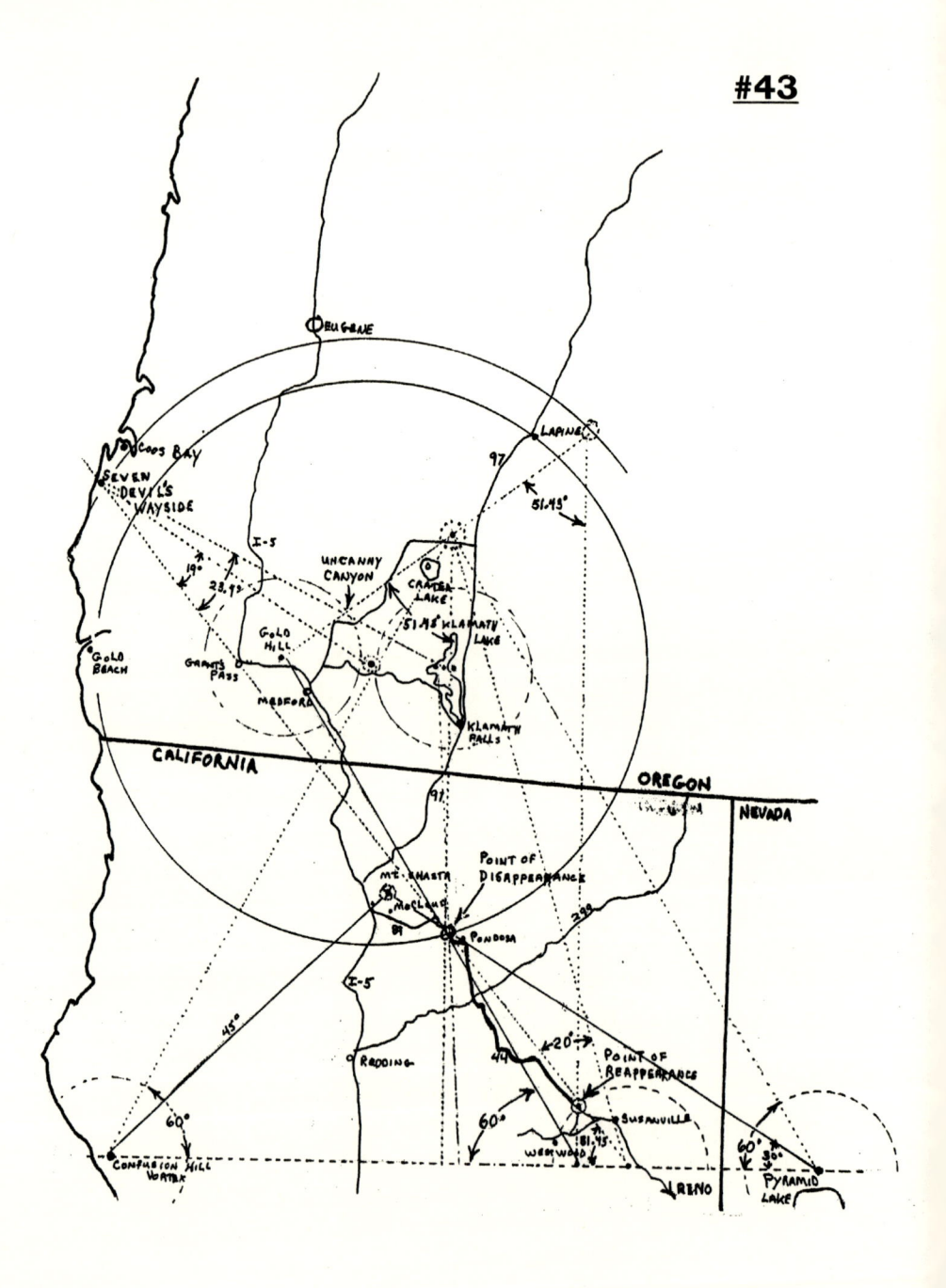

At a diameter of 216 miles the greater vortex is big enough that when a car hits a million to one shot starting position at the beginning of the harmonic disturbance, it and its passengers get carried along to the place where the shaking stops.

I'm sure glad there was a road at that point.

While in transit, what happened to time? Was the transport done in an instant, or in a manner that makes no sense, did it take a long period, and only seemed like an instant? John and I were so hungry it could have been two days since we had eaten, even though it had been less than an hour by our watches. Instead of taking up residence two hours ahead, did we hang around in hyperspace long enough to resume viability two *days* later, on a Thursday that was two days behind in the universe split that had simply caught up with us, but we identified as the same Thursday we had left?

One of the things we didn't check was the growth of our beards, but maybe it wouldn't have mattered.

Perhaps someday, now that I'm able to draw the road map, I'll figure out the mechanics and the timing of our jaunt across hyperspace, but until then I'll just have to continue using up asphalt miles like everyone else.

My working theory is that the car at a certain ground speed breached an infinity boundary in the same fashion that I breach lines of demarcations every day in the House of Mystery Vortex. I think there must be such things as infinity boundaries, and that they exist as a way to segment and make sensible an otherwise endless vortex. Three vortexes of increasingly larger sizes form the basic reality structure. One, two, three, and then at right angles, four, five, six, followed by the last contrary right angle, seven, eight, and nine. These three vortex structures then combine into the same three-vortex right angle form epitomized in the *Ankh* shape (Ill. #23).

Demarcation lines are simply cut-off points formed at the edges of the orthogonal spinning of the vortex spirals. Remembering that the Fibonacci points within the natural vortexes only count out to the number 13, and then widen to the next 13, and so on is a clue to how the demarcation lines hold reality in check. The Fibonacci Sequence itself is an infinite structure, but because it repeats itself to the number 13, no matter how large the next structure, it is a limited procedure that still allows an infinite progression. If the sequence is allowed to progress without regard to number size, infinity would be a smooth, seamless progression to infinitely larger numbers and nothing would, or could happen in between them.

If reality is dealt with without breaking it up into little pieces, or into small vortexes giving way to larger ones at right angles, it seems there will be no reality as we know it. It would instead be a perfect line to forever, and on such a line we could not exist in our present form.

The past, present, and future tense in our language is therefore only a convenience to which Reason has ascribed importance. The concept of linear time helps us make appointments, keep track of gray hairs, and helps nail down the lid of our perceived reality.

Reason loses its grip as soon as we intuitively understand that the statement, *now*, is always correct no matter when it is stated.

Perception seems to be dependant on being able to encapsulate vortexes.

Encapsulating vortexes seems to be the key to taming infinity, and perhaps to opening it up to manipulation.

At the House of Mystery Vortex recently, I was the recipient of a devastating experience that tends to lend credence to my last statement. I include this account not for its sensational nature, but more to show the kind of thing that can happen when vortexes become misaligned. At least, for the space of less than half a minute, that's what I think happened, and it totally unnerved me.

It had been my morning custom to place a compass on a certain spot in the gift shop where I could check it during the day. At this spot I had noticed a slight change in the north-pointing needle that occurred over a long period. Some days there was no movement at all, while on others the needle would move by anywhere as much as two to six degrees of arc over several hours. I was becoming aware that internal parts of this otherwise stable vortex were in motion within itself. The scenery, if not in motion, was at least contracting and expanding like the slow beating of a heart.

On this morning the compass was pointing almost due north. I made a note of it, and then went do the set-up chores to get ready for any early customers. Twenty minutes later when I returned to the compass it was still rock-solid on north. I was about to turn away when the needle positioned itself almost twelve degrees of arc to the east. I say it "positioned itself", because I have no memory of having seen it move!

I picked the instrument up, shook it, and then put it back down. It was still off by about 12-degrees. We have more than one compass around the shop, so I put another one about a foot from the first, and it too was off by 12-degrees. I had no magnets in my pockets, nor was there a mass of metal near the devices. I felt no tremors. It was past the spring equinox. There had been no nearby earthquakes. The full Moon was days away. No trumpets blared. The immediate world appeared normal, but north had moved by a huge amount!

I headed for the front yard with a pair of dowsing rods. Another of those things, which I check on a continuing basis, is that gap in the demarcation line just outside the gift shop door. In the past I have never found anything other than a gap at this point, even though the gap is constantly expanding and contracting. At this moment, though, it was shut tight. Even though it was closed, it registered differently on either side of the position of the missing gap. Later I found a new gap had opened at the top of the hill in the middle of the small concrete platform.

When I reentered the shop the compasses had returned to only being off by a "normal" two-degrees. Maria came in about this time, and I told her what had happened. We tossed around theories, even jokingly blaming her brother who was visiting that day, but no good explanation came to the discussion. I checked the line outside once an hour, but it remained closed.

A couple of days later I discovered that two of our demonstrations were not working very well, while others seemed to have increased in intensity. By the fifth day, it was apparent that the inner, primary vortex was moving down that 23-degree line from the axis position. Also, by this time those two demonstrations no longer functioned at all. Throughout all this, the demarcation line remained closed near the gift shop, and wide open at the top of the hill.

I had never before missed the guidance of Litster, but now I was wishing for his help. This was just my second year in the Vortex. He had spent more than thirty years. If this occurrence was a periodic thing, I wanted to know how long it lasts.

On the seventh morning, Bryton and I were alone at the Vortex without customers, so I used the free time to climb up the hill and into the brush with a compass, dowsing rods, and a magnet on a string. I thought looking at some of the other aspects we don't show might shed light on this new mystery. I first checked the position of the equivalent of the Queen's Chamber on the ground south of the old shack. This seemed to register no problem, so I thought to check circumstances on the line of demarcation at what I call the subterranean chamber equivalent.

This "basement" position of the Vortex exists on a steep side hill, and to face toward the apex position, or upper platform 165 feet away, I have to place my back to the slope of the hill. This creates a strange impulse to fall backward uphill, and I found myself fighting the impulse more aggressively than at other visits to this position.

I started to bring the compass up to my eyes to take a reading toward the "apex" upper platform. A strange feeling stopped me from completing the motion. Without the compass, my eyes told me that something was out of whack. I was directly opposite of the upper platform "apex", and always when I had sighted across the diameter of the Vortex from this position, a huge Douglas fir tree beside the house blocked the platform from view.

The tree *used* to block that view, but this time the platform was in plain sight through leafless trees! I could see the platform beyond the tree to its right.

The scenery had shifted on me, and it was not a subtle shift! I didn't get a chance to check, but the difference was at least five-degrees.

I didn't get a chance to check because something else was out of the ordinary.

Me.

A hair or two stood up on the back of my neck. *Things* looked normal, but something felt alien, and that feeling melted quickly into what I can only describe as panic. Immediately every hair on my neck stood straight up. I could fathom no logical reason for this crazy emotion.

I was completely, and without rational foundation, terrified, and was welded to the spot.

To make matters worse, just below my position, about 25 feet away, a man stood with his back toward me. I didn't see him walk up, or even magically appear. He was just there, and this somehow struck me with a new wave of that intense, irrational fear.

The man's left hand rested on a knurled walking stick, and he studied a fairly large magnetic compass in his outstretched right hand. A pile of gray hair adorned the top and back of his head. He wore what looked like a heavy wool suit coat with matching brown pants tucked into high leather boots.

My thoughts seemed divorced from the unreasonable feeling of terror, which was making my skin pulsate. This was an area of the woods where Maria doesn't let patrons roam, yet when I tried to ask him if I could be of assistance, I couldn't even clear my throat. My real intent was to crawl into a hole and pull the ground in after me. Without any reason, I was frozen in a silent spasm of utter, senseless dread of a sort I've never experienced before.

Apparently the intruder was unaware of me, and that suited me just fine. If I could have made my legs function, I would have fled. Perhaps ten seconds into this sighting, he looked up from the compass and peered toward the assay shack. As if from an outside command, my head raised to gaze where he was looking.

A hole developed in my stomach, all that nutty fear fell into it, and dragged me along. The old board fence around the shack didn't look right. It took the beat of at least two seconds to focus on a slight skein of snow on the roof, and this sight brought on another round of instant terror.

The temperature of the world in which I embarked on my short hike was in the low forties; chilly, but not cold enough to produce snow!

I saw him glance down at his compass. This movement evidently caused me to look at the compass I had forgotten I was holding. The sight of it couldn't have been more frightening if I had just discovered a snake in my hand. I gasped and dropped it. At light-speed my thoughts built a scenario of the instrument clattering as it hit the ground, thus alerting the man to my presence.

With a reaction I can only regard as superhuman, I snatched the compass out of mid-air. This is a feat I have since tried to duplicate with other objects without success. The fear magnified with a vengeance so intense I was knocked backward and staggered to catch my balance. I was sure all this commotion had betrayed my position to the enemy, and with gargantuan effort I raised my eyes to meet whatever was out there.

The man was still visible, but somehow in two or three seconds, he had gotten over beside the shack, which was probably 70 feet away. He was turned toward me, and I suddenly realized that perspective had gone completely insane.

There were two shacks; a big shack, and a smaller shack superimposed on the other. In front of the small shack with snow on the roof, the man was looking right at me. My body felt huge - a thousand feet high, and it tingled with a strange, heavy vibration. The scene of the man near the assay shack was disappearing as if it was being pulled into a hole in the air. He seemed a thousand yards away, yet I saw his eyes open wide.

A voice entered my right ear, and only my right ear. The sound appeared to come from six inches away. It was flat, yet almost breathless.

"*Oh Jesus*!"

I felt a dull thud in my solar plexus, and then the strange bloating anxiety bled away. My breath was coming in steam-engine huffs, and I sat heavily on the moss that carpets the side hill. For long moments I let my breath slow, and then I looked back up at the shack.

The sight was normal. The fir tree now blocked the view of the upper platform.

I intended to tell Bryton what had happened, but halfway back to the gift shop I decided to keep such an improbable thing as this to myself, at least until I could think about it. Because of its dubious nature, I later made the decision to keep the story out of this book, but was persuaded to recount it by an insistent editor who I had entrusted with the incident.

Was it Litster in another time that I saw?

Did seeing me, and seeing the world rotate before his eyes convince him that humanity wasn't ready for what he had learned?

I can pose the questions, but the only answer I really have involves that intense fright that nearly consumed me.

I'm sure it was body fear.

My mind in that strange encounter was normal. Intellectually I was sharp, and I managed to remember everything. I think, like the house cat, or the deer at the line of demarcation, my body sensed mortal danger, and knew that one step in any direction would have plunged me into that world.

I think of how the men on Flight 19 must have felt when not just a patch of woods changed before their eyes, but an entire world. I can imagine the immediacy of their fear.

The following day while taking people through the area, I noticed the Vortex had reverted to its familiar, dependable self. The broom fairly leaped from my hand to stand like a rock, the demarcation lines were sharp, and the group easily saw the instant passage from one side to another. The Vortex seemed rejuvenated, and felt normal; at least as normal as such an abnormality can ever be.

The day before, what I had been thinking of as my favorite vortex had nearly eaten me alive, and seven days had gone by since the big 12-degree change signaling the start of the whole episode. I'm still debating what I might do should I ever see the compass take such a huge swing again. Will I tempt fate, and on the sixth day again place myself on that side hill? The pull is strong to do so, but the abject terror that accompanied the last experience is a perhaps a bit stronger. Maybe I will, like Odysseus before the encounter with the Sirens, have myself tied to the living mast of a tree.

Perhaps the moment will not ever repeat, or I'll miss the timing, but I think I'd like to try just to prove to myself that the experience was real. Is the world in which we live so easily bent that wispy things like thoughts might open such portals? It was, until recently an idea worthy only of a science fiction story, but now that I've stood at the edge and peered over...I wonder?

Can the world be influenced in this fashion? I know that magnetic fields can be manipulated with such minor influences as pencil lines. I've also had a bit of experience with thoughts causing a change in the aspect configurations of magnets, but how much force, or agreement is needed up here at the level of the macrocosm to affect big changes?

With this question asked I shouldn't be surprised that a possible answer lies in another encounter that started at the House of Mystery.

I man I met at the Vortex, and who has gone on to help me greatly with certain parts of my life, insisted I meet a person who had some photographs he thought I needed to see. Later I did meet this person, and viewed the pictures that had been billed as nothing short of spectacular. Regrettably, I must couch this narrative in careful language, because the photographs are the property of another who doesn't want a name, or even the location of where the pictures were taken to become public.

Because of the build-up, when two eight by ten glossies where pulled from a manila envelope, I was expecting something fantastic. What I first saw, however, was a pair of what looked like mundane identical vistas that were apparently taken at the same time and place by two different cameras. I studied them intently but was completely baffled about what was supposed to be so amazing about them.

One of the pictures was of a superior quality to the other. Both showed a narrow border of water at the bottom, an even thinner band of treed shoreline with dwellings of some sort, and in the background a low, rather unimpressive brown and barren hill. The pictures were eighty per cent sky. Dense clouds swept on a shallow angle from the left horizon to the right like a fat contrail, and then broken off above this were dozens of fluffy popcorn clouds floating against the blue sky.

At this meeting were three others beside myself, and while I searched the photos for some clue as to what miraculous vision was hidden in them, everyone was silent. Finally, I lifted my head, and directed a quizzical gaze at the party assembled about the table.

"You're going to have to help me," I said.

"What if I told you," my friend offered, "that these pictures were taken three years apart?"

It took a second to digest this statement, and then I looked back down at the set of photos. It took less than a second to now understand why these artifacts were placed in such high regard.

The simple query formed itself:

If the two pictures were taken three years apart, then how was it possible for the skyscape to be *perfectly identical in every detail?* I immediately began checking the shoreline, and sure enough some of the trees could be identified as slightly larger than their twins in what had to be the first photo. A few seconds later, I spotted a house in the later picture that was not in the earlier one. I knew all this could be faked, and probably rather easily since my new friend was something of a computer genius. When I glanced back up at the anxious faces around me, though, I had the feeling they were not putting me on.

They remained silent, and I spent a couple more minutes on the photographs. I picked out two or three little puffs of cloud in each picture and compared them. They were precisely the same in size, configuration, and placement within the two scenes.

Did the photographer, I wondered, snap the first picture of a future skyscape, or was the second picture taken of a past skyscape? And no matter which might be the case, did the skyscape represent a portal that opened into one of those worlds or both? Was the second picture somehow a three-year-old memory of the first picture that was through psychic ability mentally pasted onto the negative of the second picture?

Either the photos were faked, or I was looking at more evidence that the world isn't hinged to the doorframe too tightly.

Because of the people I was with, I choose to believe the pictures were not tampered with.

I have decided to carry around one of those throwaway cameras in the Vortex. I sure wish I'd had one the day my little pet tried to gobble me up. If an occasion to use it presents itself, I hope I'm not immobilized with fear like the last time.

If portals to other places and times can open on this planet, and if an interstellar geometric link does exist between planets of different star systems, it seems reasonable that the other planets in our neighborhood have their counterparts strung about the universe as well.

In December of 1999 I was talking with a friend about the Mars Lander that NASA had just lost. He knew of my Bermuda Triangle theory, and joked that NASA, by trying to find water by landing that thing near the south pole of Mars inadvertently dropped it through the "Byrd" portal of the Red Planet. In view of my recent experience at the Vortex, and the evidence of those photographs, I am now seriously reexamining the quality of my friend's joke. NASA may have had a greater success than they know. Their machine might be broadcasting all kinds of information right now, but not about Mars. The messages, however, won't be getting through any time soon.

NASA will never get the Mars Lander back, and I think my consuming fear while on that side hill acknowledged something similar.

It seems certain that a portal in the continuum opened for me that day at the Oregon Vortex and briefly displayed somewhere and somewhen else. Even though my mind wanted to investigate, my body recognized the improbability of a round trip, and refused to budge. All my research tells me that the world is open-ended, and that if we can achieve a kind of quantum consciousness that is also open-ended the world can present some pretty amazing experiences.

When the world changes its view of us, we change our view of the world. Man, like the Greek philosopher Protagoras claimed 2,500 years ago, is the measure of all things. *Man is the Golden Vortex.* Our consciousness is synchronized with the vortex superstructure of space-time, and if our timing is good we can go anywhere and anywhen we will.

THE CONSCIOUS LIBRARIES

THE CLASSIC LIBRARY

1 Gianfranco Spavieri *Science And Myth*

THE POPULAR LIBRARY

1 Nick Nelson *The Golden Vortex*

Conscious Books
can be ordered from Ingram at any bookstore
or online at amazon.com or barnesandnoble.com

Printed in the United States
967600002B